T0323494

WOMEN'S POLITICAL LEADERSHIP FOR SUSTAINABLE DEVELOPMENT

This book posits that women's political leadership is vital for transitions to a sustainable future. It investigates the unsustainability of the current social order, offers strategies for achieving sustainable development, and explores the structure and agency variables that enable women political leaders to successfully drive political innovations for a greater societal transformation.

This book sheds light on the genesis of the current capitalist social order, the transformational role of the state, political leadership, political innovations, and particularly women leaders in driving sustainable development. The book analyses three case studies of women leaders who have successfully implemented political innovations for sustainable statehood and development on national, regional, and local governance levels: Jacinda Ardern, Carole Delga, and Valérie Plante. From these case studies, the author demonstrates which agency and structural prerequisites are crucial for women political leaders to become a driving force behind creating the conditions needed for a sustainable future.

Taking both a theoretical and an empirical approach, this is key reading for graduate students and researchers interested in political leadership, gender and politics, political innovations, sustainability sciences, and transition research. It will also be of interest to political leaders, and those advising them, looking to understand the leadership styles, skills, and strategies needed to successfully drive progressive political agendas for sustainable statehood and development.

Anna-Katharina von Stauffenberg is a political scientist and former strategy consultant who founded a Government Technologies startup based on the insights in this book. She lives in Münster, Germany.

Leadership: Research and Practice Series

In Memoriam
Georgia Sorenson (1947–2020), Founding Editor

Series Editor
Ronald E. Riggio, *Henry R. Kravis Professor of Leadership and Organizational Psychology and former Director of the Kravis Leadership Institute at Claremont McKenna College.*

Navigating Leadership
Evidence-Based Strategies for Leadership Development
Susanne Braun, Tiffany Keller Hansbrough, Gregory A. Ruark, Rosalie J. Hall, Robert G. Lord, and Olga Epitropaki

Snapshots of Great Leadership, Third Edition
Jon P. Howell, Isaac Wanasika and Maria J. Mendez

Heroic Leadership, Second Edition
An Influence Taxonomy of 100 Exceptional Individuals
Scott T. Allison and George R. Goethals

A Pluralistic Approach to Leadership
Interdisciplinary Perspectives
Nathan W. Harter

Women's Political Leadership for Sustainable Development
Driving Political Innovations
Anna-Katharina von Stauffenberg

For more information about this series, please visit: www.routledge.com/Leadership-Research-and-Practice/book-series/leadership

WOMEN'S POLITICAL LEADERSHIP FOR SUSTAINABLE DEVELOPMENT

Driving Political Innovations

Anna-Katharina von Stauffenberg

Routledge
Taylor & Francis Group

NEW YORK AND LONDON

Designed cover image: Mary Long via Getty Images

First published 2025
by Routledge
605 Third Avenue, New York, NY 10158

and by Routledge
4 Park Square, Milton Park, Abingdon, Oxon, OX14 4RN

Routledge is an imprint of the Taylor & Francis Group, an informa business

ISBN: 978-1-032-83083-4 (hbk)
ISBN: 978-1-032-82727-8 (pbk)
ISBN: 978-1-003-50766-6 (ebk)

DOI: 10.4324/9781003507666

Typeset in Sabon
by SPi Technologies India Pvt Ltd (Straive)

CONTENTS

PART III
Cases of women's political leadership for sustainable development 131

PART IV
Practical research implications 217

SERIES FOREWORD

Ronald E. Riggio

This latest contribution to the *Leadership: Research and Practice* book series is, I think, a very important one. It deals with two very prominent, and well-researched, areas related to the leadership challenges of today. The first is the concern for the rapidly degrading physical and social environment in which we live. The second issue is the fact that our prototype of effective leaders – in business, but especially in politics – is based on a masculine "great man" model. In analyzing dominant political leadership, author von Stauffenberg argues that the dominant capitalist approach works against sustainable development, which involves protecting our precious environment and caring for all members of society. So, shifts are needed. We need to move way from reliance on the traditional (and masculine-fueled) capitalist model to one that is focused more on prioritizing sustainability. Moreover, the best, recent examples of this form of political leadership for sustainable development have been women political leaders. So, a shift also needs to occur in terms of how politicians lead, and women leaders, such as New Zealand's Jacinda Arden, France's Carole Delga, and Canada's Valerie Plante offer templates for this new form of leadership for sustainability. In addition to critiquing the status quo in political leadership, the author offers a way forward. This is, in essence, a valuable contribution to our understanding of world politics, the challenges we face as human beings in a fragile ecosystem, but also to the future of our understanding of what exemplary leadership for the future should look like.

Ronald E. Riggio, Ph.D.
Henry R. Kravis Professor of Leadership
and Organizational Psychology
Kravis Leadership Institute
Claremont McKenna College

INTRODUCTION

The leadership we need

Anna-Katharina von Stauffenberg

> The vital attributes of a leader…are courage and character – courage to choose a direction among complex and difficult options, which requires the willingness to transcend the routine; and strength of character to sustain a course of action whose benefits and whose dangers can only be incompletely glimpsed at the moment of choice.
>
> (Kissinger, 2022, p. xvi)

Societies of the Global North are in a predicament today: we are living through an epochal transformation as our current routines and, more importantly, the entire social order are losing their legitimacy in the face of social, economic, political, and ecological crises. However, in the words of Antonio Gramsci, "the crisis consists precisely in the fact that the old is dying and the new cannot be born; in this interregnum a great variety of morbid symptoms appear" (Hoare & Nowell-Smith, 1971, p. 276).

Scientific evidence points to the dangers of remaining in the "old" and our inertia's "morbid symptoms". Still, the "new" and courses towards it are even more contested in this inherently political transition phase, which requires a fundamental redistribution of values, in which some may lose whilst others may gain. Respectively, this "new" lingers, and, as Henry Kissinger (2022) addresses in his latest book, leadership tends to slack in long periods of tranquillity and only in adverse times do people, out of necessity, turn to those leaders they almost forgot. If this holds, then now should be the time for leaders who attempt to raise society to their visions instead of managing the immediate. Leaders who show the courage to transcend routines and have the strength of character to take us on this

DOI: 10.4324/9781003507666-1

contested journey towards a "new" whose dangers and benefits we cannot yet know of.

This "new" is particularly relevant to capitalist societies of the Global North, which are foremost responsible for many of the crises we face today and, therefore, should lead the way towards realising a good life for all and conserving non-human nature. There is a need for the State to move to the forefront of pursuits towards sustainable development, as it remains the most potent human mechanism for collective action (Deutsch, 1970) and the only institution that structures political, economic, and social interactions, and distributes resources across society (Duit et al., 2016). Thereby, politics is concerned explicitly with realising societal goals, setting new priorities, and potentially transforming our current social order (Deutsch). Since sustainable development involves processes of self-steering and new priorities, much of the responsibility for realising it thus rests with governments and politicians (Meadowcroft, 2011). In line with this argumentation, political leaders may take on a central role in promoting transformations toward sustainable development. In democratic regimes, they are charged with defending the public interest, potentially have the knowledge, resources, and competencies for strategic leadership, and can legitimately channel political demands from the State, economy, and society into the political process (Ottens & Edelenbos, 2018). What we seem to require then is political leadership for sustainable development.

However, political sciences have paid little attention to this type of leadership, possibly because political scientists have preferred to reason in terms of processes, structures, and institutions (Elgie, 2015). All the while, political challenges are changing vastly in the fast-paced, complex multi-governance networks of the 21st century, making effective political leadership ever more critical. This book aims to shed light on the transformative potential that political leaders, and women political leaders, in particular, may have in driving sustainable development, which strategies they ought to follow, and which structure and agency variables may be decisive for their endeavour.

The roots of unsustainable development

Capitalism has had and still has detrimental effects on the web of life, including both humans and non-human nature (Dörre, 2019; Jaeggi & Fraser, 2020; Lessenich, 2019; Moore, 2015). Following a Neo-Marxist tradition, this book conceptualises capitalism as an institutionalised social order and life form. It is characterised by the economic foreground conditions of class division, the institutionalised marketisation and commodification of wage labour, the dynamic of capital accumulation, and allocative markets (Jaeggi & Fraser, 2020). In addition, the non-economic background conditions that support the capitalist economy's functioning are of particular interest: the transfer from goods production to social reproduction, from human to non-human nature, from economy to polity, as well as racism, imperialism, and expropriation (Jaeggi & Fraser). The general logic is a permanent compulsion for capital accumulation and economic growth (Dörre, 2019; Lessenich, 2019; Marx, 1986). This builds on the expropriation and exploitation of ever-new non-capitalist milieus, including territories, forms of production, lifestyles, social relations, consumption patterns, knowledge, and the environment's resources (Dörre; Lessenich). This Imperial Mode of Living enables a "good life" for some at the cost of others, including non-human nature (Brand & Wissen, 2018).

The consequences of the capitalist Imperial Mode of Living are vast. We have crossed seven out of eight globally quantified planetary boundaries, thereby driving our planet's ecosystem toward collapse (Rockström et al., 2023). This manifests in the likes of human-induced climate change, displacing more than 20 million people (IFRC, 2020, p. 10) or a vast range of plant and animal species at threat of extinction (LMD, 2019). In economic terms, capitalist logics also lead to recurring crises. Between 1970 and 2011 alone, there were 147 banking, 211 currency, and 66 sovereign crises, including the global financial crisis in 2008 (Pineault, 2019a). The outbreak of the COVID-19 pandemic and the Russian-Ukraine War further exposed the fragility of global supply chains, leading to economic and social crises worldwide (Rume & Didar-Ul Islam, 2020; Zemelyte, 2022, July 8). Socio-economically speaking, capitalist relations have further continuously decreased average wages since the 1980s (IMF, 2017), and income inequality has risen to historical highs in most OECD countries over the past three decades (Thévenot, 2017). Under these increasing pressures, it becomes ever more evident that democratic institutions and capitalist accumulation logics contradict themselves (Jessop, 2018), and trust in political institutions and the State is faltering. In 2023, less than 50 percent of the OECD countries' population reported confidence in their national governments (OECD, 2023). Meanwhile, democratic party support is declining just the same (Berman & Snegovaya, 2019), whilst right-wing parties with their typical ideologies of radicalism, nationalism, populism, and extremism are on the rise (Golder, 2016). The capitalist "now" has become increasingly fragile, but as previously mentioned, the "new" has yet to emerge.

As the capitalist social order led to recurring crises since its inception, the notion of sustainable development eventually evolved. Its origins date back to 17th century Germany. Carl von Carlowitz called for sustainable forest management, where individuals and businesses ought to cut down only as many trees as could be restored in a single year to the benefit of both the economy and the environment (Heinrichs et al., 2016, p. 1). This notion reached its height in 1972 when the Club of Rome issued its report "Limits to Growth" (Michelsen et al., 2016, p. 19). They examined the most significant problems society faced at the time, which are still topical today, including the degradation of the environment, poverty despite growth and plenty, the loss of faith in institutions, and economic disruptions (Meadows et al., 1972). The report further demonstrated that if the present growth trends in population, industrialisation, pollution, and resource depletion continued at the same rate, humanity would reach the planet's limits to growth within the next one hundred years. Meadows et al. (1972, p. 24) thus called for an alteration of these trends by halting growth and creating "a condition of ecological and economic stability that is sustainable far into the future". Soon after, in 1987, the Brundtland Report presented today's most well-known definition of sustainable development: development that meets the needs of the present without compromising the ability of future generations to meet their own needs (Michelsen et al., 2016, p. 19).

Since these reports were issued and the normative goal of sustainable development proclaimed, the concept has been interpreted along different paradigms and criticised for this variation (Meadowcroft, 2007). Some believe that the capitalist social order can manage the paradox of environmental sustainability and continued economic growth, whilst simultaneously promoting quality of life and reducing social inequities, by incorporating natural capital principles, a cautious technology treatment, and green consumerism (Gladwin et al., 1995; Jacobs, 2013; OECD, 2012; World Bank, 2012). Others criticise capitalism for hindering liberty, equality, and solidarity through profit-seeking motives, whilst simultaneously depleting the natural environment (Baer, 2018). They conclude, that to achieve sustainable development, capitalism needs to be transformed (Daly, 1993; Jackson, 2009; Kallis et al., 2012; Pineault, 2019b; Victor, 2012) or even overcome (Baer, 2018; Foster, 2011; Gorz, 2012; Jessop, 2019; Kovel & Löwy, 2001).

Proponents of both views assume the necessity and feasibility of a steered transition or transformation toward sustainable development. This assumption leads to the structure-agency duality (Giddens, 1979) and the question of whether the institutionalised capitalist social order has greater power over agents or if power remains for agents to change it. Adopting a Critical Realist perspective, accepting the existence of independent structures influencing actors and actors shaping these structures just the same (Mukumbang, 2023), I uphold that the capitalist social order has vast influence over society but suppose that actors can work towards overcoming it. Seeing that capitalism has not always been the natural order of things (Moore, 2015), it indeed appears feasible that we may change or even overcome it.

Following the premise that agents may change capitalism, both previously mentioned approaches hold that a transition or transformation towards sustainable development will only be possible via a strong State. Indeed, States played a central role in the evolution of capitalism, e.g., by enabling private property laws and creating the capitalist class (Jaeggi & Fraser, 2020). However, the State has been torn between securing economic growth and societal wellbeing ever since (Polanyi, 2017), and it is up for debate whether it can live up to the task.

In the latest stages of the capitalist social order's evolution, there was a development from government to governance as more stakeholders got involved in the steering of society, such as large corporations and civil society organisations (Peters & Pierre, 2006). Some uphold that the State has lost power in this evolution (Adger & Jordan, 2009). Others suggest that State power has merely transformed to include different roles and functions (Adger & Jordan), such as collaborator, steward, and funder (Virtanen & Tammeaid, 2020). A third governance debate revolves around a normative view, namely governance for sustainable development (Patterson et al., 2017). Duit et al. (2016) attest to the central role of the State in this type of governance because it remains the only democratic institution that structures political, economic, and social interactions, maintains legal frameworks, is backed by coercive power, and deploys resources through expenditures and bureaucratic apparatuses. In their view, States stand at the juncture of the domestic and international political order and remain the "most powerful human mechanism for collective action that can compel obedience and redistribute resources with legitimate authority" (Duit et al., p. 4). Consequently, if the State indeed remains the central steering institution, and sustainable development involves processes of societal self-steering, much of the responsibility for realising it rests with the State and governments (Meadowcroft, 2011).

However, the State's strength and scope do not yet allow for this type of governance (Gough & Meadowcroft, 2011; Heinrichs, 2017, 2022; Heinrichs & Laws, 2014; Mazzucato, 2018; WBGU, 2011). They must both be extended for it to take on activist functions (Fukuyama, 2004) and potentially contribute to sustainable development. There is already a vast range of suggestions of what this new type of statehood can look like: a "Green State" (Meadowcroft, 2006), a "Decarbonised Welfare State" (Gough & Meadowcroft, 2011), a "Formative State" (Heinrichs, 2017), a "Sustainability State" (Heinrichs & Laws, 2014), or "Sustainable Statehood" (Heinrichs, 2022). What unites these concepts is that this type of State's most important parameter for performance evaluation may no longer be economic growth but rather navigating society into a promising future, which entails one version or another of fulfilling human needs within planetary boundaries.

Suppose sustainable statehood is a precondition for sustainable development, and politics is concerned explicitly with realising societal goals and new priorities via the State (Deutsch, 1970). In that case, much of the responsibility for creating sustainable statehood and bringing about sustainable development rests with governments and politicians (Meadowcroft, 2011). What we thus seem to require to bring about a sustainable "new" is political leadership that explicitly aims to drive sustainable development.

The missing link: Women's political leadership for sustainable development

Political leadership has only become an area of serious academic investigation since the mid-1940s (Elgie, 2015). A prominent strand of this research builds on an Interactionist foundation, concerned with leadership outcomes and why some leaders are more successful than others (Elgie). However, the phenomenon of political leadership for sustainable development has not yet been sufficiently explored in this field. Still, there are fundamental concepts on which we can build. The literature points out that the public expects political leaders to be political entrepreneurs who provide "innovation..., not reproduction... not re-presentation but a presentation of something new, a creation of something which has not existed before" (Körösényi, 2005, p. 375). In line with this notion, political innovations may play a decisive role in sustainable statehood, defined as "intentional efforts to transform political institutions designed to make authoritative political decisions (polity), the political processes that lead to such decisions (politics) and the content of the resulting policies (policy)" (Eva Sørensen, 2021, p. 2). Governance and transition literature add to this perspective, demonstrating the potentially transformative power of political leaders on local, regional, and national levels of multi-level governance networks (Fischer & Newig, 2016; Peters & Pierre, 2006).

Still, the missing link between political leadership, transition, and governance research, seems to be the conjunction of sustainable statehood, political leadership, and political innovations with a normative orientation towards sustainable development. This book contributes to the existing literature by exploring political leaders aiming to implement political innovations for sustainable development, i.e., to conceptualise the phenomenon of political leadership for sustainable development. This type of leadership appears necessary, if not vital, for bringing about a sustainable "new".

Yet another shortcoming of political leadership research is the adoption of a feminist lens. Since the 1940s, when scholars first established political leadership research as a discipline, patriarchal structures, and respective theories of "great men" dominated (Elgie, 2015), leaving little to no room for exploring women's roles in the literature and mirroring actual practice. Despite significant progress, in 2024, there were only 17 women heads of government and 19 women heads of state (UN Women, 2024). Whilst this represents progress, the representation of women in politics is still far from equal. Recent political leadership research suggests that women leaders may take on a particular role in driving sustainable development because women are perceived as more honest, less entangled in power games, and thus well set up to cater to demands for change (Campus, 2013). Political leadership expert Ludger Helms (2016) further posits that there may be a nexus between women political leaders and transformational leadership, while Michael Genovese and Janie Steckenrieder (2013) suggest that the emergence of a woman head of government may be both effect and cause of social change. Exploring how women political leaders, in particular, can succeed at implementing political innovations for sustainable development may thus be of particular interest to both research and practice.

This research recognises that women remain a political minority, oppressed along their sex, and under pressure to comply with gender expectations. It is the socially constructed gender binary that led to the discrimination of women and non-binary gender identities. At the same time, a lack of research on women executive political leaders remains. Therefore, the research recognises that anyone can possess both traditionally assigned feminine and masculine psychological characteristics but nonetheless explores *women's political leadership for sustainable development* in particular to fill the research gap.

Grasping the emergent leadership phenomenon

Adopting a Critical Realist approach, this book seeks to explore the decisive causal mechanisms that affect women's political leaders' pursuits of implementing political innovations for sustainable development (Mukumbang, 2023). Through theoretical and empirical research, the book seeks to uncover the hidden generative mechanisms and political leaders' actions that enable them to transform the currently unsustainable social order (Mukumbang).

Based on this approach, the structure-agency duality becomes central to the investigation of the phenomenon of women's political leadership for sustainable development, which we may think of as a holon: a molecule that is whole in itself but at the same time part of a cell (Volckmann, 2010). The analysis thus revolves around the cell, that is the leaders' context and the molecule of the political leader herself, to understand this multidimensional phenomenon shaped by various agency and structure variables.

First, it is imperative to understand the cell that is the leaders' context. As previously outlined, capitalism, as an institutionalised social order, appears to be the source of unsustainable development. Thus, the book approaches the phenomenon of political leadership for sustainable development by shedding light on the vertical evolution of capitalism and respective structures that need to be altered or overcome by political leaders to bring about sustainable development. In line with this understanding, it is vital to explore different paradigms and strategies for achieving it.

Next, we need to fathom the State as an institution, its role in multi-level governance networks, the degree to which it relies on the capitalist social order, the extent to which it may contribute to sustainable development, and finally, the political innovations necessary for sustainable statehood.

Only when we have grasped this context of political leadership can we dive into the specific structure-agency variables determining the outcomes of women's political leaders seeking to implement political innovations for sustainable statehood and development. Since the phenomenon has not yet been explicitly considered in research, it is imperative to extend an investigation of the literature to further disciplines focusing on transformative leadership, transitions, social change, and innovation. Finally, leadership research adopting a feminist lens is of particular relevance to the endeavour. There is still a need to expand the research perspective on women political leaders and thus the research will focus on exploring how structure and agency variables may differ for women in particular. From this basis, the phenomenon of *women's political leadership for sustainable development* and how said leaders can succeed at implementing political innovations for sustainable statehood can be conceptualised.

To make the phenomenon's conceptualisation more robust, multiple embedded case studies are empirically explored to shed light on the vast range of structure and agency variables that determine said leaders and their outcomes. The cases centre around women political leaders in executive political positions on local, regional, and national levels of democratic political systems in capitalist societies of the Global North, as they have the potential power to change respective structures. Along with the conceptualisation of the phenomenon, as an outcome, the leaders must have implemented political innovations for sustainable statehood.

On a national level, New Zealand's former Prime Minister, Jacinda Ardern, implemented a variety of political innovations since she was appointed to office in 2017. These include, amongst others, a new Wellbeing

Framework and Budget, moving the wellbeing of New Zealanders into the centre of the government's attention rather than economic growth. On a regional level, the Regional President of Occitanie in France, Carole Delga, elected to office in 2016, made her region the first in the world to follow a Green Deal based on the European Union's example. Thereby she and her regional government pursue an eco-social transition to ensure social and environmental justice. Finally, on a local level, I explore the case of Valérie Plante, mayor of Montréal, in Québec, Canada. She was elected to office in 2016 and has implemented a variety of mission-oriented strategic frameworks to drive the city's ecological and social transition towards sustainable development. Considering the cases of individual women political leaders, we must, however, be aware of their idealisation. Following the most recent studies in leadership, leadership is a collective effort shared across individuals who collectively contribute to successful political outcomes. Still, executive positions allow for significant leeway in driving the implementation of such innovations, and thus exploring their role in the process is feasible.

The book's structure

The central aim of the book is to shed light on how women political leaders drive sustainable development via political innovations and sustainable statehood. The first chapter, Chapter 1, explores how the current capitalist social order came to be, what characterises it, and what its shortcomings are to understand why sustainable development is necessary. It showcases a vertical analysis of capitalism, i.e., its historical regime developments (Jaeggi & Fraser, 2020), focusing on how capitalist foreground and background characteristics evolved, what the impacts on humans and non-human nature were, and the role States took in these processes. The review explores the following five phases: (1) Feudalism and Mercantilism, (2) the Industrial Revolution, (3) Fordism, (4) Post-Fordism, and (5) the time since the global financial crisis in 2007/2008. Finally, the general logic of capitalism and its unsustainable development are explored. This review provides an in-depth understanding of the structural barriers hampering sustainable development, which political leaders may potentially resolve.

Chapter 2 investigates what sustainable development is and how we can achieve it. The degree to which environmental wellbeing and social equality concerns are perceived varies significantly along paradigms. Therefore, the origins of the concept are explored, how paradigms determine its conception, and the strategies taken towards it. Most importantly, this section sheds light on the results these strategies may yield regarding long-term social and environmental flourishing.

Seeing that States and governments may play a key role in promoting strategies for sustainable development, Chapter 3 determines how the State may come true to these claims, exploring the current state of governance, the legitimation of the State along its reciprocal relationship with the economic, social and political spheres, and how different actors may issue demands for sustainable development towards it. The chapter further reveals the institutional requirements necessary for sustainable statehood, the State's potential pursuit of activist functions for sustainable development, and finally, the role political leadership plays in establishing sustainable statehood.

Chapter 4 explores the structures that may influence political leaders in their pursuit of establishing sustainable statehood, touching upon the parliamentary, administrative, and public arenas and the potential decisiveness of structures over agency.

Chapter 5 dives deeper into leadership styles that drive social change and transformation, as well as skills necessary to implement innovations.

Chapter 6 establishes the phenomenon of women's political leadership for sustainable development and uncovers the potential structure and agency variables that specifically enable or hinder women political leaders. As a result, a theoretical framework for analysing real-life case studies of the phenomenon is presented.

In Chapters 7–9 case studies provide insights into the phenomenon and uncover decisive variables and causal patterns.

Chapter 10 derives generalisable findings from a cross-case analysis on decisive structure and agency variables and causal patterns and contrasts the empirical with the prior theoretical findings.

Finally, the concluding chapter recapitulates all findings, reveals future potentials for further research and ends with a brief outlook of what we may make of the book's contribution.

To conclude, the book's contributions is fourfold: it (1) conceptualises the phenomenon of political leadership for sustainable development, (2) sheds light on the transformative potential of political leadership and its contribution to sustainable development, (3) reveals the structure and agency variables that are decisive and particularly enabling for women political leaders' quests, and finally, (4) highlights the transformative potential of women political leaders in particular.

References

Adger, W. N., & Jordan, A. (2009). *Governing sustainability*. Cambridge: Cambridge University Press.

Baer, H. A. (2018). *Democratic eco-socialism as a real utopia*. New York, NY: Berghahn Books.

Berman, S., & Snegovaya, M. (2019). Populism and the decline of social democracy. *Journal of Democracy*, *30*(3), 5–19. https://doi.org/10.1353/jod.2019.0038

Brand, U., & Wissen, M. (2018). What kind of great transformation? The Imperial Mode of Living as a major obstacle to sustainability politics. *GAIA – Ecological Perspectives for Science and Society*, *27*(3), 287–292. https://doi.org/10.14512/gaia.27.3.8

Campus, D. (2013). *Women political leaders and the media*. Basingstoke: Palgrave Macmillan. https://doi.org/10.1057/9781137295545

Daly, H. (1993). Steady-state economics: A new paradigm. *New Literary History*, *24*(4), 811–816. https://doi.org/10.2307/469394

Deutsch, K. W. (1970). *Staat, Regierung, Politik [State, government, politics]*. Freiburg, Germany: Rombach.

Dörre, K. (2019). Risiko Kapitalismus. Landnahme, Zangenkrise, Nachhaltigkeitsrevolution [Capitalism as a risk. Land seizure, crisis of pliers, sustainability revolution]. In Dörre, K., Rosa, H., Becker, K., Bose, S., & Seyd, B., *Große Transformation? Zur Zukunft moderner Gesellschaften [Great transformation? About the future of modern societies]* (pp. 3–34). Wiesbaden, Germany: Springer Fachmedien.

Duit, A., Feindt, P. H., & Meadowcroft, J. (2016). Greening the Leviathan: The rise of the environmental state? *Environmental Politics*, *25*(1), 1–23. https://doi.org/10.1080/09644016.2015.1085218

Elgie, R. (2015). *Studying political leadership*. Hampshire: Palgrave Macmillan.

Fischer, L.-B., & Newig, J. (2016). Importance of actors and agency in sustainability transitions: A systematic exploration of the literature. *Sustainability*, *8*(476), 1–21. https://doi.org/10.3390/su8050476

Foster, J. B. (2011). Capitalism and degrowth: An impossibility theorem. *Monthly Review*, *62*(8), 26–33. https://doi.org/10.14452/mr-062-08-2011-01_2

Fukuyama, F. (2004). *State-building: Governance and world order in the twenty-first century*. Ithaca, NY: Cornell University Press.

Genovese, M. A. & Steckenrieder, J. S. (2013). *Women as political leaders. Studies in gender and governing*. London: Routledge.

Giddens, A. (1979). *Contemporary social theory*. London: Macmillan Education.

Gladwin, T. N., Kennelly, J. J., & Krause, T.-S. (1995). Shifting paradigms for sustainable development: Implications for management theory and research. *Academy of Management Review*, *20*(4), 874–907. https://doi.org/10.5465/amr.1995.9512280024

Golder, M. (2016). Far right parties in Europe. *Annual Review of Political Science*, *19*(1), 477–497. https://doi.org/10.1146/annurev-polisci-042814-012441

Gorz, A. (2012). *Capitalism, socialism, ecology*. London: Verso.

Gough, I., & Meadowcroft, J. (2011). Decarbonizing the welfare state. In Dryzek, J. S., Norgaard, R. B., & Schlosberg, D. (Eds.), *Oxford Handbook of climate change and society*. Oxford: Oxford University Press.

Heinrichs, H. (2017). Der gestaltende Staat im Kontext gesellschaftlichen Wandels [The formative state in context of societal change]. Umweltbundesamt. https://www.umweltbundesamt.de/sites/default/files/medien/1410/publikationen/2017-11-29-texte_107-2017_gestaltender-staat_0.pdf

Heinrichs, H. (2022). Sustainable statehood: Reflections on critical (pre-)conditions and design options. *Sustainability*, *14*(15): 9461. https://doi.org/10.3390/su14159461

Heinrichs, H., & Laws, N. (2014). "Sustainability state" in the making? Institutionalization of sustainability in German federal policy making. *Sustainability*, *6*(5), 2623–2641. https://doi.org/10.3390/su6052623

Heinrichs, H., Martens, P., Michelsen, G., & Wiek, A. (2016). *Sustainability science. An introduction*. Dordrecht, Netherlands: Springer Science + Business Media.

Helms, L. (2016). Democracy and innovation: From institutions to agency and leadership. *Democratization*, *23*(3), 459–477. https://doi.org/10.1080/1351034 7.2014.981667

Hoare, Q., & Nowell-Smith, G. (1971). *Selections from the prison notebooks*. London: Lawrence & Wishart.

IFRC. (2020). *World disaster report 2020. Executive summary*. International Federation of Red cross and Red Crescent Societies. https://media.ifrc.org/ifrc/wp-content/uploads/2020/11/IFRC_wdr2020/IFRC_WDR_ExecutiveSummary_EN_Web.pdf

IMF. (2017). *IMF Annual Report 2017*. https://www.imf.org/external/pubs/ft/ar/2017/eng/pdfs/AR17-DEU.pdf

Jackson, T. (2009). *Prosperity without growth?* London: Sustainable Development Commission.

Jacobs, M. (2013). Green growth. In Falkner, R., *Handbook of climate and environmental policy* (pp. 197–214). Oxford: Wiley Blackwell.

Jaeggi, R., & Fraser, N. (2020). *Kapitalismus. Ein Gespräch über kritische Theorie* [Capitalism. A conversation about critical theory]. Berlin, Germany: suhrkamp.

Jessop, B. (2018). Elective affinity or comprehensive contradiction? Reflections on capitalism and democracy in the time of finance-dominated accumulation and austerity states. *Berliner Journal für Soziologie [Berlin Journal of Sociology]*, *28*, 9–37. https://doi.org/10.1007/s11609-018-0371-9

Jessop, B. (2019). Kapitalismus, Staat, Transformation: Neosozialismus oder demokratischer Ökosozialismus [Capitalism, state, transformation: Neosocialism or democratic ecosocialism]. In Dörre, K., & Schickert, C. (Eds.), *Neosozialismus [Neosocialism]* (pp. 97–110). München, Germany: oekom Verlag.

Kallis, G., Kerschner, C., & Martinez-Alier, J. (2012). The economics of degrowth. *Ecological Economics*, *84*, 172–180. https://doi.org/10.1016/j.ecolecon.2012.08.017

Kissinger, H. (2022). *Leadership. Six studies in world strategy*. London: Allen Lane.

Körösényi, A. (2005). Political representation in leader democracy. *Government and Opposition*, *40*(3), 358–378. https://doi.org/10.1111/j.1477-7053.2005.00155.x

Kovel, J., & Löwy, M. (2001). *An ecosocialist manifesto*. Capitalism, Nature and Socialism. https://www.cnsjournal.org/about/an-ecosocialist-manifesto/

Lessenich, S. (2019). Mitgegangen, mitgefangen. Das große Dilemma der Großen Transformation [Serves you right. The great dilemma of the great transformation]. In Brie, M. (Ed.), *Futuring: Perspektiven der Transformation im*

Kapitalismus über ihn hinaus [Futuring: Transformation perspectives within capitalism and beyond] (pp. 57–74). Münster, Germany: Westfälisches Dampfboot.

LMD. (2019). *Atlas der Globalisierung [Atlas of globalisation]*. Berlin, Germany: Le Monde Diplomatique.

Marx, K. (1986). *A reader*. Cambridge: Cambridge University Press.

Mazzucato, M. (2018). *The entrepreneurial state. Debunking public vs. private sector myths*. London: Penguin Randomhouse.

Meadowcroft, J. (2006). Greening the state. *Politics and Ethics, 2*(2), 109–118. https://doi.org/10.1177/1743453X0600200203

Meadowcroft, J. (2007). Who is in charge here? Governance for sustainable development in a complex world. *Journal of Environmental Policy & Planning, 9*(3–4), p. 299–314. https://doi.org/10.1080/15239080701631544

Meadowcroft, J. (2011). Engaging with the politics of sustainability transitions. *Environmental Innovation and Societal Transitions, 1*(1), 70–75. https://doi.org/10.1016/j.eist.2011.02.003

Meadows, D. L., Meadows, D. H., Randers, J., & Behrens III, W. W. (1972). *The limits to growth*. New York, NY: Universe Books.

Michelsen, G., Adomßent, M., Martens, P., & von Hauff, M. (2016). Sustainable development – background and context. In Heinrichs, H., Martens, P. Michelsen, G., & Wiek, A. (Eds.), *Sustainability science. An introduction* (pp. 5–30). Dordrecht, Netherlands: Springer Science + Business Media.

Moore, J. (2015). *Capitalism in the web of life*. London: Verso.

Mukumbang, F. C. (2023). Retroductive theorizing: A contribution of critical realism to mixed methods research. *Journal of Mixed Methods Research, 17*(1), 93–114. https://doi.org/10.1177/15586898211049847

OECD. (2012). *Inclusive green growth: Towards the future we want*. https://www.oecd.org/greengrowth/futurewewant.htm

OECD. (2023). *OECD survey on drivers of trust in public institutions – 2024 results*. https://www.oecd.org/governance/trust-in-government/

Ottens, M., & Edelenbos, J. (2018). Political leadership as meta-governance in sustainability transitions: A case study analysis of meta-governance in the case of the Dutch National Agreement on Climate. *Sustainability, 11*(1), 110. https://doi.org/10.3390/su11010110

Patterson, J., Schulz, K., Vervoort, J., van der Hel, S., Widerberg, O., Adler, C., Hurlbert, M., Anderton, K., Sethi, M., & Barau, A. (2017). Exploring the governance and politics of transformations towards sustainability. *Environmental Innovation and Societal Transitions, 24*, 1–16. https://doi.org/10.1016/j.eist.2016.09.001

Peters, B. G., & Pierre, J. (2006). Governance, government and the State. In Hay, C., Lister, M., & Marsh, D. (Eds.), *The state. Theories and issues* (pp. 209–222). New York, NY: Palgrave McMillan.

Pineault, É. (2019a). A moloch demanding the whole world a sacrifice. The structures of financial capital in the early 21st century. In Dörre, K., Rosa, H., Becker, K., Bose, S., & Seyd, B. (Eds.), *Große Transformation? Zur Zukunft moderner Gesellschaften [Great transformation? About the future of modern societies]* (pp. 119–147). Wiesbaden, Germany: Springer Fachmedien.

Pineault, É. (2019b). From provocation to challenge: Degrowth, capitalism and the prospect of "Socialism without growth": A commentary on Giorgios Kallis. *Capitalism Nature Socialism, 30*(2), 251–266. https://doi.org/10.1080/104557 52.2018.1457064

Polanyi, K. (2017). *The great transformation.* (13th ed.). Berlin, Germany: suhrkamp.

Rockström, J., Gupta, J., Qin, D., Lade, S. J., Abrams, J. F., Andersen, L. S., Armstrong McKay, D. I., Bai, X., Bala, G., Bunn, S. E., Ciobanu, D., DeClerck, F., Ebi, K., Gifford, L., Gordon, C., Hasan, S., Kanie, N., Lenton, T. M., Loriani, S., ... Zhang, X. (2023). Safe and just Earth system boundaries. *Nature, 619,* 102–111. https://doi.org/10.1038/s41586-023-06083-8

Rume, T., & Didar-Ul Islam, S. M. (2020). Environmental effects of COVID-19 pandemic and potential strategies of sustainability. *Helyion, 6*(9), 1–8. https://doi.org/10.1016/j.heliyon.2020.e04965

Sørensen, E. (2021). Political innovations: Innovations in political institutions, processes and outputs. In Sørensen, E. (Ed.), *Political innovations. Creative transformations in polity, politics and policy* (pp. 1–19). New York, NY: Routledge.

Thévenot, C. (2017). Inequality in OECD countries. *Scandinavian Journal of Public Health, 45*(18), 9–16. https://doi.org/10.1177/1403494817713108

UN Women. (2024). *Facts and figures: Women's leadership and political participation.* https://www.unwomen.org/en/what-we-do/leadership-and-political-participation/facts-and-figures

Victor, P. A. (2012). Growth, degrowth and climate change: A scenario analysis. *Ecological Economics, 84,* 206–212. https://doi.org/10.1016/j.ecolecon.2011.04.013

Virtanen, P., & Tammeaid, M. (2020). *Developing public sector leadership.* Cham, Switzerland: Springer Nature.

Volckmann, R. (2010). Integral leadership theory. In Couto, R.A. (Ed.), *Political and civic leadership: A reference handbook* (pp. 121–127). Thousand Oaks, CA: SAGE Publications.

WBGU. (2011). *World in transition. A social contract for sustainability.* https://www.wbgu.de/en/publications/publication/world-in-transition-a-social-contract-for-sustainability#section-downloads

World Bank. (2012). *Inclusive green growth: The pathway to sustainable development.* https://doi.org/10.1596/978-0-8213-9551-6

Zemelyte, B. (2022, July 8). *Russia-Ukraine war: 'Not all refugees are treated the same'.* Aljazeera. https://www.aljazeera.com/news/2022/7/8/russia-ukraine-amnesty-interview

PART I

The need for sustainable development

1
UNDERSTANDING THE GLOBAL NORTH'S UNSUSTAINABILITY

In the 19th century, societies of the Global North embarked on what economist Angus Deaton (2013) calls the Great Escape, leading to prosperity for many. This Escape closely links to the evolution of the capitalist social order in the 16th century (Polanyi, 2017) and its dominance ever since. Many use *capitalism* to describe the Global North's economic systems. However, this does not come true to the social constructions' multiplicity. As philosopher Friedrich Nietzsche declared, "all concepts in which an entire process is semiotically concentrated defy definition; only something which has no history can be defined" (1994, p. 53). Accordingly, political economist Wolfgang Streeck (2015) suggests that what we see today, we can only understand if we know what it looked like yesterday, and on which path it is moving.

To understand how political leaders may drive sustainable development, it is thus essential to understand the historical evolution and manifestations of capitalism, which characteristics and logics the concept entails, what is unsustainable about it, and what a possible future may look like. During the evolution of capitalism over the past 300 years, whenever one capitalist regime encountered barriers or crises, a new regime replaced it in a dialectical process (Jaeggi & Fraser, 2020). The book will thus briefly explore these regimes along the following five major phases: (1) Feudalism & Mercantilism, (2) Industrial Revolution, (3) Fordism, (4) Post-Fordism, and (5) the time since the financial crisis in 2007/2008.

In the review, (Neo-)Marxist theories of class, status, redistribution, and recognition are merged with feminist theories, cultural theory, post-colonial, and ecological thinking to give a comprehensive overview of the

DOI: 10.4324/9781003507666-3

social order's consequences. The ideologies that drove capitalist regimes' evolution, the configuration of their economic systems, and the State's role in these developments are discussed, since one of the propositions is that States may contribute to alleviating its harms and creating a sustainable future. Finally, capitalism's consequences for the web of life, where human and non-human nature stand in a dialectical relationship (Moore, 2015) are touched upon. This depth of analysis is vital to understanding which levers political leaders may use to make our social order sustainable. However, the book does not attempt to capture the full range of historical, political, economic, social, and environmental developments. Instead, it only sheds light on the complexity of respective interconnections and roughly explores the capitalist social order as a general phenomenon. This approach is valid as far as capitalist logics and the challenges they bring about are similar to a degree in all capitalist social systems across the globe (Streeck, 2015). Still, we cannot neglect multiple modernities (Sachsenmaier et al., 2002), varieties of capitalism (Amable, 2003) and different societal reactions to capitalism in each country's specific institutional and cultural constellation.

Capitalism as an institutionalised social order

Before diving into capitalism's evolution, we must understand the logics shaping it. As the following review will show, it does not just include economic practices and institutions. It is an institutionalised social order that provides for social, economic, and cultural practices and gives rise to various affiliated institutions forming the capitalist socio-cultural fabric (Jaeggi & Fraser, 2020). In their critical theory of capitalism, Rahel Jaeggi and Nancy Fraser (2020) suggest four essential foreground conditions for capitalist economic relations.

Class division between owners and producers

In capitalist societies, private individuals, i.e., capitalists, own capital, e.g., money and ground, with which they produce goods in large quantities (Fulcher, 2004). Individuals who only have their labour power to sell to capitalists make the former dependent on the latter (Fulcher). This class division required breaking down previous societal structures in which most people had access to means of subsistence and production, e.g., food, housing, clothing, tools, land, and work, without participating in labour markets (Jaeggi & Fraser, 2020). With capitalism, the majority was excluded from these means (Jaeggi & Fraser), as will be shown in more detail in the following sections.

Institutionalised marketisation and commodification of wage labour

Capitalists exchange goods on markets, which act as a referential system, signalling and controlling prices in their pure state (Fulcher, 2004). Labour markets are essential to these relations. Through them, capitalists and non-capitalists form contracts to exchange labour power for wages (Fulcher). In this relation, labourers are free in a double sense: free to work legally because they are not serfs or enslaved and, theoretically, simultaneously free to starve when they do not enter labour contracts (Jaeggi & Fraser, 2020).

Allocation of productive inputs and social surplus through the market

Capitalism is more than a market society where participants exchange goods, as such markets existed before capitalist societies (Jaeggi & Fraser, 2020). Jaeggi and Fraser respectively differentiate between the purpose of markets for distribution and allocation. Earlier market societies only had the former but not the latter. Distributive markets offer material goods for personal consumption. Allocative markets employ common social resources in collective projects, such as production, accumulation of surpluses, research and development, or infrastructure investments. The latter is characteristic of capitalism, and steers accumulated wealth and collective societal energies (Jaeggi & Fraser.).

Dynamic of capital accumulation

Capitalism thrives on infinite capital accumulation and everything capitalists do must have the goal of further accumulation (Jaeggi & Fraser, 2020). This is due to the social relation of competition (Sutterlütti & Meretz, 2018). Competition makes investing money as capital necessary to reproduce it. That is part of the structurally imposed demands of value realisation: if producers realise less utilisation and, therefore, fewer profits than their competitors, they have less capital to invest into potential competitive advantages. In the long run, these producers will lose to their competition. Accordingly, production's purpose must be producers' economic utilisation and respective profitability. At the same time, satisfying human needs becomes a means to reach this goal rather than the goal itself (Sutterlütti & Meretz). Capital's propulsion to continuous self-expansion and the competition dynamic then create the compulsive economic rationality of repeatedly producing a value add (Lessenich, 2019). This value add is realised by exploiting "Cheap Nature", i.e., by devaluing specific work and actively constructing and appropriating unpaid or cheap labour performed by humans and non-human nature outside the commodity system (Moore, 2015, pp. 53–87).

The economic system is essential to the capitalist social order and encompasses the formerly explored economic foreground characteristics (Jaeggi & Fraser, 2020). These build on four non-economic background conditions enabling the capitalist economy's functioning (Jaeggi & Fraser).

Transfer from the production of goods to social reproduction

Production through labour exploitation is essential to capitalist markets as a motor that drives accumulation (Jaeggi & Fraser, 2020). Capital expands as capitalists do not appropriately remunerate labourers' work. In turn, because capitalists can pay them less than their work is worth, these workers must obtain a substantial part of their social reproduction or livelihood from sources other than their income: self-sufficiency (e.g., gardening, sewing), informal reciprocity (e.g., reciprocal help, transaction of natural produce), and support by the State (e.g., social services, public goods). The quantitative estimate for unpaid work, still overwhelmingly delivered by women, varies between 70 and 80 percent of the world's GDP (Moore, 2015, p. 64). As such, a substantial part of goods and activities are created and occur outside of the economy and wage labour market – at home, in neighbourhoods, in civil society organisations, and public institutions such as schools (Jaeggi & Fraser). Commodified and non-commodified work interweave functionally, as they are dependent on one another and enable the capitalist markets' functioning (Jaeggi & Fraser).

Transfer from human to non-human nature

With the scientific revolution of the 17th century, the Cartesian duality started shaping the dichotomy between "nature" as the antithesis to "humanity" (Moore, 2015). The duality created a mechanical worldview where humans are separate from nature. The latter is external, and its value is valorised. Capitalism aggravated this duality, positing that humans can overexploit nature because it produces free raw materials and represents a sink for waste. Capitalists do not pay any or the total price for nature's reproduction costs. Thus, capitalists profit from nature's added value and the value they retrieve from the exploitation of wage labour. Nature in the form of resources and its ability to sustain and renew itself thus forms a critical background condition for production and capital accumulation (Moore).

Transfer from economy to polity

State power is another capitalist background condition (Jaeggi & Fraser, 2020). The social order relies on the State to establish and enforce its constitutive norms. It requires a legal framework that supports private businesses and exchange processes on markets, e.g., by guaranteeing property rights and contracts. Only through the State can capitalists pursue their economic interests free from political assaults or patronages. Thereby it also shifts its externalisations costs, e.g., social benefits, onto the State (Jaeggi & Fraser), as we will explore more in-depth in the following review.

Racism, imperialism, and expropriation

From its inception, capitalism strongly relied on the social practices of exploitation and expropriation (Jaeggi & Fraser, 2020). Exploitation forms the basis for capital accumulation, as capitalists do not remunerate labourers appropriately. Expropriation thereby allows for exploitation and represents a form of accumulation. In capitalist societies, the likes of labour, land, animals, tools, mineral reserves, energy, children, and the sexual and reproductive capacities of adults have been regularly expropriated and are thus indispensable for accumulating capital. Without expropriation, there is no capital accumulation, and without expropriation, there can be no exploitation (Jaeggi & Fraser).

Capitalism further creates a status hierarchy (Jaeggi & Fraser, 2020). On the one hand stand exploited citizens who can dispose of their labour power, whose reproductive costs capitalists remunerate and who are protected by the State. On the other hand, stand unfree, dependent subjects with no political protection, such as enslaved or colonised subjects, Indigenous people, indebted day labourers or convicted offenders who can be expropriated and exploited without remuneration. From the beginning, this status difference went hand in hand with the distinction of race. Racialised members of society predominantly did not have political protection and, by nature, were deemed exploitable. This difference was politically constituted because States provided or refused their protection and controlled racialised categories and status hierarchies by differentiating between citizens, foreigners, and subjects. Via these mechanisms, States provide an indispensable background condition for capital accumulation (Jaeggi & Fraser).

Capitalist regimes differ in how these economic foreground and non-economic background conditions delineate and interrelate (Jaeggi & Fraser, 2020). In the following exploration, these relations are recapitulated because, as we will see, every capitalist regime developed from the crisis of these conditions in a previous regime and sought to overcome them. But every regime led to a new crisis it could not solve, and thus one by one, they dialectically superceded each other in the course of history (Jaeggi & Fraser).

The unsustainability of Capitalist regimes: From Mercantile to Financial Capitalism

Mercantile Capitalism

During Feudalism, the social order was not yet capitalist, but we will briefly touch upon this era to show that capitalism has not always been the order of things. In this period, States did not yet exist but rather patronage relations between feudal lords, vassals, knights, servant farmers, and kings bound by informal contracts (Benz, 2008). The economic system's success primarily built on exploiting humans and non-human nature through agricultural practices (Moore, 2015) and artisans who worked in shops under the authority of municipalities (Polanyi, 2017). There were no labour markets (Jaeggi & Fraser, 2020), municipalities severely restricted imports, and guilds eliminated competition and limited production so it would not outstrip demand (Polanyi). The economic system focused on the trade of goods for other goods to satisfy basic human needs (Fulcher, 2004). In Marxist terms, this relation equaled "C-C", the trade of one commodity (C) for another (C) (Fulcher).

During the Mercantile era, merchants started pursuing foreign trade activities, and the first merchant capitalist class rose (Polanyi, 2017). They traded exotic goods and specialty products from afar. Capitalist economic relations then meant investing in excursions to obtain foreign goods and selling them for a profit (Polanyi) or "M-C-M": Money (M) was invested into commodities (C) for the sake of profit and, therefore, more money (M) (Marx, 1986). In this case, profit resulted from scarcity and the difference between the price paid for a good and the price it fetched at the market (Fulcher, 2004).

Still, farmers and their work comprised the economic system's most significant share which depended on humans' and animals' muscle power (Polanyi, 2017). The regime was "somatic" because the only possibility of increasing existing energy, productive forces, and value at the time was through conquests, the annexation of land, and the confiscation of additional labourers in the Old and New World (Jaeggi & Fraser, 2020). Conquests, raids, and hunting of coloured and Indigenous inhabitants in the entire periphery of Asia, Africa, and the New World formed the regime's basis. At the same time, it depleted the environment's resources without renewing what it was using up. From the beginning, capitalism built on expropriation to create profits (Jaeggi & Fraser).

During this era, wars required more significant financing, resources, and centralised management, whilst increasing trade made unified legislation, monetary systems, and country-wide taxes necessary (Benz, 2008). Respectively, the Absolutist State and parliamentary governmental systems evolved. In the case of Absolutism, the State became the sole holder of power over society and a central authority for managing economic processes associated with a territory (Benz). Whilst municipalities were trying to protect their local markets from foreign merchants, Absolutist States started to push the mercantile system onto them (Polanyi, 2017). They consequently destroyed local and inter-municipal trade and paved the way for a national domestic market that soon became dominant. With every measure States took to free the market of particularistic restrictions, customs barriers and prohibitions, it exposed existing trade relations to unregulated competition and merchants interested in skimming the markets rather than stabilising them. Thus simultaneously, States started intervening in the economic system to hinder monopolies and regulate competition (Polanyi).

Industrial Capitalism

Eventually, liberal and revolutionary thinking evolved among the new bourgeoisie, which had formed from new trade relations and corresponding profits (Jaeggi & Fraser, 2020). Their concentration and intellectual exchange in new city centres led to revolutions that helped bring about the new Industrial Capitalist regime (Jaeggi & Fraser).

The State and economic system

The State took on a vital role in the evolution of the Industrial Capitalist regime. With the invention of steam engines, a new, more complex economic system evolved, requiring factories, significant investments, and the availability of a broad range of production factors (Polanyi, 2017). Capitalists could only guarantee the availability of production factors if they were purchasable. Following this logic, States consequently turned labour, ground, and money into traded commodities in the market economy (Polanyi). They also created the capitalist classes' private property (Jaeggi & Fraser, 2020) by rejecting property and customary laws to commodify grounds (Polanyi). Enclosure Acts violently evicted peasants from their lands, creating the proletariat and powerful landowners. In addition, States lifted the traditional Law on Settlements, so people were now free to settle anywhere. Former farmers and artisans had to move towards new industrial centres to find work and sell their labour power because jobs in industrial production came to be their only alternative (Polanyi). This marked the beginning of labour markets, as a group of people could not dispose of anything but their labour power to earn a living (Berger, 2019).

In the 19th century, as business volumes increased, the State further created fiduciary currencies to coexist with metallic currencies (Polanyi, 2017). A lack of money would have otherwise led to decreased business activities and an economic downturn. States accepted metallic currencies as a means of payment for taxes and other purposes, and the new currency became a means of payment with purchasing power in its own right. The leading industrial nations eventually set the "gold standard" as an internationally standardised currency system to expand and facilitate international trade. International currency thereby regulated markets and marked the complete commodification of money (Polanyi).

This new regime built on the economic dogma of Liberalism, which followed economist Adam Smith's theories of the homo oeconomicus and the invisible hand of the market (Polanyi, 2017). The former states that humans are naturally inclined to barter, trade and maximise gains and individual self-interest (Polanyi). Thomas Hobbes (2017) laid the basis for the theory and concluded that individuals must expect competition from every other individual because everyone has equal opportunities to take what they want. The solution to this conflict of interest is to attack and discriminate against others before one becomes a victim himself (Hobbes). Following this logic, the market became the ultimate measure of all things, and everyone had to partake in competition (Demirović, 2008).

In line with this ideology, the civilisation of the 19th century became economical in that the primary motivation and justification of all actions became the pursuit of profits rather than livelihood itself (Polanyi, 2017). Max Weber (2018, p. 23) called this the new "capitalist spirit". This spirit meant that capitalism became an ethical maxim for the conduct of life that entailed the acquisition of money as an end to itself. The trade relations "M-C-M", i.e., investing money into commodities to gain more money, became the economy's driving force (Polanyi). If individuals used market activities for ends other than profit maximisation, the system would falter, and the community would run into hard times (Jacobsen, 1991). Market participants, therefore, were responsible for bystanders' wellbeing through the pursuit of profit maximisation (Jacobsen). Personal freedom and individual profit-seeking were interconnected and assigned a positive connotation from the outset (Biebricher, 2012). Furthermore, Liberalism built on the belief that free markets and an unlimited amount of material goods created by the current economic system could solve all of humanity's problems (Polanyi). Respectively nothing had to hinder the formation of markets. Governments should not regulate demand and supply, adjust prices, or allow income generation from anything other than sales (Polanyi).

The evolution of Industrial Capitalism shows that national markets and the capitalist social order did not evolve due to capitalist emancipation from State control (Polanyi, 2017). On the contrary, it resulted from an active and sometimes violent intervention on the State's behalf to guarantee the ownership of production means and economic development (Jaeggi & Fraser, 2020). State and local government regulations, e.g., land enclosures, the definition of private property, and access of capitalist merchants to local markets, accelerated Industrial Capitalism's evolution (Jaeggi & Fraser).

With the Industrial Revolution, the development of economies now fully depended on capitalists (Benz, 2008). Their influence stood in contrast to citizens' subordinated political position. Thus, eventually, Absolutist rulers had to acknowledge the conception of citizens as free individuals with natural rights to equality, self-determination, and property. Finally, "governments" and "citizens" replaced the Absolutist State. As fragmented State systems were increasingly disadvantageous to the economy's modernisation, and there was a need to unite enlightened citizens with varying and often contrasting ideologies, the Nation-State simultaneously developed. The concept of the "nation" then encompassed a socio-culturally and politically justified community of people (Benz).

The consequences of Industrial Capitalism

New constitutions and legislation offered new freedom to most, and the new economic system provided many with wealth and life necessities (Deaton, 2013), but it also had its downsides. In this era, States laid the foundation for social classes by turning the rural population into "free" labourers to be exploited in wage labour relations (Jaeggi & Fraser, 2020). They could not dispose of anything but their labour power to earn a living and did not, or only rarely, had the chance to become capitalists themselves (Berger, 2019). Thus, the new economic system was socially unequal from the outset, as agents with differently equipped resources met (Bourdieu, 2002). Those who ruled over a substantial share of capital had power over the field (Bourdieu).

Recently urbanised and proletarianized citizens, including women and children, were forced to pursue poorly paid and dangerous jobs in factories and mines (Jaeggi & Fraser, 2020). Workers and their families lived in overcrowded parishes with high water and air pollution, leading to cholera epidemics, typhoid, and other respiratory and intestinal diseases (Hobsbawm, 1969). According to historians, the spread of factories and society's dependence on them turned inhabitants into nomads without self-respect (Polanyi,

2017). The market's competitive principles destroyed their social life, neighbourhood relations, communities (Polanyi), and relations between humans and non-human nature (Moore, 2015).

States followed a "laissez-faire" approach, leaving regulation to the markets, treating labourers as goods, the market determining their price and competition their chances, with no wage determination, no support for the unemployed, and no means of subsistence (Polanyi, 2017). Part of this approach was the belief in "trickle-down effects", which assumed that a general abundance would eventually trickle down to the masses. However, this did not happen. The redistribution of wealth brought about by the new social order instead caused an increase in poverty, directly correlating with the expansion of world trade (Polanyi).

The new social order divided social reproduction from economic production, constituting them as different spheres (Jaeggi & Fraser, 2020). One was spatially placed at home, gendered, because it related to women, and the other in factories, related to men. The latter was considered productive and thus renumerated, and the former was not. Thereby capitalist relations disguised and devalued women's labour and structurally subordinated those enrolled in reproductive social work to those who earned wages, even though socially reproductive tasks were vital for wage labourers' existence. Through this division, the Liberal regime created a substantial gender difference and a new ideal of social reproduction as women's main field of activity (Jaeggi & Fraser). In addition, women were further disadvantaged because the new Liberal State exempted them from legal rights (Benz, 2008).

Industrial Capitalism introduced a new socio-ecological accumulation regime by commodifying nature and introducing fossil energy (Jaeggi & Fraser, 2020). The invention of the coal-fired steam engine led the way to the first exosomatic regime, which turned coal into mechanical energy (McNeill, 2000). The extended use of coal had extreme effects on the web of life. For example, around 1870, the United Kingdom used around 100.000 coal-fired steam engines (McNeill, p. 72). These produced extensive amounts of smoke and sulphur dioxide, which polluted the surrounding air and water, making the middle of England known as the "black land". In addition, copper smelting caused acid rain, destroying the surrounding vegetation (McNeill). Aside from that, workers in the industrial centres required vast amounts of food. Thus, farmers and agricultural businesses started following unsustainable, profit-focused agricultural practices without paying attention to the dire consequences for the ecological system (Jaeggi & Fraser, 2020).

Expropriation and eco-imperialism were constant characteristics of regime (Jaeggi & Fraser, 2020). The new industrial centres required vast amounts of cotton for textile factories and cheap sugar, tobacco, coffee, and tea to stimulate workers. Capitalists sought to expropriate racialised enslaved people and natural resources to obtain inexpensive or free production inputs and keep costs to a minimum. Respectively, they increased the conquest of peripheric societies in the Global South and strengthened their colonial domination. At the same time, the continued expropriation at the periphery interlinked with profitable exploitation in the central territories. Nations, such as the United States, expanded their inner colonies through racialised slavery and, after the State abolished it, indebted day labourers (Jaeggi & Fraser).

When States eventually granted White male workers rights, they further racialised the notions of dependency and freedom (Jaeggi & Fraser, 2020). Free White exploitable citizen-workers stood in contrast to subordinated Black and Indigenous subjects. These mechanisms systematically interweaved because industrial labourers' exploitation in the cities would not have been profitable without expropriating populations and land at the periphery (Jaeggi & Fraser).

In this regime, capitalists thus expropriated land, animals, and people, subordinating humans and extra-human nature to market laws (Jaeggi & Fraser).

By the end of the 1920s, after the First World War, the prestige of economic Liberalism had reached its peak (Polanyi, 2017). The Great Depression of 1929 struck millions of people with inflation and expropriated entire classes and nations. The United Kingdom and the United States left the gold standard to regain control over their currencies and return to Protectionist politics. This development significantly influenced the worldwide economy and led to national currency declines. Countries such as Germany, France, Belgium, and Austria could no longer participate in foreign trade, their import industries declined, employment broke down, and so did their domestic economies (Polanyi). This transition, along with that from an agricultural to an industrial society, brought about a cultural crisis that led to a state of anomy (Reckwitz, 2019). This anomy turned into violent polarisation in vast parts of Europe in the 1930s (Reckwitz) and tied to a democratic crisis: liberal democracies fell into a defensive state, and Fascists gained power, leading to World War II (Polanyi, 2017). Eventually, a new regime emerged from these developments.

Social Capitalism

The State and economic system

The time post-World War II was defined by war debts, reparations, drastic inflation rates, and mass unemployment (Ptak, 2017). As a result of class struggles and alliances of trade unions and labour parties, a social-corporatist paradigm evolved, aiming at creating a new social order, restoring social welfare, and overcoming the societal disintegration caused by the wars (Reckwitz, 2019). State-led democracies aimed to create a fully developed industrial society characterised by homogeneity with an active State that sought to tame the capitalist economic system and its inherent crises and distribute wealth equally within a "society of equals" (Reckwitz, p. 255). The result was an actively politically promoted middle-class society that disrespected cultural differences, individualities, and deviant behaviour from its ideal patriarchal hierarchy and small family model (Reckwitz).

The regulatory paradigm further strove to correct market results (Polanyi, 2017). John Maynard Keynes' "General Theory" stated that endogenous factors and, therefore, the market itself was responsible for crises in the economic system during the 1920s. He suggested capitalism, unregulated by systematic economic policy interventions, led to stagnation and decreased economic growth. During the depression, people started saving, and spending less on goods and services, thus reducing economic growth and overall welfare (Polanyi). Appropriate fiscal and monetary policies could solve this crisis: taxation during good times and spending during recessions (Biebricher, 2012). Most countries of the West consequently started regulating their economies. They developed social Welfare States (Biebricher) via solid democratic institutions and economic policies that redistributed wealth from the top down (Streeck, 2015) to unite private with social property and ensure economic development with social rights (Lessenich, 2019).

As the State took on greater responsibilities, crises in the new economic system became the State's problem because it had legally agreed to guarantee its citizens social benefits (Andersen, 2012). Economic crises thus represented political crises that endangered States' abilities to act as welfare providers. Respectively, they developed instruments to steer economic development (Andersen). The economy built on a macroeconomic accumulation regime based on mass production and consumption (Jessop, 2005). Industrial production became "Fordist" along Henry Ford's factory designs, allowing for standardised mass production. It also involved the technical division of labour along Taylorist production to secure economies of scale. Each firm then typically controlled all states of accumulation, from producing raw materials to marketing (Jessop).

The Welfare State was a "Fordist State" which had to sustain Fordism as an accumulation regime and social mode of economic regulation (Jessop, 1991). On the one hand, it secured full employment in relatively closed national economies (Jessop, 2005). It also generalised mass norms to reinforce effective domestic demand favourable to the Fordist development model (Jessop, 2005). Furthermore, the State implemented scientific and technological policies to ensure future economic growth and took on the responsibility of overcoming the risks of modern technologies (Benz, 2008).

At the same time, the State became responsible for securing livelihoods, protecting citizens from the risks and consequences of Industrialisation, and providing public goods not produced by private businesses (Andersen, 2012). Consequently, during the post-war period and before the 1970s, the balance of power between classes became as balanced as ever during capitalism (Jessop, 2005). States raised taxes significantly to finance these efforts, and tax extraction reached between one-third and one-half of economies' GDP after World War II (Andersen, p. 4). This was a process of increased inclusion of all members of society into the State's sphere, thereby expanding State tasks and civil rights (Benz, 2008). The latter included the entitlement to work, a home, education, and care in case of sickness or inability to work (Benz).

By taking on these control functions, the relationship between the State, economy, and citizens changed fundamentally, and the State actively shaped society (Benz, 2008).

Consequences of Social Capitalism

The new predominant understanding of wellbeing and a good life explicitly focused on mass consumption, individual success, the ideal of a family income, and conformity (Jaeggi & Fraser, 2020). Most of the population now depended on wages to satisfy their needs and with the rise of new middle classes, many were lifted out of poverty by the Fordist economic model's success (Jessop, 2005). These developments significantly affected consumption patterns, as the desire for the automobile and industrialised food, the use of plastics, and spatial structures that privileged the separation of the workplace, living, and leisure, spread (Brand & Wissen, 2018).

During Fordism, the notion of social reproduction and gender changed once more (Jaeggi & Fraser, 2020). Whereas Industrial Capitalism separated the spheres of production and social reproduction, working-class women strongly supported the new ideal and democratic norm of family incomes. It meant paying men enough to care for their families whilst women stayed home to become full-time housewives. These developments, along with others, such as men having the right to quit jobs for their wives, institutionalised women's dependency on their husbands (Jaeggi & Fraser).

During Fordism, the division between expropriation and exploitation became less clear (Jaeggi & Fraser, 2020). One example is segmented labour markets in the United States. At some point, machines replaced African Americans working in agriculture, and many moved to cities in the North to find work. However, once there, they were used for menial tasks and paid much less than White citizens. During this time, expropriation overshadowed exploitation because capital did not pay the total costs for these labourers' social reproduction. Simultaneously, the State denied African Americans political protection, social insurance, voting rights, and full citizenship, making them subject to further racial segregation (Jaeggi & Fraser).

Whilst Industrial Capitalism had built on the looting of the Global South, the era after World War II led to a wave of liberation struggles and decolonisation (Jaeggi & Fraser, 2020). Still, Western Imperialism in these regions did not end. As some colonies reached political independence, foreign governments and multinational corporations started exploiting citizens under precarious working conditions. Therefore, countries of the Global North continued to channel value and profits from the former colonies to their nations. In addition, post-colonial States started using their limited resources to drive Industrialisation and catch up with the world economy, often expropriating their citizens, especially Indigenous inhabitants. Thus, just like Industrial Capitalism, the success of Social Capitalism was built on expropriation and exploitation (Jaeggi & Fraser).

The Fordist model built on the ever-increasing use of non-renewable energy and resources (Brand & Wissen, 2018). Oil became the key driver of the new regime and exponentially increased carbon emissions with dire environmental consequences (Jaeggi & Fraser, 2020). At the same time, humanity started reengineering entire landscapes (McNeill, 2000). For one, governments started realising gigantic water projects because channelling water meant power and wealth, e.g., for increasing agricultural needs. Thereby the earth's water system and its surroundings were often entirely reshaped. Half of all deforestation also occurred in the 20th century (McNeill, p. 246), and heavy metals and substances such as plastic particles have been detectable in nature since this time (McNeill, p. 154). Finally, cars became catalysts for the dissection of landscapes for highways and vast amounts of carbon dioxide (Jaeggi & Fraser).

In the 1970s, a range of economic crises started with the collapse of oil prices, shaking the trust in government regulation of the economy (Reckwitz, 2019). The Fordist model had reached saturation, and tendencies towards deindustrialisation and post-industrialisation were increasing. Besides, the globalising economy demanded more flexibility, especially after the 1980s. With slowing economic growth, the expansion of the Welfare State also reached its limits. The rise of the knowledge economy and simple services eroded the socio-cultural basis of this industrial society, and the working class became increasingly disenchanted with politics. After 30 years of immense growth and societal welfare, capitalist societies faced high unemployment, stagflation, and tremendous State debts (Reckwitz).

Eventually, vast parts of society no longer desired a regulated system requiring equality, conformism, and uniformity (Reckwitz, 2019). This led to a cultural legitimation crisis that started with the anti-authoritarian student protests of the 1960s. Due to this shift in values and socio-cultural transition, the new highly qualified Fordist middle class now pushed for individual self-realisation (Reckwitz). Women from the middle classes also started perceiving family income and their household roles as outdated (Jaeggi & Fraser, 2020). Capital fractions started rebelling against corporate and capital gains taxes that financed the Welfare State. The "youth" became a new political subject as universities drastically expanded and strong environmental movements started developing, focusing on wildlife, air pollution, and the disposal of toxic wastes. African Americans and other racially discriminated groups also stood up for their rights. Eventually, movements fighting racism, imperialism, sexism, consumerism, and paternalism joined in their strive for emancipation (Jaeggi & Fraser). A new societal vision that was no longer homogenous and egalitarian but rather diverse and multicultural became the new imperative and brought about the transition to a new regime (Reckwitz).

Financial Capitalism

The State and economic system

The Financial Capitalist era marks the domination of Neoliberalism and the end of the Fordist Welfare State, which was aching under the burden of welfare services, slowed productivity, rigidities, and dysfunctions (Jessop, 1994). By the 1980s, State sectors in most Western European countries and the United States consumed nearly 50 percent of the gross domestic product (Fukuyama, 2004, p. 3). Neoliberals counteracted this development by dramatically scaling back the State and turning it into a "Growth State" (Lessenich, 2019), "Competition State" (Genschel & Seelkopf, 2014), "Schumpeterian Workfare State" (Jessop, 2005) or "post-Fordist State" (Jessop, 1991).

The neoliberal agenda included the consolidation of State budgets, stable monetary policy, the opening of markets to foreign direct investments, the liberalisation of financial markets and foreign trade, the protection of property rights, the deregulation of the economy, and the privatisation of State property (Biebricher, 2012). Nations either adopted this agenda because they were in a crisis and needed support from the International

Monetary Fund and World Bank who tied their rescue packages to this program, or they democratically instated them (Biebricher). Thereby Neoliberals supported Liberal assumptions about the functioning of market mechanisms and the "homo oeconomicus" theory previously discussed (Ptak, 2017). They suggested that politics should focus on deregulation reforms to strengthen the markets (Biebricher).

Respectively, they held that if instabilities or crisis tendencies showed in the economic system, it was only because political institutions broke the free market rules via interventions (Ptak, 2017). In addition, "rational choice theory" posited that humans and their social connections represent acts of exchange and could be entirely economised (Ptak). This led to the privatisation of formerly State-run businesses and social services to create high-performance competitive societies and represented a switch from social justice to the justice of chance and orientation towards individual gain and self-interest (Demirović, 2008).

Thereby Neoliberals propagated their agenda as a welfare philosophy from the outset, suggesting that capitalists' profits would trickle down to provide welfare gains for the masses (Demirović, 2008). The State was to favour freedom and prohibit wealth redistribution (Biebricher, 2012) since actors' knowledge, discipline and efforts, sheer luck, and coincidence determined who gained from the market (Altvater, 2008). Finally, democracy was perceived as a potential economic threat and only acceptable if it remained restricted and acted as a market-type institution (Ptak, 2017). This position manifested in the development from government to governance, which refrained from top-down State intervention and favoured the inclusion of private businesses' in the steering process (Ptak).

The new post-Fordist economic system (Jessop, 1994) built on flexible production, growing productivity, expanding demand for differentiated goods and services, increasing profits based on the full utilisation of flexible capacities, reinvestments in more flexible production equipment, techniques, and products, and boosting economies of scope (Jessop, 1994). The production process was based on micro-electronics, information and communication technologies, and flexible machines, systems and labour (Jessop, 2005). Competition revolved around non-price factors, such as improved quality and performance for individual products and customer responsiveness via customisation. As a social mode of economic regulation, post-Fordism involved supply-side innovations and flexibility through, e.g., a shift to enterprise- or plant-level collective bargaining, rising incomes for polyvalent skilled workers, and poorly paid peripheral workers recruited from politically marginalised social groups such as ethnic minorities, rural-urban migrants and illegal immigrants (Jessop, 2005).

The post-Fordist State promoted these developments via creatively destructive interventions to push product, process, organisational, and market innovations in open economies (Jessop, 1991). A key aim was to strengthen the structural competitiveness of national economies in light of globalising markets by intervening on the supply-side and subordinating social policy to the needs of labour market flexibility and international competition. In turn, domestic full-employment, contrary to the Fordist Welfare State, was deprioritised in favour of global competitiveness from newly industrialised countries such as China. States played a crucial role in technological intelligence, promoting innovative capacities, and ongoing research and development activities. Almost all States of the Global North became involved in managing internationalisation by creating appropriate frameworks for their economies. That led to the paradox of them losing control over their national economies whilst giving rise to large multinationals who further reduced States' political power within national borders (Jessop, 1991). The post-Fordist State then no longer represented a national State because it pushed for internationalisation rather than insulating its national economy (Jessop, 2005). It was also no longer a State of national sovereignty because international economic organisations, such as the EU, WTO, and IMF, reduced its scope for Protectionism and constantly exposed it to the need to compete for international capital via market-friendly policies (Jessop, 2005).

The new economic flexibility allowed for enhanced specialisation by small firms and producer networks and gave rise to new financial markets (Deutschmann, 2008). In traditional Industrial Capitalism and the early stages of Financial Capitalism, capital was appropriated mainly ex-post, i.e., through capital investment in means of production and labour and the consequent sale of produced goods on markets (Deutschmann). This dynamic changed with the disintegration of capital controls and the liberalisation of investment flows (Ptak, 2017). Private bank credits started circulating internationally, and more flexible forms of credits and a broadening range of financial instruments dominated markets (Jessop, 2005). The market's credit function shifted to an investment function with the free trade of stocks, bonds, securities, and foreign currencies (Deutschmann). The time-consuming route through labour processes and production thus no longer had to be awaited. Through capital market liberalisation, stock exchange speculators could now evaluate investments ex-ante and use valuation differences for profit. That resulted in a disembedding of product and capital markets. Investors could invest in a company without the intention of gaining profits from its operations but purely from reselling its shares after a predicted increase in share prices. Valuation differences could also be rated and turned into new products such as derivatives (Deutschmann). Financial

Capitalism thus represented a shift in how wealth was created (Pineault, 2019). In a Marxist tradition, this meant a switch to "M-M", or "interest-bearing capital", which ties itself to the productive accumulation process of industrial capital expressed in "M-C-M". In Marxist terms, capital as "M-M" is alienated and rendered independent of its inner substance in a complete objectification and derangement (Pineault).

With the priority of financial markets over all other markets, politics started orienting itself along the interests of large banks and investment companies (Klein, 2013). Locations and States with the best possible basis for business and investments started competing by offering low taxes, low labour costs, subventions, and inadequate environmental regulations (Altvater, 2008). That created a "race to the bottom", resulting in investment, hedge, pension, and private equity funds accumulating significant monetary, economic, and political power. These institutions could now pressure governments for better market conditions (Altvater). Hence, national States started to act as guardians of business locations rather than constitutions, as they turned into "Growth States" that subordinated social interests and values to the logic of growth (Lessenich, 2019, p. 59). At the same time, due to intense competition, high expectations for investment returns put pressure on institutional investors themselves (Dörre, 2019). That resulted in an endless search for ever-new investment possibilities and excessive growth of financial assets (Dörre).

To conclude, Financial Capitalism entails the institutional and socio-cultural embedding of the financial sector and its speculative dynamic (Dörre, 2019). Since the 1970s, vast spheres of the lifeworld were privatised and thus made subject to financial markets, including care facilities, hospitals, and vital products such as food and pharmaceuticals (Pineault, 2019). With increasing power, financial markets subordinated essential industries and nature to speculation and the maximisation of shareholder value. Economist Éric Pineault (p. 119) describes this as the "financialisation of everyday life" and it profoundly changed capitalist economies and societies and mediates almost all economic processes today. Of course, the degree to which financialisation has done so varies across countries (Pineault).

Consequences of Financial Capitalism

Like its predecessors, the Financial Capitalist regime eventually ran into a multidimensional crisis: a socio-economic and sociocultural crisis that also turned into one of democracy (Reckwitz, 2019) and the planet (Rockström et al., 2009).

Financial Capitalism redefined social reproduction by making it impossible for families to finance themselves on a single income (Jaeggi & Fraser,

2020). Instead, it introduced a new ideal of double-income earner families. Considering social welfare cutbacks, almost everyone in the low-income and middle classes now had to work and use their time once dedicated to social reproduction for productive paid labour (Jaeggi & Fraser).

In the same light, Neoliberalism further institutionalised gender-based discrimination (Jaeggi & Fraser, 2020). It particularly disadvantaged women who are most often employed in poorly paid service sectors and must still fend for themselves and their families, overseeing most care work. Overwhelmed but well-off workers in the Global North also typically pass social reproduction, care and support work on to those from impoverished regions who are most often female immigrants. The regime thus further concealed the number of unpaid labour hours and shifted burdens from the Global North to the Global South and ex-Communist countries (Jaeggi & Fraser).

Whilst State-managed Social Capitalism had lifted many out of poverty and created a broad middle class, Financial Capitalism started disintegrating it again around the 1990s (Reckwitz, 2019). Post-Fordism and consequent post-industrialisation led to a structural shift of wage labour from industry to services. In countries like the United States, 50 percent of labourers had worked in industrial sectors in 1960, but only 26 percent in 2015 (Reckwitz, p. 78). This development is similar in all capitalist countries of the Global North that outsourced large parts of their industrial sectors to the Global South. On the one hand, this led to a significant increase in demand for highly qualified labour in the knowledge economies, e.g., for research and development or business services such as consulting, marketing, media services, and the digital economy. On the other hand, the new economic configuration required a significant expansion of simple services that do not require high formal qualifications, such as security, gastronomy, logistics, and maintenance services. This caused a new social divide between the professional class with its "lovely jobs" and those in the service class with "lousy jobs" (Reckwitz, p. 80).

The new upper middle class is central to the past decades' societal development (Reckwitz, 2019). They depend on employment but have average or above-average economic capital, concentrate in urban spaces, have high mobility, and prioritise a life of postmaterialism and self-realisation that goes hand in hand with emotional competence, tolerance, diversity, emancipation, and ecological awareness. The old middle class partially remains in place. However, their incomes stagnated, society no longer privileges their values, and they lost prestige. They live in smaller cities and rural areas with low individual mobility and focus on values of order, discipline, social embeddedness, and a traditional, gender-segregated work and family ethos. They are politically conservative and often sceptical of globalisation. Because they cannot rise in terms of material status, they feel culturally devalued by the new middle class. They are one of the essential supporters of right-wing populism, with its critique of elites, large cities, and globalisation (Reckwitz).

In the historical core states, poorly paid, precarious service jobs replaced trade union-organised industrial work, while social welfare services simultaneously decreased (Jaeggi & Fraser, 2020). The new precarious class did not exist before the post-Fordist era (Reckwitz, 2019). Their incomes are close to the poverty line, and some move outside the labour market and depend on social services, living in structurally weak, deindustrialised, rural regions. The service proletariat typically lives in metropolitan areas with its expanding service sector (Reckwitz). Racial minorities and immigrants are often exploited in these new jobs, where they are paid less than they need to get by and typically depend on debts to manage everyday life, under the constant threat of being expropriated (Jaeggi & Fraser). Simultaneously, the financial sector thrives on this relationship by offering various loans (Jaeggi & Fraser). Social systems do not protect them well, and they have low cultural capital, no status, and no safety net (Reckwitz). This class is both socially declassified and culturally devalued, feels socially outpaced, and has a feeling of negative self-worth (Reckwitz). Neoliberal social reforms threaten them with poverty whilst social protection was changed to principles of neediness, leading to social degradation and systemic misanthropy (Ther, 2019). That, in turn, again aggravated protest votes for right-wing parties, and many have become disenchanted with politics and hold the State accountable (Ther).

Finally, the upper class lives off their financial capital, which they significantly increased since the 1980s (Reckwitz, 2019). These developments in social classes have led to an ever-greater polarisation that has often become detrimental to the value of solidarity and causes substantial political unrest (Reckwitz).

A large share of industrial exploitation now also occurs outside the historical core States in the BRICS States and periphery (Jaeggi & Fraser, 2020). In these areas, expropriation overtakes exploitation as the critical driver for profits and capital accumulation because it universalises it, especially in free export zones where businesses pay workers less than they need for social reproduction. At the same time, global financial institutions such as the IMF imposed austerity measures on indebted post-colonial States, which also represents accumulation by expropriation, as often, large corporations confiscate Indigenous populations' and farmers' lands (Jaeggi & Fraser).

Instead of a gap between expropriated and exploited, we now have a continuum: on the one hand, stand growing masses of unprotected subjects that governments and corporations can expropriate, and on the other, thinning-out numbers of protected exploited citizen-workers (Jaeggi & Fraser, 2020). And in the middle, we find a new hybrid form of citizen-workers that can be both exploited and expropriated. This hybridity is becoming the norm and highly racialised because people of colour are still disproportionately represented at the expropriation end. Across the globe, they are still likelier to be poor, unemployed, homeless, hungry, sick, imprisoned, enslaved for sex, accepted as collateral damage, or turned into war refugees (Jaeggi & Fraser).

Regarding eco-imperialism, the Global North's post-materialism also substantially influences the Global South's environment (Jaeggi & Fraser, 2020). The North's ability to specialise in IT, services, and finance builds on the Global South's materialism, e.g., mining, agriculture, and industry. As a result, the South must carry an even more disproportionate burden of environmental degradation and pollution than before. Extreme air pollution in cities, hyper-predatory exploitation in the countryside, and increased vulnerability to harmful influences from climate change lead to a more significant number of environmentally induced migrants and refugees (Jaeggi & Fraser).

Whereas Financial Capitalism promised economic growth and welfare for the masses, its predominance goes hand in hand with macroeconomic trends of slowing growth and secular stagnation (Pineault, 2019). Interest rates are at historic lows, real wage growth has stagnated, and productivity has slowed (Pineault). Statistics reveal that the global economy is slowing down, and economic growth is merely shifting to countries of the Global South (The Economist, 2019, April 19). In countries like the United States, households depend on debt to maintain their consumption levels, and many economists have linked financialisation to these developments. They suggest that it slows real accumulation and leads to the faster recurrence of a cycle of economic upswing, overproduction, crisis, recession, and stagnation (Pineault).

In 2007/2008, the deregulation of banks and the financial industry eventually led to a housing bubble and stock market crash in the United States, which caused a global financial crisis (Ther, 2019). During the crisis, companies were "too big to fail", as States depended on them to generate employment and collect taxes (Culpepper, 2015). States saved banks and big businesses and protected managers and shareholders from financial losses (Culpepper). This led to the "zombification of the economy", as an increasing share of companies kept existing because central banks lowered interest rates during the crisis (Stelter, 2020). These companies could still pay their interest rates but did not have enough capital to invest, innovate, and train their employees, putting a further strain on economic growth (Stelter). The savings also led to public disenchantment with the

State, which had failed to appropriately regulate financial markets and protect society from the consequences. Instead States partially shifted the financial burdens onto the public via austerity measures (Culpepper). Thereby they turned to "Neoliberal Authoritarian Constitutionalism" (Bruff, 2013) and "Authoritarian Crisis Constitutionalism" (Oberndorfer, 2015), turning themselves into "Austerity States" (Jessop, 2018) or "Consolidation States" (Streeck, 2015). Respective measures had particularly adverse effects on social welfare (Andersen et al., 2012).

Since the 1970s, States appeared to no longer protect democracy but rather markets (Streeck, 2015), leading to a state of post-democracy (Bader et al., 2011). Governmental actions aim at improving investment conditions and competitiveness in a globalised world and shifted power relations within the State in favour of transnationally oriented capital. The increasing transfer of decision-making processes to informal committees, supranational institutions, or transnational public-private networks further weakened national parliaments' power. Simultaneously, the representation relations of those depending on wages, organising through parties, associations, and trade unions, increasingly strained (Bader et al.).

These developments have led to the public's disenchantment with democracy and politics (Jessop, 2018). Less than 50 percent of the OECD countries' population have reported confidence in their national governments since 2006 (Ortiz-Ospina & Roser, 2020). The higher income inequality in a nation, the lower trust in the State (Ortiz-Ospina & Roser). Due to this lack of confidence in governments and public institutions, voter turnouts stagnate or regress in the Global North (Solijonov, 2016). The public's loss of faith in political parties typically relates to their involvement in the past decades of neoliberal politics and saving big businesses during the financial crisis (Berman & Snegovaya, 2019).

The frustration of the old middle and precarious working classes with the consequences of the financial crisis also led to protest events such as the election of Donald Trump or Brexit (Ther, 2019). Citizens voted for protest parties and right-wing populists promising protection from neoliberal developments, such as free trade agreements and foreign competition on the labour market, whilst preserving national values and traditional family images (Ther). Economic grievances associated with the current social order are also often blamed on outgroups, such as immigrants, reinforcing the identification with right-wing parties (Golder, 2016).

At the same time, the disenchantment with the Financial Capitalist regime led to the rise of new political parties and social movements promoting human, nature, and animal rights, peace, global climate justice, transition movements from urban gardens to local currencies (Foran, 2019), post-capitalism (Mason, 2016) and degrowth (Victor, 2012). The new middle class mainly drove these developments in a move from "old" politics of economic growth, public order, national security, and traditional lifestyles to "new" politics of environmental quality, social equality, alternative lifestyles, minority rights, and participation (Müller-Rommel, 2019).

Between the late 1970s and 1980s, a wide range of severe risks and human-induced catastrophes confronted Western societies (Wiesenthal, 2019). Massive forest diebacks and various industrial accidents like Chornobyl decreased the public's trust in industrial progress and the controllability of complex technologies (Wiesenthal). The public realised that humanity could not progress further by exhausting more fossil resources and increasing environmental damage and recognised ecological protection as a growing concern (Michelsen et al., 2016). This recognition reached its height in 1972 when the Club of Rome issued its report "Limits to Growth" (Meadows et al., 1972). It demonstrated that if the present growth trends in population, industrialisation, pollution, and resource depletion continued at the same rate, humanity would reach the planet's limits to growth within the next one hundred years. Scientists called for altering these trends by halting growth and creating "a condition of ecological and economic stability that is sustainable far into the future...a state of global equilibrium" (Meadows et al., p. 24). Roughly ten years later, in 1987, the Brundtland Report presented the most well-known definition of sustainable development as development that must meet the needs of the present without compromising the ability of future generations to meet their own needs (Michelsen et al., 2016, p. 19).

Despite these warnings, as the world population increased rapidly since the 1970s, humanity further re-engineered the world's land surface and substantially degraded the environment via unsustainable material production and consumption patterns (Steffen et al., 2007). These developments led to a new geological epoch called the Anthropocene. This epoch is the first in which humanity's actions significantly altered the earth system (Steffen et al.). Political scientist Elmar Altvater (2018) demands that this epoch be renamed "Capitalocene" since it closely ties to the capitalist social order. The Board of the Millennium Ecosystem Assessment concluded that human activity is putting such strain on the planet's ecosystem that we can no longer take for granted that it can sustain future generations (WBGU, 2011). Indeed, we are risking the Earth's capability to provide a stable life-support system and threatening our existence (WBGU).

After roughly five decades, just like its predecessors, the public increasingly called the Financial Capitalist regime into question, as it created social, economic, and ecological crises it could no longer resolve. Even the regimes' proponents openly admitted that liberal markets, the free movement of capital and the technological revolution paid off only for a few

(Dörre, 2019). Some even suggested that we are confronted with a crisis of capitalism because it no longer satisfies human needs and has gone too far (Dörre). Respectively, a new regime replaced it and it is the first to revolve around sustainability. The subsequent chapter dives deeper into the logic of this new regime.

References

Altvater, E. (2008). Globalisierter Neoliberalismus [Globalised neoliberalism]. In Butterwegge, C., Lösch, B. & Ptak, R. (Eds.), *Neoliberalismus. Analysen und Alternativen [Neoliberalism. Analyses and alternatives]* (pp. 50–68). Wiesbaden: VS Verlag.

Altvater, E. (2018). Kapitalozän. Der Kapitalismus schreibt Erdgeschichte [Capitalocene. Capitalism writes planetary history]. *Luxemburg.* https://zeitschrift-luxemburg.de/kapitalozaen

Amable, B. (2003). *The diversity of modern capitalism.* Oxford: Oxford University Press.

Andersen, J. G. (2012). *Welfare states and welfare state theory.* Aalborg, Denmark: Centre for Comparative Welfare Studies.

Andersen, T. M., Basso, G., Degryse, C., Dolls, M., Eichhorst, W., Hemerijck, A. C., [...] & Vandenbroucke, F. (2012). The welfare state after the Great Recession. *Intereconomics*, 47(4), 200–229. https://www.intereconomics.eu/contents/year/2012/number/4/article/the-welfare-state-after-the-great-recession.html

Bader, P., Becker, F., Demirović, A., & Dück, J. (2011). Die multiple Krise – Krisendynamiken im neoliberalen Kapitalismus [The multiple crisis – crisis dynamics in neoliberal capitalism]. In Demirović, A., Dück, J., Becker, F. & Bader, P. (Eds.), *VielfachKrise [Multiple crisis]* (pp. 11–28). Hamburg, Germany: VSA Verlag.

Benz, A. (2008). *Der moderne Staat [The modern state]* (2nd ed.). München, Germany: Oldenbourg Wissenschaftsverlag.

Berger, J. (2019). Warum Kapitalismus? [Why capitalism?]. In Dörre, K., Rosa, H., Becker, K., Bose, S., & Seyd, B. (Eds.), *Große Transformation? Zur Zukunft moderner Gesellschaften [Great Transformation? About the future of modern societies]* (pp.75–95). Wiesbaden, Germany: Springer Fachmedien. https://doi.org/10.1007/978-3-658-25947-1_4

Berman, S., & Snegovaya, M. (2019). Populism and the decline of Social Democracy. *Journal of Democracy*, 30(3), 5–19. https://doi.org/10.1353/jod.2019.0038

Biebricher, T. (2012). *Neoliberalismus zur Einführung [Introduction to neoliberalism]* (3rd ed.). Hamburg, Germany: Junius Verlag.

Bourdieu, P. (2002). *Der Einzige und sein Eigenheim [The one and his private home].* Hamburg, Germany: VSA Verlag.

Brand, U., & Wissen, M. (2018). What kind of great transformation? The Imperial Mode of Living as a major obstacle to sustainability politics. *GAIA – Ecological Perspectives for Science and Society*, 27(3), 287–292. https://doi.org/10.14512/gaia.27.3.8

Bruff, I. (2013). The rise of authoritarian neoliberalism. *Rethinking Marxism*, 26, 113–129. https://doi.org/10.1080/08935696.2013.843250

Culpepper, P. D. (2015). Structural power and political science in the post-crisis era. *Business & Politics, 17*(3), 391–409. https://doi.org/10.1515/bap-2015-0031

Deaton, A. (2013). *The Great Escape. Health, wealth, and the origins of inequality*. Princeton, NJ: Princeton Unviersity Press.

Demirović, A. (2008). Neoliberalismus und Hegemonie [Neoliberalism and hegemony]. In Butterwegge, C., Lösch, B. & Ptak, R. (Eds.), *Neoliberalismus. Analysen und Alternativen [Neoliberalism. analyses and alternatives]* (pp. 17–33). Wiesbaden, Germany: VS Verlag.

Deutschmann, C. (2008). *Kapitalistische Dynamik. Eine gesellschaftstheoretische Perspektive [Capitalist dynamics. A social theory perspective]*. Wiesbaden, Germany: VS Verlag.

Dörre, K. (2019). Risiko Kapitalismus. Landnahme, Zangenkrise, Nachhaltigkeitsrevolution [Capitalism as a risk. Land seizure, crisis of pliers, sustainability revolution]. In Dörre, K., Rosa, H., Becker, K., Bose, S., & Seyd, B. (Eds.), *Große Transformation? Zur Zukunft moderner Gesellschaften [Great transformation? About the future of modern societies]* (pp. 3–34). Wiesbaden, Germany: Springer Fachmedien.

Foran, J. (2019). System change, not climate change: Radical social transformation in the twenty-first century. In Berberoglu, B. (Eds.), *The Palgrave Handbook of social movements, eevolution, and cocial transformation*. Cham, Switzerland: Palgrave Macmillan.

Fukuyama, F. (2004). *State-building: Governance and world order in the twenty-first century*. Ithaca, NY: Cornell University Press.

Fulcher, J. (2004). *Capitalism. A very short introduction*. Oxford: Oxford University Press.

Genschel, P., & Seelkopf, L. (2014). The Competition State: The modern State in a global economy. In Leibfried, S., Huber, E., Lange, M., Levy, J. D., & Stephens, J. D. (Eds.), *The Oxford Handbook of transformations of the State* (pp. 253–268). Oxford: Oxford University Press.

Golder, M. (2016). Far right parties in Europe. *Annual Review of Political Science, 19*(1), 477–497. https://doi.org/10.1146/annurev-polisci-042814-012441

Hobbes, T. (2017). *Leviathan*. London: Penguin Books.

Hobsbawm, E. J. (1969). *Industry and empire: From 1750 to the present day*. London: Penguin Books.

Jacobsen, R. (1991). Economic efficiency and the quality of life. *Journal of Business Ethics, 10*(3), 201–209. https://doi.org/10.1007/bf00383157

Jaeggi, R., & Fraser, N. (2020). *Kapitalismus. Ein Gespräch über kritische Theorie [Capitalism. A conversation about critical theory]*. Berlin, Germany: suhrkamp.

Jessop, B. (1991). The welfare state in the transition from Fordism to Post-Fordism. In Pedersen, O. K., Jessop, B., Kastendiek, H., & Nielsen, K. (Eds.), *The politics of flexibility: Restructuring the State and industry in Britain, Germany and Scandinavia* (pp. 82–104). Cheltenham: Edward Elgar.

Jessop, B. (1994). The transition to post-Fordism and the Schumpeterian workfare state. In Borrows, R., & Loader, B. (Eds.), *Towards a Post-Fordist Welfare State?* (pp. 13–37). London: Routledge.

Jessop, B. (2005). Fordism and Post-Fordism: A critical reformulation. In Scott, Allen J. and Storper, Michael (Eds.), *Pathways to industrialization and regional development* (pp. 42–62). London: Routledge.

Jessop, B. (2018). Elective affinity or comprehensive contradiction? Reflections on capitalism and democracy in the time of finance-dominated accumulation and austerity states. *Berliner Journal für Soziologie [Berlin Journal of Sociology]*, 28, 9–37. https://doi.org/10.1007/s11609-018-0371-9

Klein, D. (2013). *Das Morgen tanzt im Heute: Transformation im Kapitalismus und über ihn hinaus [Tomorrow dances in the today: Transformation within capitalism and beyond]*. Hamburg, Germany: VS Verlag.

Lessenich, S. (2019). Mitgegangen, mitgefangen. Das große Dilemma der Großen Transformation [Serves you right. The great dilemma of the great transformation]. In Brie, M. (Ed.), *Futuring: Perspektiven der Transformation im Kapitalismus über ihn hinaus [Futuring: Transformation perspectives within capitalism and beyond]* (pp. 57–74). Münster, Germany: Westfälisches Dampfboot.

Marx, K. (1986). *A reader.* Cambridge: Cambridge University Press.

Mason, P. (2016). *Postcapitalism. A guide to our future.* London: Penguin Randomhouse UK.

McNeill, J. R. (2000). *Blue Planet.* Frankfurt, Germany: Campus.

Meadows, D. L., Meadows, D. H., Randers, J., & Behrens III, W. W. (1972). *The limits to growth.* New York, NY: Universe Books.

Michelsen, G., Adomßent, M., Martens, P., & von Hauff, M. (2016). Sustainable development – background and context. In Heinrichs, H., Martens, P. Michelsen, G., & Wiek, A. (Eds.), *Sustainability science. An introduction* (pp. 5–30). Dordrecht, Netherlands: Springer Science + Business Media.

Moore, J. (2015). *Capitalism in the web of life.* London: Verso.

Müller-Rommel, F. (2019). *New politics in Western Europe. The rise and success of Green parties and alternative lists.* New York, NY: Routledge.

Nietzsche, F. (1994). *On the genealogy of morals: A polemic.* Cambridge: Cambridge University Press.

Oberndorfer, L. (2015). From new constitutionalism to authoritarian constitutionalism. In Jäger, J., & Springler, E. (Eds.), *Assymetric crisis in Europe and possible futures* (pp. 184–205). London: Routledge.

Ortiz-Ospina, E., & Roser, M. (2020). *Trust.* https://ourworldindata.org/trust

Pineault, É. (2019). A Moloch demanding the whole world a sacrifice. The structures of financial capital in the early 21st century. In Dörre, K., Rosa, H., Becker, K., Bose, S., & Seyd, B. (Eds.), *Große Transformation? Zur Zukunft moderner Gesellschaften [Great transformation? About the future of modern societies]* (pp. 119–147). Wiesbaden, Germany: Springer Fachmedien.

Polanyi, K. (2017). *The great transformation.* (13th ed.). Berlin, Germany: suhrkamp.

Ptak, R. (2017). Grundlagen des Neoliberalismus [Basics of neoliberalism]. In Butterwegge, C., Lösch, B., & Ptak, R. (Eds.), *Kritik des Neoliberalismus* (3rd ed.) *[Critique of neoliberalism]* (pp. 13–78). Wiesbaden, Germany: Springer VS.

Reckwitz, A. (2019). *Das Ende der Illusionen. Politik, Ökonomie und Kultur in der Spätmoderne [The end of illusions. Politics, economy and culture of late modernity]*. Berlin: suhrkamp.

Rockström, J., Steffen, W., Noone, K., Persson, Å., Chapin, F. S., III, Lambin, E. F., Lenton, T. M., Scheffer, M., Folke, C., Schellnhuber, H. J., Nykvist, B., de Wit, C. A., Hughes, T., van der Leeuw, S., Rodhe, H., Sörlin, S., Snyder, P. K.,

Costanza, R., Svedin, U., … Foley, J. A. (2009). A safe operating space for humanity. *Nature, 461*(7263), 472–475. https://doi.org/10.1038/461472a

Sachsenmaier, D., Eisenstadt, P. S. N., & Riedel, J. (2002). *Reflections on multiple modernities: European, Chinese, and other interpretations.* Leiden, Netherland: Brill.

Solijonov, A. (2016). *Voter turnout trends around the world.* International Institute for Democracy and Electoral Assistance. https://www.idea.int/sites/default/files/publications/voter-turnout-trends-around-the-world.pdf

Steffen, W., Crutzen, P. J., & McNeill, J. R. (2007). The Anthropocene: Are humans now overwhelming the great forces of nature? *AMBIO: A Journal of the Human Environment, 36*(8), 614–621. https://doi.org/10.1579/0044-7447(2007)36[614:taahno]2.0.co;2

Stelter, D. (2020). Mit Corona droht die völlige Zombifizierung [Covid threatens complete zombification]. *Ágora 42, 3,* 9–13.

Streeck, W. (2015). *Gekaufte Zeit [Purchased time].* Berlin, Germany: suhrkamp.

Sutterlütti, S., & Meretz, S. (2018). *Kapitalismus aufheben [Abolishing capitalism].* Hamburg, Germany: VSA Verlag.

The Economist. (2019, April 9). *The world economy is slowing down.* The Economist.https://www.economist.com/graphic-detail/2019/04/09/the-world-economy-is-slowing-down

Ther, P. (2019). *Das andere Ende der Geschichte. Über die große Transformation [The other end of history. About the great transformation]* (2nd ed.). Berlin, Germany: Suhrkamp.

Victor, P. A. (2012). Growth, degrowth and climate change: A scenario analysis. *Ecological Economics, 84,* 206–212. https://doi.org/10.1016/j.ecolecon.2011.04.013

WBGU. (2011). *World in transition. A social contract for sustainability.* https://www.wbgu.de/en/publications/publication/world-in-transition-a-social-contract-for-sustainability#section-downloads

Weber, M. (2018). *Die protestantische Ethik und der Geist des Kapitalismus [The Protestant ethic and spirit of capitalism].* Hamburg, Germany: Nikol Verlag.

Wiesenthal, H. (2019). Institutionelle Transformationen gestern – und morgen? [Institutional transformations yesterday – and today?]. In Dörre, K., Rosa, H., Becker, K., Bose, S., & Seyd, B. (Eds.), *Große Transformation? Zur Zukunft moderner Gesellschaften [Great transformation? About the future of modern societies]* (pp. 367–382). Wiesbaden, Germany: Springer Fachmedien.

2

CRAFTING STRATEGIES FOR A SUSTAINABLE SOCIAL ORDER

The many interpretations of sustainable development

In the light of economic crises, social inequality, and intensified ecological crises caused by the capitalist social order, sustainability, and sustainable development became the imperative of the new regime. The concepts' origins date back to 17th-century Germany when Carl von Carlowitz called for sustainable forest management, where individuals and businesses ought to cut down only as many trees as could be restored in a single year to the benefit of both the economy and the environment (Heinrichs et al., 2016, p. 1). Today, sustainable development is a multidimensional concept emphasising social, ecological, and economic dimensions, or in more advanced versions, an additional cultural dimension (Michelsen et al., 2016). Still, the concept is open-ended, and its social understanding depends on time, culture, and knowledge (Michelsen et al.). Accordingly, different actors lay their' interpretations out along differing paradigms, and respective belief and value structures about how the world works (Milbrath, 1984). Paradigms form the source of systems from which shared agreements about the nature of reality form, and the mainstream paradigm functions as the discursive face of politics, thereby influencing both structures and agency (Fraser, 2015, p. 15). Strategies for solving environmental and social concerns within a dominant paradigm vary depending on how one perceives them. Understanding these varying paradigms and approaches to sustainable development is essential for understanding what strategies political leaders for sustainable development ought to follow.

DOI: 10.4324/9781003507666-4

Since the Enlightenment and Industrial Revolution, the dominating paradigm has been the growth-based and human-centred technocentric paradigm (Quaddus, 2011). Fundamental beliefs revolve around the need for unlimited growth and free markets, technological optimism, and the environment as a resource to be exploited by the superior species of humankind. This paradigm parallels Adam Smith's homo oeconomicus theory and the Liberal thinking I previously addressed. Technocentrism thereby accepts environmental and social concerns to some degree, but a need to change the current regime is not a matter of discussion. Instead, technological innovation can alleviate environmental issues and further growth can eradicate social inequality (Quaddus). That goes hand in hand with a weak conception of sustainability which holds that we can substitute different kinds of capital and that, e.g., we can further exploit nature and substitute natural capital with artificial capital (Michelsen et al., 2016). Judging from this paradigm, the status quo already leads to sustainable development.

A second fundamental paradigm is that of Sustaincentrism (Gladwin et al., 1995). Sustaincentrism perceives human activities as interwoven with natural systems, and the economy in a stewardship role of governing business, society, and ecology. The goal of this stewardship is to manage the paradox of environmental sustainability and continued economic growth on a finite planet. Sustaincentrism seeks sustainable development through a strong economy that meets social and environmental needs and guarantees all three's flourishing (Gladwin et al.). This paradigm follows a stronger conception of sustainability because it recognises that we must preserve natural capital to maintain human welfare through sustainable economic growth (Michelsen et al., 2016). Rather than maintaining the status quo, Sustaincentrism seeks to "tame" capitalism's harms, e.g., by introducing egalitarian, democratic, or solidary values into the system to make it function less purely capitalistic (Wright, 2019). The result of this strategy is a capitalist regime with substantially modified rules, which, however, does not eliminate its immanent logic (Wright).

The third relevant paradigm is Socio-Ecocentrism (Baer, 2018). This paradigm builds on Socialist demands for liberty and equality and the belief that we must overcome capitalism so that humanity may flourish (Honneth, 2017). It merges these Socialist with Ecocentric views, seeing humans as part of nature, recognising our interdependency, and seeking to transform capitalism to create a world where both humans and non-human nature can flourish (Quaddus, 2011). Socio-Ecocentrism recognises the equal value, interrelatedness, and inherent worth of humanity and the environment (Baer). It criticises capitalism for hindering liberty, equality, and solidarity within society through profit-seeking motives whilst simultaneously depleting the natural environment (Baer). This aligns with a strong conception of sustainability, where nature needs to be protected for its intrinsic value regardless of substitutability debates (Michelsen et al., 2016). To achieve sustainable development, proponents see the necessity to transform or overcome capitalism by "eroding" it, e.g., by building more democratic, egalitarian, participatory economic relations in the spaces and cracks of the capitalist system, both top-down and bottom-up (Wright, 2019). Actors following this strategy aim for these alternatives to become sufficiently prominent in the lives of individuals and communities, so they can eventually displace capitalism from its dominant role (Wright).

Figure 2.1 lays out the paradigms, their varying conceptions of sustainability and sustainable development, and their respective strategies for managing capitalist harms.

Earlier sections of this chapter showed the technocentric Financial Capitalist regime's crisis tendencies. Respectively, it argued that we must recognise increasing social and environmental concerns and that the current regime is not sustainable. The normative position of this book thus upholds that we need to "tame" and reform or even "erode" and transform capitalism to solve the various crises we face. Since only Sustaincentrism and Socio-Ecocentrism come true to these claims, the following sections will neglect Technocentrism and focus on exploring sustaincentric and socio-ecocentric approaches to sustainable development.

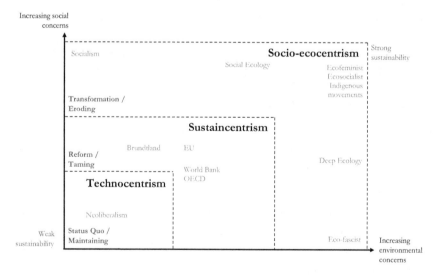

FIGURE 2.1 Paradigms and approaches to sustainable development (based on Hopwood et al., 2005, p. 41).

The logic of Sustainable Capitalism

The Sustainable Capitalist regime evolved from Financial Capitalism and follows the "taming" or reform approach laid out above. It is particularly promoted by international institutions such as the OECD (2012), World Bank (2012), and European Union (EC, 2019, December 11), who push for inclusive green growth agendas. The following section explores the logic in detail.

Sustainable development through economic growth

Sustaincentrists diverted the definition of sustainable development to primarily suit economic demands: economic development today must ensure that future generations are not left worse off than present generations (Barbier, 2011). Therefore per-capita welfare may not decline over time, requiring continuous economic growth. Respectively, proponents recognise GDP as the primary indicator of social welfare, assuming that if economic growth is secured, social welfare will increase, and natural capital can be replenished or substituted (Barbier).

Improving market mechanisms

Sustaincentrists predominantly hold market mechanisms responsible for capitalist economies' failure to alleviate environmental harms (World Bank, 2012). Thus far, economists have treated natural capital as free of charge, and there was no incentive to value it adequately in an economic sense (Borel-Saladin & Turok, 2013). Respectively, green growth agendas recognise that GDP does not include the pricing of natural capital and externalities such as pollution, loss of ecosystems, and the social costs of environmental ills. Thereby natural capital, which provides valuable services, is over-exploited and significantly depleted (Borel-Saladin & Turok). Market mechanisms such as pricing may improve the valuation of natural capital and ecosystem services and make their benefits more visible (OECD, 2012). If markets reflect the actual value, economic activity will achieve environmental objectives and provide incentives for further efficiency gains and innovations while encouraging more sustainable production and consumption patterns and generating fiscal revenues to finance critical social and environmental projects (OECD).

Enhancing State regulation and spending

A failure of past attempts at sustainable growth stems from a lack of policies and regulations (Bowen & Fankhauser, 2011). In the transition to an inclusive green economy, the agendas of organisations such as the World

Bank (2012) and OECD (2012) thus typically call for governments to redirect the economy from employing harmful means to greener practices (Borel-Saladin & Turok, 2013). They should promote innovation, steer investments toward green infrastructure and technologies, and provide public goods (OECD). Central interventions and measures include efficiency and production standards, CO_2 tax incentives, CO_2 emissions permits, public infrastructure provisions, informative campaigns, increased research and development efforts, and environmentally harmful subsidy reforms (Borel-Saladin & Turok).

Promoting innovation

Sustaincentrists hold that economic growth can alleviate environmental crises through green technological innovations. Said innovations reduce emissions, decrease natural resource depletion, produce substitutes for natural capital (Barbier, 2011), open opportunities for creative entrepreneurs, intensify competition, and challenge established and outdated ideas (Bowen & Fankhauser, 2011). These developments lead to innovative products that stimulate sustainable supply and demand (Bowen & Fankhauser). For one, introducing natural capital and environmental degradation pricing changes the relative prices of production factors and the composition of productive assets, disrupting the existing revenue distribution (De Perthuis & Jouvet, 2015). The idea is that businesses will change their ways when they realise that existing assets have become too expensive, and the cost of pollution hampers their performance. The pricing mechanism will trigger new investments in sustainable practices to rebuild natural capital. These investments will lead to creative destruction, generating green innovations and reorienting conventional growth towards green growth (De Perthuis & Jouvet). In addition, technological innovations will achieve eco-economic decoupling, i.e., resource use and environmental pressures will decouple from growth (OECD, 2012).

Making growth inclusive

Innovation will also lead to new jobs, ensuring increased incomes (OECD, 2012). Rising incomes, in turn, go hand in hand with receding poverty, increasing literacy, and decreasing child mortality, and therefore greater wellbeing and equality (World Bank, 2012). Still, innovation will also put jobs in declining industries at risk (OECD; World Bank). Inclusive green growth agendas thus try to spread the burdens equally via education and vocational training, the reallocation of workers from declining to growing sectors, and tax and benefits system reforms so the costs of environmental policies do not reduce workers' purchasing power (OECD; World Bank). Simultaneously, various measures ought to protect those affected by climate change in the Global South (Borel-Saladin & Turok, 2013). These include restoring natural ecosystems, reducing vulnerability to natural disasters, increasing livelihood security, and countries of the Global North compensating for ecosystem services in the Global South (Borel-Saladin & Turok).

Exemplary operationalisation

There are many attempts at "taming" the capitalist social order in the Global North. These include the Paris Agreement, which aims to unite nations to combat climate change and limit the global temperature rise to 1.5°C (UNFCCC, 2020a). Another attempt is the European Green Deal, which seeks to make the European Union climate-neutral via a resource-saving circular economy, green finance, and profitable private investments in green economy sectors (Schramm, 2020). The Deal is a

> new growth strategy that aims to transform the EU into a fair and prosperous society, with a modern, resource-efficient and competitive economy where there will be no net emissions of greenhouse gases in 2050 and where economic growth is decoupled from resource use.
>
> *(EC, 2019, December 11, p.2)*

Finally, there are various examples of local and national cases of green economies, such as Costa Rica (GIZ, 2015) and Vancouver (VEC, 2018).

Increased acceptance of the need for sustainable development

The current Sustainable Capitalist regime has advantages and disadvantages that need to be reviewed to evaluate whether it can bring about sustainable development or whether political leaders for sustainable development must go further than the "taming" measures mentioned earlier. From a strategic point of view, Sustainable Capitalism and visions of inclusive green economies are successful because they moved the most pressing environmental and social concerns onto the agendas of heads of State and governments (Barrett & Stavins, 2003; EC, 2019, December 11; UNFCCC, 2020b, April 14). They also moved it onto the agendas of global economic elites and their central institutions (UNEP, 2011a; UNEP, 2011b; OECD, 2011; World Bank, 2012) and raised awareness and acceptance of sustainable development within society (Borel-Saladin & Turok, 2013). They thereby changed the dominant paradigm from Technocentrism to Sustaincentrism, which ecological scientists and environmentalists had pushed for decades (Jänicke, 2012). Overall, it is the most effective strategy for sustainable development currently being adopted on a large scale (Borel-Saladin & Turok). Still, there are counter-arguments to consider.

GDP is not an indicator of wellbeing

Sustaincentrism builds on economic growth, which closely ties to the primary indicator of the gross national product (GDP), which represents the most universally accepted goal, where the fastest-growing system is considered the best (Daly, 1993). However, GDP is flawed, as it does not account for externalities (Daly, 2013). Instead, it counts the consumption of natural capital and efforts to revert economic activities' externalities, such as pollution, as income (Daly, 1991). In this sense, GDP and current accounting systems are asymmetric and a "gilded index of far-reaching ruin" (Daly, 1991, p. 816).

Furthermore, GDP does not measure direct indicators of societal wellbeing such as health, friends, and family (Jackson, 2009) or the capacity for self-determined actions and free time (Brand, 2016). Experts thus demand new measures that assess and monitor what citizens care about (Stiglitz et al., 2009), such as Herman Daly's (2013) General Progress Indicator (GPI). Daly's investigation demonstrates that whilst GDP and GPI positively correlated up until 1980, GDP continued to rise after but GPI levelled off. Thus, Daly concludes that increasing throughput, measured by real GDP, no longer increases social and environmental welfare (Daly).

Lack of wellbeing and social inequality remain

Economic growth is no longer a panacea for inequality. Whilst top incomes have been increasing since the 1980s, middle- and bottom-class incomes have remained stagnant in real terms (IMF, 2017; UNDP, 2017). Economic growth and the expansion of middle classes in countries of the Global South happened at the expense of market participants in the OECD countries (Dörre, 2019). Inequality, measured with the Gini coefficient, has risen to a historical high in most OECD countries over the past three decades (Thévenot, 2017). The main winners of globalisation remain capital elites (Dörre). Being born in a wealthy country thus no longer protects one from income and status loss, social relegation, precariousness, or social exclusion. Overall, social and class inequalities have reached a level that even Liberals call out as a brake on further growth (Dörre). In 2017, the global top 10 percent owned more than 70 percent of global wealth, whilst the bottom 50 percent owned less than 2 percent (UNDP, p. 131). These developments may be tied to the unleashing of financial markets and increased capital concentration among the wealthy (UNDP).

In the same line of argument, the distribution of emissions and environmental degradation's unavoidable consequences are unequally distributed between social classes and groups (Candeias, 2014). The wealthiest 1 percent of the global population was responsible for 15 percent of the cumulative carbon emissions over the past 25 years and the poorest 50 percent for 7 percent (Oxfam, 2020, September 21, p. 2). Still, the burdens are shared mainly by those who emit the least (WMO, 2021). For example, between 2010 and 2019, weather-related events displaced an estimated 23.1 million people in the Global South (WMO, p. 35). Many remain displaced because environmental conditions cease to improve with increasing climate change (WMO). On the other hand, technological innovations promoted in the Global North typically require rare minerals from countries in the Global South, sourced under dire social and environmental conditions (Bader et al., 2011). Cheap and often unsustainably produced natural and human resources are simply exploited, further excelling social inequality and environmental degradation in these countries (Bader et al.). Sustainable Capitalism thereby leads to selective adaptation, where privileged members of society maintain their lifestyles of materialistic abundance whilst the less privileged pay the price (Davis, 2010).

Flawed promotion of innovation

A critical argument tied to the inclusive green economy is that they attest to a central role of innovation and decoupling. Still, studies reveal that relative decoupling typically takes place when one resource is simply substituted for another, when businesses externalise environmental impacts to another region of the world, or when GDP increases but does not lead to income gains for the lower and middle classes who do not raise their consumption levels (Brand & Wissen, 2018). Studies further show no evidence for real absolute decoupling, which is necessary in the context of planetary boundaries and scarce resources (Ward et al., 2016).

In addition, the current capitalist regime configuration hinders innovation. Monopolistic corporations hold immense power over markets and use it to prevent competition (Pineault, 2019a). To do so, they, amongst others, stabilise their dominant market positions with patents or buyouts of potentially disruptive start-ups. At the same time, their shareholder value model hinders extensive investments into research and development and, thus, disruptive innovations (Pineault).

Finally, innovation is said to decrease resource use but tends to ignore the Jevons Paradox or rebound effects (Umweltbundesamt, 2019). Whilst innovation may increase resource efficiency, it will typically also reduce costs for those products and, in turn, may increase consumption. Thereby the actual savings are cancelled out (Umweltbundesamt). The intensification and promotion of consumerist lifestyles through green alternatives may even outstrip all progress (Heinrichs & Biermann, 2016). This is because growth economies build on a treadmill of overproduction and overconsumption (Pineault, 2019b). Inclusive green growth visions do not address sufficiency, which is necessary to create genuine wellbeing beyond the symbolic value of materialistic products, decrease consumption, and release pressure on the environment (Jackson, 2009). The mass production of cheap products leads to excess capacities and a devaluation of products in a continual search for new, better, or more affordable products (Jackson). The system fuels constant market demand, e.g., customers keeping fashion items half as long as 15 years ago (Edge, 2020). Consumers have a restless desire for innovation, which perfectly fits producers' need to sell new goods on the market. These are the self-reinforcing processes that drive growth. Still, this may also cause anxiety and undermine wellbeing because the pressure to purchase new goods in the "iron cage of consumerism" is too great (Jackson).

Maintaining an environmentally destructive economic system

Inclusive green economies represent a form of crisis management within the capitalist social order (Brand et al., 2019a). Neoliberals expanded their crisis management to developing "market-friendly" solutions (Brand et al.), turning the socio-ecological crisis, rising emissions, as well as resource scarcity and depletion into new markets for accumulation (Bader et al., 2011). Thereby inclusive green economies commodify nature further, focusing on controlling risks and follow-up costs rather than eliminating their causes (Bader et al.; Brand, 2016). This stems from a human-first perspective, which emphasises that humanity must primarily protect natural assets to continue to provide the resources and environmental services on which human wellbeing relies (OECD, 2011). That is despite the premise that infinite economic growth and finite natural resources are not reconcilable due to thermodynamic laws (Daly, 1991). As the human population and consumption grow, they assimilate an ever-larger proportion of the earth's ecosystem for production and waste disposal. If we consume all valuable resources and fill all of nature's sinks with waste, eventually there will be no more resources or sinks left (Daly).

Some proponents of inclusive green economies, such as the European Commission, aim to overcome this equation by creating a circular economy (EC, 2019, December 11). However, this type of economy still consumes resources and produces waste and emissions (Corvellec et al., 2022). Significant structural obstacles to this type of economy remain, including a flawed conception of innovation and the difficulty of closing material loops (Corvellec et al.). Until we achieve a circular economy and potentially a Regenerative Capitalist regime (Fullerton, 2015, April 20), growth will increase ecological costs faster than production benefits, ultimately creating antieconomic growth (Daly, 1993). Scientists have already shown that the human ecological footprint outpaces biological carrying capacity (Global Footprint Network, 2019) and that we have surpassed the critical level of seven out of eight globally measured planetary boundaries (Rockström et al., 2023).

In addition, a lack of understanding of nature remains. Natural capital depreciation is often irreversible, new ecosystems cannot replace depleted or degraded ones, and ecosystems collapse abruptly without prior warning (Barbier, 2011). Human-made capital cannot substitute for all depleted natural capital or ecosystem services because most biological processes, such as photosynthesis, cannot be technologically replaced (Daly, 1993). Thus, there is a point beyond which the earth's system will collapse under the demands of its ever-growing economic subsystem (Daly). Due to our actions, total plant biomass on Earth reduced twofold relative to before the start of human civilisation (Bar-On et al., 2018, p. 6508). We have significantly altered three-quarters of land-based environments and about 66 percent of marine environments (Ritchie & Roser, 2019). Looking at the biomass of animals on the planet in gigatons of carbon (Gt C), livestock today makes up around 0.1 Gt C, and humans 0,06 Gt C (Bar-On et al., p. 6507). In contrast, wild mammals, fish, and birds only make up 0.0016 Gt C (Bar-On et al., p. 6507), and many face extinction (LMD, 2019).

Maintaining a destructive social order

In the previous chapter and sections, I shed light on a broad range of symptoms caused by past and current capitalist regimes. To conclude on these observations, the general logic and characteristics that drive all of these regimes are highlighted.

Modern capitalist societies may only stabilise if they retain their focus on permanent economic growth and technological acceleration (Dörre, 2019; cf. Marx, 1986; cf. Lessenich, 2019; cf. Rosa, 2019). Without growth, capitalist economies go into crisis (Rosa, 2019). That leads to a central conflict of modern society: the battle for the distribution of reproduction and accumulation may defuse but never entirely halt, as growth and accumulation represent a collective individualised way of living (Lessenich, 2019) and a structurally inscribed logic that individuals agree to independent of their own will (Marx). Indeed, society often remains unaware of the logic of growth that enslaves them because they are embedded in social practices and norms (Lessenich, 2019). They cherish unlimited mobility, never-ending streams of consumption, or functioning public services. Their lifestyle intrinsically links to norms about material welfare, social advancement, self-realisation, and individual and collective potential. Capitalist societies thrive on a liberal moral economy that presents their actions as ethically neutral. Inhabitants of these societies may not escape via individual free will because they are structurally bound to their material and ideological interests in an enforced complicity and state of participative compulsory integration. Habitual living conditions, long rehearsed everyday life practices, and acquired living standards can only be maintained through the constant reproduction of respective structures (Lessenich), giving them the ultimate power over themselves (Sutterlütti & Meretz, 2018). That is the "compulsive character of self-alienated society" (Horkheimer & Adorno, 2017, p. 29), a dynamic where members of society simultaneously become rulers and ruled (Lessenich) and part of what Max Weber called a masterless slavery (Thielemann, 2000). Members of society no longer have decisive power over historical developments and, at the same time, take gains from welfare created by externalisation. Thus, some conclude that there may not be a "correct" way of life because even the weakest participants can only secure or improve their condition at someone's or something's cost (Lessenich). It appears that to survive, the objective necessity is to accept and submit to the system (Thielemann).

To generate further growth, capitalists must continuously increase productivity and expand their markets (Urban, 2018). A continuous tendency for "land grabbing" of non-capitalist milieus characterises this drive for expansion. Land grabbing, in this sense, can be external by tapping into countries, regions, or new economic sectors. It can also be internal, exploiting social relations, individual lifestyles, and consumption patterns by privatising public goods or expropriating public goods such as social welfare services (Urban). States play a significant role in this compulsion to expand as they enable accumulation through expropriation (Harvey, 2006). Land grabbing and respective expropriation damage commodified fields and sectors through externalisation costs (Urban). Brand and Wissen (2018) call this the Imperial Mode of Living (IML), or "good living for parts of humanity at the cost of others" (Brand & Wissen, p. 288). As laid out earlier, this mode of reproduction has characterised capitalist societies since Mercantilism (Lessenich, 2019), where exploitation initially took place in the classic, forceful colonisation and respective enslavement of inhabitants (Boatca, 2015). Today this social relation is embedded in modern legal institutions that allow for unequal economic and ecological trade within global labour, production, and trade regimes (Boatca). Both nature and weak social actors, such as Indigenous inhabitants, women, and migrants, can be exploited as cheap resources (Biesecker & von Winterfeld, 2013).

Capitalist regimes outsource the collateral damages and subsequent costs of capital exploitation as far away as possible from where they were caused, i.e., to an extended economic and social space (Lessenich, 2019). These costs include financial costs, environmental costs caused by production, the social costs of consumer goods and service industries, and the political and legal costs of often half-legal or even criminal capitalist activities in the countries of the Global South. To not carry these costs themselves, capitalist nations typically close off their economic and social spheres from the constructed outside either through the prevention of uncontrolled immigration from the rest of the world or the self-interested recruitment thereof. Finally, externalisation's legitimacy and social acceptance rely on the consequent hiding of the connection between appropriation, exploitation, degradation, and outsourcing from societal knowledge. Thereby, the knowledge of externalisation is externalised itself. Capitalists either hide these costs from collective societal consciousness or address them, detached from responsible actors, e.g., via specialised networks such as scientific institutions or NGOs (Lessenich).

Finally, German sociologist Klaus Dörre (2019, p. 4) concludes that capitalist regimes find themselves amid a socio-eco-economic "Zangenkrise," translated to "crisis of pliers". The most important means of overcoming economic crises remains economic growth. Still, growth leads to social detriments and ecological destruction, destroying society's means of living and society itself. This crisis represents the intersection of two significant long-term developments (Dörre). On the one hand, the era of fast, permanent economic growth with high growth rates is ending (Galbraith & Dörre, 2018). On the other, growth rates based on fossil fuels remain high enough because countries of the Global South are adapting their production methods and increasing energy and resource use (Dörre). This "Zangenkrise" consists of continuously weak economic growth rates with a simultaneous "keep it up" mentality. Economic growth's ecological and social destruction has thus become the most significant conflict of our time (Dörre).

Beyond Sustainable Capitalism

Judging by the evaluation of the Sustainable Capitalist regime, we can expect that a new regime will eventually replace it. Proponents of the Socio-Ecocentric paradigm are already promoting a wide variety of alternatives. They, rather than "taming" capitalism, seek to transform or erode it altogether. Since these alternatives require transformative changes to the current regime, it is helpful to understand the possibilities of how to achieve them. Some Left thinkers assume that there cannot be a revolutionary leap into something entirely different and that transformational strategies must always start with reforms (Brand et al., 2019b). French social philosopher André Gorz differentiates between reforms and non-reformist reforms (Baer, 2018). The former makes minor improvements to the current regime. In contrast, the latter represents the means to the end of a greater vision, aiming at making permanent changes in structures and power alignments (Baer). By being promoted within the current regime but aiming for a transformation, non-reformist reforms may then turn into "revolutionary real politics [revolutionäre Realpolitik]" (Brand et al., p. 252).

Some of these alternative views, which may be approached via non-reformist reforms, are briefly outlined in the following paragraphs.

Steady-state economy

Herman Daly (1993) developed the concept of a steady-state economy (SSE) as an alternative economy that achieves sustainable development in a "full world". The fundamental goal of this vision is to overcome the dominant growth paradigm. In this economy, resource throughput levels remain constant, to not deplete the environment beyond its regenerative and pollute it beyond its absorptive capacities (Daly, 1993). A fundamental premise for this steady state is that the number of human bodies and the stock of material wealth must remain constant (Daly, 2013). To attain and maintain this state, Daly (2013, pp. 51–52) calls for three critical State institutions: (1) a distributive institution that puts minimum and maximum limits on income and maximum limits on wealth, ensuring that private property is evenly distributed, (2) transferable birth licenses which are issued equally and made transferable on a respective market, and (3) resource depletion quotas, which governments will auction. The steady-state economy aims to go beyond "taming" capitalism but still builds on the existing capitalist logics of markets, price systems, and private property. Thereby it remains close to Sustaincentric approaches.

The new economics of prosperity

Economist Tim Jackson (2009) builds on the concept of the SSE. Still, he argues that the economy is part of the problem and that addressing consumerism's social logic is vital for sustainable development. In line with this argument, he conceptualises a model of new economics of prosperity (NE) that builds on the premise that humans need more than material needs and financial security to flourish. Prosperity, in his conception, goes well beyond material sustenance and allows humans to thrive whilst reducing their environmental impact. The concept includes social and psychological dimensions such as the ability to give and receive love, be respected, have valuable work, trust in one's community, and a sense of belonging (Jackson).

Jackson (2009) also assigns a vital role to the State in maintaining macroeconomic stability, co-creating a new culture of consumption, and shaping society's behaviour. He argues that capitalist governments are conflicted between securing a sustainable future and holding macroeconomic stability, as long as the latter depends on growth. Freeing society from growth would thus free governments from this compulsion and redirect their efforts towards the common good. Jackson suggests a variety of steps for this new macroeconomic model. Amongst others, they include resource and emissions caps, investments in jobs, assets, and infrastructures, increasing financial and fiscal prudence, replacing GDP with measures for prosperity, avoiding unemployment by reducing the total and the average number of working hours, and providing a basic income (Jackson, pp. 103–107).

Whilst NE builds on the concept of the SSE and capitalist mechanisms, it goes further than the SSE in that it seeks to overcome capitalist logics, including freeing society from overconsumption based on a new set of values rather than just restricting resource throughputs.

Degrowth

Degrowths' (DG) vision builds on similar premises as the SSE and NE. It focuses on the scale of the economic process, arguing that it needs to degrow, i.e., its throughputs must shrink (Pineault, 2019b). This process involves shaking off consumerism's cultural fetish and hegemonic ideology and enabling equitable and democratic transitions to smaller economies with less production, consumption, and material throughput (Pineault). In this new system, proponents consider the following principles as essential: ending exploitation, enabling direct democracy, localising production, sharing and reclaiming the commons, focusing on relationships, investing in public goods, care, and diversity, decommodifying land, labour, and value, emphasising reproduction and care, as well as solidarity and interpersonal relations (Kallis, 2015).

To achieve this vision, DG prioritises a heavy bottom-up approach and voluntarist solutions (Foster, 2011). Proponents stress social movements' roles in testing out transition projects and driving these transitions from the bottom up by incrementally replacing parts of the current system (Kallis, 2015). Such bottom-up transition projects include urban gardens, eco-communes, producer-consumer cooperatives, open-access software, decentralised renewable energy production and distribution, and new exchanges, such as community currencies and financial cooperatives (Martínez-Alier et al., 2010). At the same time, DG proponents know that broad institutional changes will be necessary to drive supplementary public policies (Kallis). They thus call for a simultaneous top-down movement by the State to foster the adoption of measures such as basic income, job guarantees (Kallis), work sharing, and resource caps (Schmelzer, 2019). In contrast to SSE and NE, degrowth is even more transformative in its approach and aims to overcome capitalist foreground and background conditions.

Ecosocialism

Ecosocialism (ES) builds on a Marxist critique of capitalism. It enhances Socialist views by including ecological insights, acknowledging that the logic of capitalist accumulation and rising capital power is incompatible with social and environmental flourishing (Jessop, 2019). ES further holds that the State will remain dependent on economic growth and a profitable private sector to fund its social and environmental reforms as long as it upholds the capitalist market economy (Eckersley, 1992).

ES seeks to limit the capitalist foreground conditions and logic of profits and markets and to subject economic development to a new social and ecological rationale (Gorz, 2012). They aim to establish a moral economy and a society where we live better while working and consuming less (Gorz). The new economy builds on extra-economic, non-monetary criteria, socio-ecological principles, and democratic decision-making processes (Löwy, 2002). The idea is that "being" will take precedence over "having," and society will strive to fulfill essential material needs but focus on non-material needs such as a sense of belonging. Production and industry are to be unalienated, re-embedded (Löwy, 2002), and radically restructured (Löwy, 2018, December 19). ES thereby envisions a combination of State and local democratic planning (Eckersley, 1992). This involves democratically controlled public enterprises, a regulated financial sector, self-managing worker cooperatives, and the continuation of a small private business sector with controlled profit accumulation (Eckersley). To achieve this, ES envisions a decisive role of the State but upholds that the State must build on direct democracy rather than representative democracy to overcome global capital dominance (Candeias, 2014). This democratic State is to employ resource caps, set prices, reflect social and political priorities through taxes and subsidies, incentivise social goods, disincentivise social ills, and make use-value the central criterium for production (Candeias).

The reconstituted lifeworld then revolves around a new culture of cooperation, self-determined activities, sharing within communities, voluntary and organised cooperation, and rights to income, decoupled from labour and working hours (Gorz, 2012). Finally, this involves deglobalisation, decentralisation, and municipalisation, and the expansion of public goods (Candeias, 2014). Ending imperial exploitation and inequality between countries of the Global South and Global North is another critical premise of ES (Löwy, 2002). In this sense, ES represents the most transformative alternative to the capitalist social order's status quo.

Exploring future potentials for sustainable development

Sustainability scientists Raskin et al. (2010) conducted a study analysing three future scenarios. The first scenario is named "Market Forces" (Raskin et al., p. 2629). In it, free market optimism remains dominant. The population will expand by 40 percent by 2050, and free trade and deregulation will drive growth, letting the global economy grow three-fold by 2050. This scenario is comparable to a "business as usual" under the Technocentric paradigm and its economic and population developments over the past decades (Raskin et al.).

The second scenario describes a "Policy Reform" future comparable to Sustainable Capitalism and visions of an inclusive green economy (Raskin et al., 2010, p. 2633). It includes a government-led redirection of growth towards sustainability goals with no significant changes to the State-centric international order, modern institutional structures, and consumerist values. In this scenario, total greenhouse gas emissions decline, growth continues in developing countries for two decades, and redistribution policies raise income in the poorest regions (Raskin et al.).

The third scenario is termed "Great Transition" (GT) (Raskin et al., 2010, p. 2630). Similar to SSE, DG, NE, and ES, it seeks a transformation of capitalism and uses comparable mechanisms. This scenario builds on a value-led change of the guiding paradigm of growth to values of solidarity, ecological resilience, and quality of life. That includes less consumerist lifestyles because notions of a "good life" turn towards qualitative dimensions of wellbeing such as leisure, relationships, and community engagement. Population stabilises more rapidly than in other scenarios due to equal gender roles and universal access to education and health care. In this scenario, the world will approach a steady-state economy by 2100 (Raskin et al.).

The "Market Forces" scenario will not significantly increase the Quality of Development Index (QDI), which measures human wellbeing, community cohesion, and environmental protection (Raskin et al., 2010, p. 2633). The second scenario, "Policy Reform" would significantly and steadily improve the QDI. Finally, the GT scenario shows the steepest long-term improvement in the QDI (Raskin et al.).

The "Policy Reform" (PT) scenario may significantly decrease annual emissions, incidences of hunger, total energy requirements, and water stress (Raskin et al., 2010, pp. 237–264). However, the effects on other aspects, such as international equity and forest cover, are less significant. In the GT scenario, international equity increases significantly in contrast to the PT scenario, whilst incidences of hunger decrease faster and slightly more. Water stress decreases considerably in both scenarios. Regarding environmental dimensions, annual emissions decrease faster in the GT scenario, total energy requirements decline substantially more, and forest cover increases strongly. The study suggests that inclusive green economies may avoid the most fundamental environmental crises. Nonetheless, critical social dimensions, such as equity, only significantly improve in a great transition envisioned by socio-ecocentric strategies that transform structures and power relations in the long run.

In this light, the vision of an inclusive green economy and its political will to part from the more destructive status quo is worth pursuing. Inclusive green growth strategies may lead to capitalism's tamed and greener form. However, it will remain selective in providing a few with higher incomes and material living standards and will not stop environmental degradation (Brand, 2014). This is because it will not significantly alter the pressure of the capitalist foreground characteristics on the background characteristics of social reproduction, non-human nature, racism, imperialism, and expropriation. Instead, it will modernise capitalism's basic structures in a transformation driven from above by dominant capital fractions who co-opt and integrate oppositional forces under their hegemony (Brand et al., 2019a). Capital groups such as insurance, automotive, regenerative energies, and investment firms actively promote inclusive green economies because they focus on technologies to solve the most pressing problems, leading to further profits (Candeias, 2014). Indeed, experts forecast the green technology and sustainability market to grow to US$417.35 billion by 2030, revealing the enormous growth and profit potential they hold for these businesses (Laricchia, 2022, July 22).

As previously addressed, inclusive green economies will lead to improvements, even if it may not be enough regarding the ecological, social, and economic crises we face. Still, its implementation may represent just one step in an overall transformation, as reforms can lead to a new paradigm and societal evolutionary change (Rosa, 2019). Transition research identifies a four-phase pattern in such transformation processes, consisting of a pre-development, take-off, acceleration, and final phase. Looking back at the evolution of capitalism, the Industrial Revolution happened over approximately 80 years (Polanyi, 2017). Transition researchers Grin et al. (2010, p. 11) further point out that transitions typically take around 40–50 years. Sustainable development has been on the agenda for about 50 years, whilst visions of an inclusive green economy have only been promoted for around 10 years. Respectively, the Sustainable Capitalist regime may be part of transformation phases 1 and 2, i.e. pre-development and acceleration, where pioneer activities and coalition building occur. These then lead to necessary regulatory changes, the anchoring of social acceptance for sustainable development, and finally, the acceleration phase. Still, the agendas around inclusive green growth also run the danger of leading to a lock-in with no further changes. It could also backlash us into the "business as usual" scenario, or, if it takes too long, our current social order could collapse altogether.

To conclude, we can, in a pessimistic way, perceive inclusive green growth reforms as capitalist greenwashing and society's unwillingness to change behaviours and mindsets to protect the environment and itself. Most optimistically, they represent a necessary step and key to a more significant transformation. Considering the emergent phenomenon of political leadership for sustainable development, respective leaders could promote both sustaincentric and socio-ecocentric approaches via reformist and non-reformist reforms, as both may be necessary steps towards a sustainable future. Regardless of the previously discussed visions and strategies, both approaches build on a strong State and respective regulations. Thus, the next chapter will show if and how States may contribute to sustainable development.

References

Bader, P., Becker, F., Demirović, A., & Dück, J. (2011). Die multiple Krise – Krisendynamiken im neoliberalen Kapitalismus [The multiple crisis – crisis dynamics in neoliberal capitalism]. In Demirović, A., Dück, J., Becker, F. & Bader, P. (Eds.), *VielfachKrise [Multiple crisis]* (pp. 11–28). Hamburg, Germany: VSA Verlag.

Baer, H. A. (2018). *Democratic eco-socialism as a real utopia.* New York, NY: Berghahn Books.

Barbier, E. B. (2011). The policy challenges for green economy and sustainable economic development. *Natural Resources Forum, 35*(3), 233–245. https://doi.org/10.1111/j.1477-8947.2011.01397.x

Bar-On, Y. M., Phillips, R., & Milo, R. (2018). The biomass distribution on Earth. *PNAS, 115*(25), 6506–6511. https://doi.org/10.1073/pnas.1711842115

Barrett, S., & Stavins, R. (2003). Increasing participation and compliance in international climate change agreements. *International Environmental Agreements: Politics, Law and Economics, 3*, 349–376. https://doi.org/10.1023/B:INEA.0000005767.67689.28

Biesecker, A., & von Winterfeld, U. (2013). Alte Rationalitätsmuster und neue Beharrlichkeiten [Old rationality patterns and new perseverances]. *GAIA – Ecological Perspectives for Science and Society, 22*(3), 160–165.

Boatca, M. (2015). *Global inequalities beyond occidentalism.* London: Taylor & Francis. https://doi.org/10.4324/9781315584867

Borel-Saladin, J. M., & Turok, I. N. (2013). The green economy: Incremental change or transformation? *Environmental Policy and Governance, 23*(4), 209–220. https://doi.org/10.1002/eet.1614

Bowen, A., & Fankhauser, S. (2011). The green growth narrative: Paradigm shift or just spin? *Global Environmental Change, 21*(4), 1157–1159. https://doi.org/10.1016/j.gloenvcha.2011.07.007

Brand, U. (2014). Transition und Transformation: Sozioökologische Perspektiven [Transition and transformation: Socio-ecological perspectives]. In Brie, M., *Futuring: Perspektiven der Transformation im Kapitalismus über ihn hinaus [Futuring: Transformation perspectives within capitalism and beyond]* (pp. 242–280). Münster, Germany: Westfälisches Dampfboot.

Brand, U. (2016). Who controls the economy? – Some critical questions. In Carius, A., Tänzler, D., Semmling, E., *The rise of the green economies. A paradigm for the developing world?* (pp. 69–81). Munich, Germany: oekom.

Brand, U., Görg, C., & Wissen, M. (2019a). Overcoming neoliberal globalization: Social-ecological transformation from a Polanyian perspective and beyond. *Globalizations, 17*(1), 161–176. https://doi.org/10.1080/14747731.2019.1644708

Brand, U., Lösch, B., Opratko, B., & Thimmel, S. (2019b). *ABC der Alternativen 2.0. Von Alltagskultur bis Zivilgesellschaft [ABC of alternatives 2.0. From everyday culture to civil society]*. Hamburg, Germany: VSA Verlag.

Brand, U., & Wissen, M. (2018). What kind of great transformation? The Imperial Mode of Living as a major obstacle to sustainability politics. *GAIA – Ecological Perspectives for Science and Society, 27*(3), 287–292. https://doi.org/10.14512/gaia.27.3.8

Candeias, M. (2014). Szenarien grüner Transformation *[Scenarios of green transformation]*. In Brie, M. (Ed.), *Futuring: Perspektiven der Transformation im Kapitalismus über ihn hinaus [Futuring: Transformation perspectives within capitalism and beyond]* (pp. 303–329). Münster, Germany: Westfälisches Dampfboot.

Corvellec, H., Stowell, A. F., & Johansson, N. (2022). Critiques of the circular economy. *Journal of Industrial Ecology, 26*, 421–432. https://doi.org/10.1111/jiec.13187

Daly, H. (1991). *Steady-state economics* (2nd ed.). Washington, DC: Island Press.

Daly, H. (1993). Steady-state economics: A new paradigm. *New Literary History, 24*(4), 811–816. https://doi.org/10.2307/469394

Daly, H. (2013). A further critique of growth economics. *Ecological Economics, 88*, 20–24. https://doi.org/10.1016/j.ecolecon.2013.01.007

Davis, M. (2010). Who will build the ark? *New Left Review, 61*, 29–46. https://newleftreview.org/issues/ii61/articles/mike-davis-who-will-build-the-ark

De Perthuis, C., & Jouvet, P. (2015). *Green capital: A new perspective on growth*. New York City, NY: Columbia University Press.

Dörre, K. (2019). Risiko Kapitalismus. Landnahme, Zangenkrise, Nachhaltigkeitsrevolution [Capitalism as a risk. Land seizure, crisis of pliers, sustainability revolution]. In Dörre, K., Rosa, H., Becker, K., Bose, S., & Seyd, B. (Eds.), *Große Transformation? Zur Zukunft moderner Gesellschaften [Great transformation? About the future of modern societies]* (pp. 3–34). Wiesbaden, Germany: Springer Fachmedien.

EC. (2019, December 11). *Communication from the Commission to the European Parliament, the European Council, the council, the European economic and social committee and the committee of the regions. The European Green Deal.* https://ec.europa.eu/info/sites/info/files/european-green-deal-communication_ en.pdf

Eckersley, R. (1992). Green versus ecosocialist economic programmes: The market rules ok? *Political Studies, 40*(2), 315–333. https://doi.org/10.1111/j.1467-9248. 1992.tb01387.x

Edge. (2020). *Fashion Industry Waste Statistics.* https://edgexpo.com/fashion-industry-waste-statistics/

Foster, J. B. (2011). Capitalism and degrowth: An impossibility theorem. *Monthly Review, 62*(8), 26–33. https://doi.org/10.14452/mr-062-08-2011-01_2

Fraser, N. (2015). A triple movement?. *New Left Review, 81*, 119–132. https:// newleftreview.org/issues/ii81/articles/nancy-fraser-a-triple-movement

Fullerton, J. (2015, April 20). *Regenerative capitalism. How universal principles and patterns will shape our new economy.* Capital Institute. https://capitalinstitute. org/wp-content/uploads/2015/04/2015-Regenerative-Capitalism-4-20-15-final. pdf

Galbraith, J. K., & Dörre, K. (2018). The great financial crisis and the end of normal. *Berliner Journal für Soziologie, 28*, 39–54. https://doi.org/10.1007/ s11609-018-0368-4

GIZ. (2015). *Bridging Costa Rica's green growth gap.* https://www.odi.org/sites/ odi.org.uk/files/odi-assets/publications-opinion-files/9997.pdf

Gladwin, T. N., Kennelly, J. J., & Krause, T.-S. (1995). Shifting paradigms for sustainable development: Implications for management theory and research. *Academy of Management Review, 20*(4), 874–907. https://doi.org/10.5465/ amr.1995.9512280024

Global Footprint Network. (2019). *Total ecological footprint.* http://data. footprintnetwork.org/#/?

Gorz, A. (2012). *Capitalism, socialism, ecology.* London: Verso.

Grin, J., Rotmans, J., & Schot, J. (2010). *Transitions to sustainable development. New directions in the study of long term transformative change.* New York, NY: Routledge.

Harvey, D. (2006). Neo-liberalism as creative destruction. *Human Geography, 88*(2), 145–158. https://doi.org/10.1111/j.0435-3684.2006.00211.x

Heinrichs, H., & Biermann, F. (2016). Sustainability: Politics and governance. In Heinrichs, H., et al. (Eds.), *Sustainability science. An introduction* (pp. 129–138). Dordrecht, Netherlands: Springer Science + Business Media.

Heinrichs, H., Martens, P., Michelsen, G., & Wiek, A. (2016). *Sustainability science. An introduction.* Dordrecht, Netherlands: Springer Science + Business Media.

Honneth, A. (2017). *Die Idee des Sozialismus [The idea of socialism].* Berlin, Germany: Suhrkamp.

Hopwood, P., Mellor, M., & O'Brien, G. (2005). Sustainable development: Mapping different approaches. *Sustainable Development, 13*(1), 38–52. https://doi. org/10.1002/sd.244

Horkheimer, M., & Adorno, T. W. (2017). *Dialektik der Aufklärung [Dialectic of enlightenment]* (23rd ed.). Frankfurt am Main, Germany: Fischer Taschenbuch Verlag.

IMF. (2017). *IMF Annual Report 2017.* https://www.imf.org/external/pubs/ft/ar/2017/eng/pdfs/AR17-DEU.pdf

Jackson, T. (2009). *Prosperity without growth?* London: Sustainable Development Commission.

Jänicke, M. (2012). Wir brauchen radikale Lösungen. Das "grüne Wachstum" und seine Kritiker [We need radical solutions. "Green growth" and its critics]. *Ecological economic activity/Ökologisches Wirtschaften, 27*(4), 20–22. https://doi.org/10.14512/oew.v27i4.1239

Jessop, B. (2019). Kapitalismus, Staat, Transformation: Neosozialismus oder demokratischer Ökosozialismus [Capitalism, state, transformation: Neosocialism or democratic ecosocialism]. In Dörre, K., & Schickert, C. (Eds.), *Neosozialismus [Neosocialism]* (pp. 97–110). München, Germany: oekom Verlag.

Kallis, G. (2015, February). *The degrowth alternative.* Great Transition Initiative. https://greattransition.org/publication/the-degrowth-alternative

Laricchia, F. (2022, July 22). *Green technology and sustainability market size worldwide from 2021 to 2030.* Statista. https://www.statista.com/statistics/1319996/green-technology-and-sustainability-market-size-worldwide/

Lessenich, S. (2019). Mitgegangen, mitgefangen. Das große Dilemma der Großen Transformation [Serves you right. The great dilemma of the great transformation]. In Brie, M. (Ed.), *Futuring: Perspektiven der Transformation im Kapitalismus über ihn hinaus [Futuring: Transformation perspectives within capitalism and beyond]* (pp. 57–74). Münster, Germany: Westfälisches Dampfboot.

LMD. (2019). *Atlas der Globalisierung [Atlas of globalisation].* Berlin, Germany: Le Monde Diplomatique.

Löwy, M. (2002). From Marx to ecosocialism. *Capitalism Nature Socialism, 13*(1), 121–133. https://doi.org/10.1080/104557502101245413

Löwy, M. (2018, December 19). *Why ecosocialism? A discussion of the case for a red-green future.* Climate & Capitalism. https://climateandcapitalism.com/2018/12/19/why-ecosocialism-a-discussion-of-the-case-for-a-red-green-future/

Martínez-Alier, J., Pascual, U., Vivien, F., & Zaccai, E. (2010). Sustainable degrowth: Mapping the context, criticisms and future prospects of an emerging paradigm. *Ecological Economics, 69*(9), 1741–1747. https://doi.org/10.1016/j.ecolecon.2010.04.017

Marx, K. (1986). *A reader.* Cambridge: Cambridge University Press.

Michelsen, G., Adomßent, M., Martens, P., & von Hauff, M. (2016). Sustainable development – Background and context. In Heinrichs, H., Martens, P. Michelsen, G., & Wiek, A. (Eds.). *Sustainability science. An introduction* (pp. 5–30). Dordrecht, Netherlands: Springer Science + Business Media.

Milbrath, L. W. (1984). A proposed value structure for a sustainable society. *The Environmentalist, 4*(2), 113–124. https://doi.org/10.1016/s0251-1088(84)80007-8

OECD. (2011). *Towards green growth.* http://www.oecd.org/greengrowth/48224539.pdf

OECD. (2012). *Inclusive green growth: Towards the future we want.* https://www.oecd.org/greengrowth/futurewewant.htm

Oxfam. (2020, September 21). *Confronting carbon inequality.* https://www.oxfam. de/system/files/documents/20200921-confronting-carbon-inequality.pdf

Pineault, É. (2019a). A moloch demanding the whole world a sacrifice. The structures of financial capital in the early 21st century. In Dörre, K., Rosa, H., Becker, K., Bose, S., & Seyd, B. (Eds.), *Große Transformation? Zur Zukunft moderner Gesellschaften [Great transformation? About the future of modern societies]* (pp. 119–147). Wiesbaden, Germany: Springer Fachmedien.

Pineault, É. (2019b). From provocation to challenge: Degrowth, capitalism and the prospect of "Socialism without growth": A commentary on Giorgios Kallis. *Capitalism Nature Socialism, 30*(2), 251–266. https://doi.org/10.1080/104557 52.2018.1457064

Polanyi, K. (2017). *The great transformation.* (13th ed.). Berlin, Germany: suhrkamp.

Quaddus, M. A. (2011). *Handbook of corporate sustainability: Frameworks, strategies and tools.* Cheltenham: Edward Elgar.

Raskin, P. D., Electris, C., & Rosen, R. A. (2010). The century ahead: Searching for sustainability. *Sustainability, 2*, 2626–2651. https://doi.org/10.3390/su2082626

Ritchie, H., & Roser, M. (2019). *Land use.* Our World in Data. https:// ourworldindata.org/land-use

Rockström, J., Gupta, J., Qin, D., Lade, S. J., Abrams, J. F., Andersen, L. S., Armstrong McKay, D. I., Bai, X., Bala, G., Bunn, S. E., Ciobanu, D., DeClerck, F., Ebi, K., Gifford, L., Gordon, C., Hasan, S., Kanie, N., Lenton, T. M., Loriani, S., ... Zhang, X. (2023). Safe and just earth system boundaries. *Nature, 619*, 102–111. https://doi.org/10.1038/s41586-023-06083-8

Rosa, H. (2019). Spirituelle Abhängigkeitserklärung [Spiritual declaration of dependency]. In Dörre, K., Rosa, H., Becker, K., Bose, S., & Seyd, B. (Eds.), *Große Transformation? Zur Zukunft moderner Gesellschaften [Great transformation? About the future of modern societies]* (pp. 57–74). Wiesbaden, Germany: Springer Fachmedien.

Schmelzer, M. (2019). Review on Giorgos Kallis Book Degrowth, Agenda Publishing (2018). *Ecological Economics, 159*, 379–380. https://doi.org/10.1016/j. ecolecon.2019.01.030

Schramm, K. (2020). Radikal bis neoliberal – aktuelle Konzepte des Green New Deal [Radical to neoliberal – current concepts of the Green New Deal]. *Journal of Marxist Renewal/Zeitschrift für Marxistische Erneuerung, 121*, 76–85.

Stiglitz, J., Sen, A. K., & Fitoussi, J. (2009). *The measurement of economic performance and social progress revisited: reflections and overview.* https://hal-sciencespo.archives-ouvertes.fr/hal-01069384

Sutterlütti, S., & Meretz, S. (2018). *Kapitalismus aufheben [Abolishing capitalism].* Hamburg, Germany: VSA Verlag.

Thévenot, C. (2017). Inequality in OECD countries. *Scandinavian Journal of Public Health, 45*(18), 9–16. https://doi.org/10.1177/1403494817713108

Thielemann, U. (2000). A brief theory of the market – Ethically focused. *International Journal of Social Economics, 27*(1), 6–31. https://doi.org/10.1108/030682 90010306435

Umweltbundesamt. (2019). *Rebound effects.* https://www.umweltbundesamt.de/ en/topics/waste-resources/economic-legal-dimensions-of-resource-conservation/ rebound-effects

UNDP. (2017). *Human Development Report 2019. Beyond income, beyond averages, beyond today: Inequalities in human development in the 21st century.* https://doi.org/10.18356/838f78fd-en

UNEP. (2011a). *Towards a green economy: Pathways to sustainable development and poverty eradication.* http://www.unep.org/greeneconomy/Portals/88/documents/ger/ger_final_dec_2011/Green%20EconomyReport_Final_Dec2011.pdf

UNEP. (2011b). *Green economy: Why a green economy matters for the least developed countries.* http://www.unep.org/greeneconomy/Portals/88/documents/research_products/Why%20a%20GE%20Matters%20for%20LDCs-final.pdf

UNFCCC. (2020a). *The Paris agreement.* https://unfccc.int/process-and-meetings/the-paris-agreement/the-paris-agreement

UNFCCC. (2020b, April 14). *What is the Paris agreement?* https://unfccc.int/process-and-meetings/the-paris-agreement/what-is-the-paris-agreement

Urban, H.-J. (2018). Ausbruch aus dem Gehäuse der Economic Governance. Überlegungen zu einer Soziologie der Wirtschaftsdemokratie in transformativer Absicht [Breaking out of economic governance's shell. Considerations about a sociology of economic democracy with transformative intentions]. *Berlin Journal of Sociology/Berliner Journal für Soziologie, 28,* 91–122. https://doi.org/10.1007/s11609-018-0358-6

VEC. (2018). *State of Vancouver's green economy 2018.* https://www.vancouvereconomic.com/focus/green-economy/

Ward, J. D., Sutton, P. C., Werner, A. D., Costanza, R., Mohr, S. H., & Simmons, C. T. (2016). Is decoupling GDP growth from environmental impact possible? *PLOS ONE, 11*(10), 1–14. https://doi.org/10.1371/journal.pone.0164733

WMO. (2021). *State of the global climate 2020.* https://library.wmo.int/doc_num.php?explnum_id=10618

World Bank. (2012). *Inclusive green growth: The pathway to sustainable development.* https://doi.org/10.1596/978-0-8213-9551-6

Wright, E. O. (2019). *How to be an anticapitalist in the twenty-first century.* London: Verso.

3

SUSTAINABLE STATEHOOD AS A PREREQUISITE FOR SUSTAINABLE DEVELOPMENT

Devising sustainable statehood

The previous chapters briefly addressed the evolution of the modern State, its role in shaping the capitalist social order, and how its position evolved in governance networks. Diving deeper into some of these developments is crucial for understanding how the State, and consequently political leadership, may contribute to sustainable development.

Governance in the 21st century

Governance is the pursuit of collective interests and the steering of society based on dialogic rationality, ongoing negotiation, reflection, and the modification of societal goals (Peters & Pierre, 2006). Regarding the State, we can view the governance debate from three main perspectives: (1) a loss of State power, (2) a transformation of State power, and (3) the normative desirability of governance for sustainable development (Adger & Jordan, 2009).

State "retreat" theorists argue that States were "hollowed out" during the post-Fordist era and that actors other than the State dominated governance processes since (Adger & Jordan, 2009; Peters & Pierre, 2006). The literature suggests that budgetary cutbacks, the forgone notion of top-down steering, growing interest among politicians to forge partnerships with non-state actors, and globalisation led to new global governance networks (Adger & Jordan). These challenge traditional nationhood and States' sovereignty over their citizens (Sørensen, 2006). Proponents often

DOI: 10.4324/9781003507666-5

bid farewell to normative ideas of political steering and planning altogether and call for liberal laissez-faire politics (Lange, 2003).

The second perspective holds that States were not hollowed out but merely transformed, developing new ways of regulation considering increasing globalisation (Sørensen, 2006). On one side, the model of a territorially defined nation-State no longer holds because States do not remain in power over the economy due to globalisation. At the same time, the latter is not stronger than the former. Instead, the historical review showed a reciprocal relationship that fluctuated in respective historical contexts. Still, the States' role changed in the post-Fordist era of the 1980s, and their activities progressed from economic management to procedural-regulatory functions. Simultaneously, decisions made beyond States' territories increasingly affect them due to the interconnectedness between institutions around the globe, resulting in expanded interstate relations, trans-governmental relations, and transnational ties in a "global polity". On the other hand, the State dispersed political authority into various government and public agencies, interacting with non-State actors who increasingly shape governance processes. Hence, regulation and control are no longer the sole preserve of the State. All these developments have led to global multi-governance networks (Sørensen). Thereby, governance is not a synonym for governments but a new process or method (Peters & Pierre, 2006). While there were undoubted cuts to State scope and strength during post-Fordism, the State's role also became "bigger" (Virtanen & Tammeaid, 2020). It shifted from a regulatory towards an enabling State seeking to improve social and economic conditions by adopting roles such as "collaborator," "steward," and "legislator" and corresponding tasks such as framing, piloting, and market forming (Virtanen & Tammeaid, pp. 48–49). To conclude, the State retains much of its power and, in theory, has significant potential to take on an active role in driving sustainable development.

The third governance debate revolves around the normative desirability of pursuing sustainable development (Adger & Jordan, 2009). Transition researchers differentiate this normative type of governance along three levels: (1) governance *for* transformations, i.e., creating conditions for transformations to emerge, (2) governance *of* transformations, i.e., actively triggering and steering corresponding processes, and (3) transformations *in* governance itself, i.e., transforming respective regimes (Patterson et al., 2017, p. 4). All the above require a dual focus on adaptive short- and transformative long-term strategies that create fundamentally new systems. Respectively, transition researchers call for transformative agendas and strategies of progressive incremental change, with small but cumulative steps contributing to new path dependencies toward a more desirable future (Patterson et al.). That goes hand in hand with the concept of "revolutionary real politics" and the non-reformist reforms I previously addressed. All these concepts correspond as far as they hold that transformations can be steered, triggered, or shaped in an interplay of top-down institutional coordination and bottom-up innovation (Patterson et al.).

Political scientists Peters and Pierre (2006, p. 215) point out that governance is goal-directed "with the need to establish collective goals and develop the means of reaching these goals." They state that "in a democratic context, those societal goals would have to be identified by some more or less inclusive process, and attaining these goals would have to be accomplished through a process that recognises individual rights and due process" (Peters & Pierre, p. 215). Actors seeking to govern transformations for sustainable development must thus establish respective collective goals but must do so democratically. In line with this conception, Duit et al. (2016) find that the State remains the only democratic institution that structures political, economic, and social interactions, maintains legal frameworks, has coercive power, and deploys resources through expenditures and its bureaucratic apparatus. States thus remain the "most powerful human mechanism for collective action that can compel obedience and redistribute resources [with] legitimate authority" (Duit et al., p. 4). Consequently, James Meadowcroft (2011) suggests that if the State remains society's central steering institution and sustainable development involves processes of societal self-steering, then much of the responsibility for realising it rests with the State.

Looking back in history, we have witnessed examples of States steering such transformations. The German Advisory Council on Global Change (WBGU, 2011, pp. 94–107) refers to four different motivational categories for transformations:

1 Motivated by a vision for a better, fairer, more peaceful future: the abolishment of slavery and the European integration.
2 Motivated by crises such as hunger and development: the "Green Revolution" and structural adaptation programs of the International Monetary Fund and World Bank.
3 Motivated by knowledge and irrefutable scientific proof of a problem: the treaties on ozone layer protection.
4 Motivated by technology or innovation, affecting far-reaching areas of life: the IT Revolution.

In these transformations, States played a vital role (WBGU, 2011). Regarding the international policy to protect the ozone layer, scientists initiated the debate. Yet bureaucrats from UNEP, the Montreal Protocol's Secretary-General, and Great Britain's and the United States's governments drove negotiations and implementation. Regarding the abolition of slavery, social groups such as the Quakers, Methodists, Baptists, and American Anti-Slavery Society initiated the transformation. Still, it was the government that finally implemented the laws. In the case of the IT Revolution, the US State had developed critical technologies for government research projects. The internet emerged from these technologies in a project by the US Department of Defence, the Advanced Research Project Agency, and the European Organisation for Nuclear Research. Finally, States also actively drove the European Integration and formation of the European Union, inspired by a vision of a more economically and politically stable Europe. The WBGU thus concludes that past transformation processes were collective acts of anticipatory change agents but that they first and foremost required a pro-active State (WBGU).

In line with the presented arguments and a State-centric approach, it is thus vital to acknowledge the State's central role in transformations. What will be critical to the strategies discussed earlier is to increase its scope and strength (Fukuyama, 2004). State scope depends on which functions the State may take on. These may range from minimal functions, e.g., property rights, defence, and law, to intermediate functions, e.g., addressing externalities, regulating monopolies, and social insurance, to activist functions, e.g., industrial policy and wealth distribution. The State's strength depends on its institutional capabilities and the degree to which it can implement its scope. That includes its ability to formulate and carry out policies, enact laws, administrate efficiently, control graft, corruption, and bribery, and maintain high transparency and accountability in government institutions (Fukuyama). Considering sustainable development as a potential State task would mean restructuring and empowering States to take on activist functions and potentially increase their strength to implement corresponding strategies. Accordingly, we must evaluate how this may be achieved.

Barriers to and opportunities for sustainable statehood

Creating a new narrative and hegemony

Sustainable development requires transformations in structures, institutions, and social practices that depend on paradigms and corresponding worldviews and shape the collective visions and strategies for the systemic changes we need (Göpel, 2016). In this sense, individual and collective sense-making and corresponding narratives are crucial for sustainable development. That, first and foremost, requires establishing a strong narrative and hegemonic project (Demirović, 2019) for why it is paramount and urgent. The State is a factor of cohesion that hegemonises varying interests and represents them in the diversity of State apparatuses. Each of these apparatuses organises and illustrates the power of a determinate fraction of society, from the treasury to unemployment agencies (Demirović). Actors may thus only realise sustainable development tasks within the State if these strategies become hegemonic. That is especially important considering legitimation (Habermas, 1988) and veto player theory (WBGU, 2011).

Legitimation is a central concept when considering State strength and scope because research on Stateness reveals that legitimation increases both (Mohamad-Klotzbach & Schlenkrich, 2017). Notions of legitimation differ among individuals and are, therefore, relative, not absolute (Deutsch, 1970). Since States are actively involved in the political, economic, and socio-cultural systems (Habermas, 1988), and dependent on the ecological system (Moore, 2015) it is subject to demands stemming from all four systems.

To succeed at issuing demands toward the State, citizens must reach a critical mass of members participating in democratic decision-making, and become citoyens, who actively shape the political will (Benz, 2008). Citoyens typically become part of collective actors, e.g., political parties, associations, and civil society organisations (Benz). The most successful State-building and institutional reforms occur when society creates strong demand because supply usually follows in one form or another (Fuku-yama, 2004). On the contrary, insufficient demand is the greatest obstacle to the States' institutional development (Fukuyama). Transition research-ers further suggest that, by diffusing niche innovations and practices, citoyens can encourage regime actors to pursue new solutions (Fischer & Newig, 2016). Some researchers even view civil society as a vital actor in transitions because it constitutes narratives and paradigms that may bring about regime changes (Fischer & Newig).

Local, regional, national, or international businesses can also become vital actors in transformations toward sustainable development by issuing respective demands (Fischer & Newig, 2016). Single entrepreneurs, start-ups, and spinoffs represent niche actors who may be enabling actors seek-ing new opportunities with products and services linked to sustainable development (Avelino & Wittmayer, 2016). Conversely, corporations are typically not interested in bringing about or supporting alternatives that may interfere with their established business efforts (Avelino & Witt-mayer). Because of their lobbying power, which ties to the reciprocal relationship between the State and the economy, corporations can act as a significant break on the State's institutional development (Culpepper, 2015). While they usually do not participate in politics directly, they do so via corporate interest groups, such as NGOs and think tanks (Arts, 2006). In recent years, there has also been a strong trend toward firms promoting their interests in international arenas as they gained standing rights in international bodies such as the EU and WTO (Arts).

Political actors may take on a unique role in sustainable development because they can issue and realise demands directly (Ottens & Edelenbos, 2018). Heads of State and governments play a decisive role in this regard, even though the extent depends on the power issued to them by the political system (Benz, 2008). Significant power also lies with members of governments and parliaments as they initiate political programs and make decisions along a majority vote after consulting in committees and public debates. Yet another decisive collective actor is regional authorities, which include a range of actors from federal States to local councils. International, transnational, and supranational organisations such as the United Nations and OECD also play a role in political demands. Whilst they are not political entities like States, they directly affect their efforts and contribute to fulfilling State tasks such as securing peace, improving living conditions, and implementing product safety standards in a globalised world (Benz).

Finally, the capitalist social order depends on and significantly impacts non-human nature. We can perceive indirect demands by nature when we see ecosystems breaking down, species going extinct, or increases in natural disasters (WBGU, 2011). However, nature cannot issue direct requests to the State. Instead, it must rely on representatives from civil society, the economy, and the State to do so.

For States to be able to expand their scope and contribute to sustainable development, the above stakeholder groups must issue demands and create a respective hegemony. A lack thereof otherwise becomes a significant barrier to sustainable development. The more collective or independent veto players emerge the more likely new visions and strategies for sustainable development will fail (WBGU, 2011). The ability of said veto players to gain power depends on the type of democracy and party constellations, the lobbying power of businesses and civil society organisations, the degree of corruption, and the influence of supranational institutions. The success, therefore, depends on the State's capacity to develop and instate a new narrative, unite the majority of actors, and offer formats for them to jointly work towards achieving this broadly accepted vision (WBGU).

Yet, even when a narrative and hegemony are in place, the primary challenge for States remains their public image (Mazzucato, 2018). Neoliberal agendas have shaped citizens' perception of the State to its disadvantage for decades. In many cases, they restricted the government's role to fixing market failures and accounting for external costs imposed on the public by the private sector. At the same time, they portrayed States as slow, large, and inert institutions that hinder markets and are unsuited to creating innovation. As a result of decades of this neoliberal narrative, explored in

Chapter 1, and corresponding cutbacks, States were downsized and had fewer resources to build competencies and capabilities for reforms and innovations necessary to drive sustainable development (Mazzucato).

In line with a new narrative, we thus need to fundamentally redefine the State's role in society as an institution that provides public value, solves problems, and invests in sustainable development (Mazzucato, 2018). There is already a vast range of suggestions of what this new State can look like: a "Decarbonised Welfare State" (Gough & Meadowcroft, 2011), a "Green State" (Meadowcroft, 2006), a "Formative State" (Heinrichs, 2017), a "Sustainability State" (Heinrichs & Laws, 2014), or "Sustainable State-hood" (Heinrichs, 2022). What unites these concepts is that this type of State's most crucial performance evaluation parameter is no longer economic growth. Instead, it must focus on navigating society into a promising future, which entails one version or another of fulfilling human needs within planetary boundaries.

Institutionalising sustainable development

A central challenge for political actors in implementing this new narrative and changing institutions and processes along them is structural, as current institutions and processes often counter the requirements for sustainable development (Osborne & Brown, 2005). State representatives and administrations in political bureaucracies usually follow past procedures and problem-solving paths, even if they no longer solve current and future problems or the problem context has changed (WBGU, 2011). In addition, different departments typically focus on specific issues, but sustainable development challenges span systematically across departments. Horizontal and vertical policy integration and fragmentation, such as federal vs. individual States or Nation-States vs. the EU, present further barriers to implementation. A lack of coherence and coordination and the fact that modern policymaking tends to follow the "good for everybody and harming nobody" maxim increases institutional fragmentation. This results in measures for sustainable development on the one side and profoundly unsustainable measures on the other (WBGU).

Sustainable development also requires policies focusing on the long-term, which contradicts short parliamentary terms and the will to stay in power (WBGU, 2011). At the same time, politicians and officeholders often shelf complex problems revolving around extensive reforms, demographic change, increasing healthcare costs, unemployment, debt, and climate change due to their complexity and because their impacts often lie in the future. To overcome these structures, the States' capacity for long-term policymaking and institutional continuity must be enhanced (WBGU).

Simultaneously, States must combine short- and long-term visions and actions because multiple transformations will intersect, overlap, and conflict, thus requiring a mixture of incremental change and longer-term transformation in various areas (Patterson et al., 2017). To succeed, new policies must focus on setting clear goals, creating macro frameworks and effective legal instruments, and involving private, public-private, and public sector actors to create more impactful solutions (WBGU).

Harald Heinrichs and Norman Laws (2014) suggest that overall, States must follow a range of institutional and procedural changes regarding sustainable development:

1. Setting strategies along fixed criteria.
2. Creating institutions specifically to deal with sustainable development.
3. Driving cooperation between parliamentary groups, ministries, and political parties on topics relating to sustainable development.
4. Prioritising sustainable development in daily business.
5. Evaluating measures along sustainable development dimensions, both ex-ante and ex-post.
6. Making investments and creating and evaluating new policies along sustainable development criteria.
7. Integrating non-state actors in driving the transformation.
8. Engaging in long-term planning for sustainable development.
9. Embedding sustainable development in the constitution.

To summarise, political leaders must create and implement a range of political innovations in the sense of "intentional efforts to transform political institutions designed to make authoritative political decisions (polity), the political processes that lead to such decisions (politics) and the content of the resulting policies (policy)" (Sørensen, 2021, p. 2). However, these innovations alone will not suffice if responsible actors do not have sufficient capacity to work with and act upon them.

Enabling leadership for sustainable development

Political innovations include changes in State structures, which pose constraints and potentials that vary by agent, depending on their strategic capacities (Jessop, 1990). Opportunities for actors to reorganise specific structures and reorient strategies are subject to structurally inscribed strategic selectivity, changes in the balance of forces in the strategic terrains of the economy, State and broader social formation, and changes in the actor's organisation, strategies, and tactics. In this way, the State represents the site, generator, and product of political strategy. If agents seek to create a new hegemony, they must analyse State apparatuses and power and its widespread approval within the State apparatus (Jessop, 2016). Success in steering the State depends on the complementarity of political strategies with deeper structures and logics (Jessop, 2016). Strategies are most likely to succeed where they address the significant structural constraints associated with dominant institutional orders, the overall balance of forces, and conjunctural opportunities via new alliances, strategies, and spatiotemporal horizons of action (Jessop, 1990). Respectively, there is no one approach to implementing demands for sustainable development within the State. Instead, political actors must understand the structures they are acting in and the actors they need to involve, creating a hegemonic project with suitable strategies. Regarding the strategies reviewed in this chapter, we may view sustaincentric approaches such as the EU Green Deal as a successful attempt at this conception because it promotes a sustainability program, but only to the extent that nation-States and businesses will accept it in the current conjuncture.

Political strategies to implement political innovations then require strategic skills in the political and administrative spheres, which are complementary and crucial for the joint pursuit of sustainable development (Braams et al., 2021). These skills include a capacity for long-term thinking and reflexivity to identify change signals and adapt efforts over time (Rotmans et al., 2001). Along political strategy theory, States need to develop their human resources through extensive training, allowing them to build systemic knowledge about respective challenges, goals, and strategies (Heinrichs & Laws, 2014). They must also foster various competencies, ranging from strategic, e.g., problem structuring, to tactical, e.g., developing agendas, to operational, e.g., mobilising actors and executing projects and experiments (Heinrichs & Laws).

In addition to leadership within the State, citoyens must also issue sufficient social demands for and engage in leadership for sustainable development. Scholars, citizens, and politicians suggest alternatives for direct representation, e.g., by creating a "fourth force" next to the legislative, executive, and judicative (Leggewie & Nanz, 2016). This force can counteract decreasing voter turnouts, declining memberships in political parties, associations, citizens' initiatives, and non-governmental organisations, as well as the disaffection with politics and politicians. Some call for civil society "future councils" in municipalities, consisting of permanent institutions of randomly selected and representative citizens. These councils cooperatively identify future challenges and develop solutions, obliging municipal councilors and administrative staff to consider their proposals in decision-making processes. These councils can also extend to a national or European level to counter the structural shortcomings of representative democracies and guarantee that States include citizens in their decisions (Leggewie & Nanz). On a similar note, others suggest "future quorums," which include the views of future generations (WBGU, 2011) or extend them to "surrogate representation" so that people who do not belong to a nation-State but are affected by its actions are also considered (WBGU).

Overcoming the dependency on capital accumulation

A final barrier to sustainable development lies within the State itself. Neo-Marxists hold that States are Capitalist States rather than States in capitalism (Borchert & Lessenich, 2016). The modern Capitalist State is bound to capitalism and democracy in a "double bind". It has both an accumulation and a legitimation function which are not external influences imposed on it but contradictory internal components. By guaranteeing capitalism's accumulation function, the State agreed to protect capital, whilst, via democracy, it decided on its societal legitimation function and to adhere to the public's will. Respectively, the Capitalist State has become dependent on taxes to create social legitimation, e.g., by supplying social services, which rely on accumulation and, thus, economic prosperity. However, the accumulation function often has legitimation costs, and similarly, legitimation produces accumulation costs. Therefore, by design, the Capitalist State is torn between its multiple contradictions, trapped in the dilemma of its double bind and the "institutional self-interest of the State" (Borchert & Lessenich, p. 27).

Going back to the sustaincentric and socio-ecocentric approaches, this implies that sustaincentric strategies reconcile the structural dilemma of the Capitalist State best because they maintain the capitalist accumulation function and tie its legitimation to social demands for sustainable development. Still, Left thinkers have started to promote mechanisms to circumvent this double bind, such as Modern Monetary Theory. The theory proposes that States with sovereignty over their currency and institutions, such as the European Union and Central Bank, may create money for investments in sustainable development, decoupled from capital accumulation (Höfgen, 2020). Still, they currently remain theories and have not been applied in practice.

The genesis of political leadership theory and practice

As touched upon in Chapter 2, actors have the power to shape State institutions. In this sense, we must understand how political leaders, in particular, may succeed at implementing political innovations for sustainable statehood.

Political leadership is an aspect of public leadership, which can be defined as

a form of collective leadership in which public bodies and agencies collaborate in achieving a shared vision based on shared aims and values and distribute this through each organization in a collegiate way which seeks to promote, influence and deliver improved public value as evidenced through sustained social, environmental and economic well-being within a complex and changing context.

(Brookes & Grint, 2010, p. 2)

Public leadership stands at the heart of good governance and is vital to accountability within governments and serving the public interest with the outcome of making society better (Page, 2016).

Politics itself is concerned with the allocation of values and who should get what, when, and how (Deutsch, 1970). We can thus broadly define a *political leader* as "one who gives direction, or meaningfully participates in the giving of direction, to the activities of a political community" (Tucker, 1995, p. 15). *Political leadership* then involves "leadership of a political community and all the activity...that may enter into the process of leadership" (Tucker, p. xv) to promote public interest.

The specific conception of political leadership evolved with time. It is only since the mid-1940s that it has become an area of academic investigation with three strands of inquiry (Elgie, 2015). The first is normative political theory which tries to establish the relationship between leadership, political life, and what constitutes good leadership. The second strand concerns the concept of political leadership, what it is, and how it should be defined. The third strand builds on an Interactionist foundation. It investigates leadership outcomes and why some leaders are more successful than others, explained in terms of the interaction between the qualities of political leaders and the context they face (Elgie). This third strand and the agency-structure duality (Giddens, 1979) are essential to this book, as the former is concerned with the success factors of political leadership, whilst the latter is concerned with what these factors may be.

Initially, Interactionist leadership research analysed leaders as positional authorities, showing how they achieved goals in their context and which leadership styles and traits helped them on the way (Komives & Dugan, 2010). Corresponding theories were mainly concerned with top-down leadership, hierarchies, and power and portrayed leaders as heroic figures and "great men" (Elgie, 1995). At the end of the 1970s, however, paradigms shifted in leadership studies. James Burns (1978) conceptualised leadership as a process that must be focused on developing followers rather than top-down management. Thereby the focus shifted from leaders' capabilities to their potential of empowering followers, collaborative methods, reciprocal relationships, and systemic approaches in complex networks (Komives & Dugan, 2010). In this state, leadership became synonymous with effective management and influence over followers and included behavioural, contingency, and leader-member exchange theories (Komives & Dugan). Parallel to this, the conception of the State changed from a top-down regulator to an organisation within complex governance networks (Sørensen, 2006), as described in Chapter 1.

Even more recently, leadership theory evolved to what may be termed *collective* (Ospina & Foldy, 2016) or *relational* (Uhl-Bien, 2006) leadership. Thereby the focus shifted away from singular leaders enabling their followers to collective dimensions of leadership and emergent processes and practices that help actors interact, co-construct meaning, and advance a shared mission they could not have achieved by themselves (Ospina & Foldy). This leadership paradigm applies to complex governance challenges that must be addressed across organisations, sectors, and actors. It implies that all group members make up the leadership phenomenon, rather than singular members, because there may be more than one person in a leadership role, leadership rotates, or it is distributed and shared (Ospina & Foldy). This view perceives leadership as a social construction that emanates from the connections and interdependencies of organisations and their members (Uhl-Bien, 2006). Collective leadership thus emerges from co-constructed meanings that help a group advance its tasks rather than from an influence relationship between the social actors' leader and follower (Ospina & Foldy).

In line with the discussed evolution, the understanding of authority associated with leadership also changed. Traditionally, leadership was viewed from a formal authority perspective because a position grants it (Heifetz, 2010). Informal authority, on the other hand, results from trust, admiration, and respect. Both forms of authority represent a social contract, where one party entrusts a second party with power in exchange for services. Today scholars suggest leadership is the ability to gain informal authority by influencing people in informal and persuasive ways without having to employ formal authority (Heifetz).

The role of political leadership in sustainable development

Political scientists have thus far not investigated political leadership regarding political innovations for sustainable development. Developing a new normative concept, derived from theoretical deductions about the kind of leadership that is necessary in the age of governance for sustainable development, is therefore feasible.

As laid out in this chapter, creating sustainable statehood by increasing the State's strength and scope requires *political innovations*. Political scientist Eva Sørensen (2020) specifies them describing innovations in polity as involving efforts to reorganise external boundaries with other States, institutional frameworks, and procedures that regulate the forming and enacting of democratically authorised decisions about what counts as public value. Innovations in politics refer to new ways for political actors to obtain democratically legitimate power. Innovations in policy can involve formulating new visions, goals, strategies, and policy programs that guide public value (Sørensen). The political leaders this book is concerned with strive to implement said political innovations with a clear normative orientation toward sustainable development. This corresponds with a socio-institutional approach in transition literature, which aims at changing cultures, structures, and practices by focusing on incumbent routines, power relations, interests, discourses, and regulations (Loorbach et al., 2017).

Political leaders may take on a central role in these socio-institutional transitions. They legitimise and delegitimise the distribution of values and directly select and channel political demands into the political process (Sørensen, 2020). In this process, the public expects political leaders to provide "innovation…, not re-production…not re-presentation but a presentation of something new, a creation of something which has not existed before" (Körösényi, 2005, p. 375). In an ideal case, political leaders become political entrepreneurs. In this sense, they do not cater to current demands but create new ones by supplying new proposals. Thus, they come true to the Aristotelian notion of Greek democracy by being an orator who shapes public opinion, a persuader that this will is good for society, and a public-opinion leader by creating respective agendas (Körösényi). Political leaders for sustainable development thus deliberately create the circumstances and possibilities for political innovations for sustainable development (Selman, 2002). In the sense of the latest notion of shared and relational leadership, we must, however, view individual leaders cautiously, since their leadership outcomes are collective rather than individual efforts. Still, executive political positions allow for significant leeway in driving the implementation of political innovations, and thus exploring the role of individual executive leaders in the process is feasible.

To analyse said leaders, we must understand the many factors influencing their efforts. Russ Volckmann (2010) suggests thinking of leadership processes as a holon: a part and a whole, all in one. A molecule that is whole in itself but simultaneously part of a cell. Thus, leadership concerns a particular leader and the context in which they act (Volckmann). First, the variables of both holons must be analysed, as agency and structure variables shape this multidimensional phenomenon. This must be done from diverse scientific angles because political sciences have paid little attention to political leadership. As political scientist Alastair Cole (1994) suggests, this may be because leadership studies are multidisciplinary, cross-cultural, and semantic difficulties with the concept remain, but more so because political scientists have preferred to reason in terms of processes, structures, and institutions. In addition, "leadership" and "governance" have tended to coexist in isolation from each other and their relationship has remained understudied (Helms, 2012).

The following chapters will therefore look at the context political leaders face, and the respective leadership styles, skills, and traits they need to promote sustainable statehood and become agents for sustainable development.

References

Adger, W. N., & Jordan, A. (2009). *Governing sustainability*. Cambridge: Cambridge University Press.

Arts, B. (2006). Non-state actors in global environmental governance: New arrangements beyond the State. In Koenig-Archibugi, M. & Zürn, M. (Eds.), *New modes of governance in the global system* (pp. 177–200). New York, NY: Palgrave McMillan.

Avelino, F., & Wittmayer, J. (2016). Shifting power relations in sustainability transitions: A multi-actor perspective. *Journal of Environmental Policy and Planning, 18*(5), 628–649.

Benz, A. (2008). *Der moderne Staat [The modern state]* (2nd ed.). München, Germany: Oldenbourg Wissenschaftsverlag.

Borchert, J., & Lessenich, S. (2016). *Claus Offe and the critical theory of the capitalist state*. New York, NY: Routledge.

Braams, R. B., Wesseling, J. H., Meijer, A. J., & Hekkert, M. P. (2021). Legitimizing transformative government. Aligning essential government tasks from transition literature with normative arguments about legitimacy from public administration traditions. *Environmental Innovation and Societal Transitions, 39*, 191–205. https://doi.org/10.1016/j.eist.2021.04.004

Brookes, S., & Grint, K. (2010). *The new public leadership challenge*. New York, NY: Palgrave Macmillan.

Burns, J. M. (1978). *Leadership*. New York, NY: Harper Row.

Cole, A. (1994). Studying political leadership: The case of Francois Mitterand. *PoliticalStudiesXLII,42*(3),453–468.https://doi.org/10.1111/j.1467-9248.1994.tb01688.x

Culpepper, P. D. (2015). Structural power and political science in the post-crisis era. *Business and Politics, 17*(3), 391–409. https://doi.org/10.1515/bap-2015-0031

Demirović, A. (2019). The Capitalist State, hegemony, and the democratic transformation toward socialism. In Ducange, J. & Keucheyan, R. (Eds.), *The end of the democratic state* (pp. 43–60). Cham, Switzerland: Springer Nature.

Deutsch, K. W. (1970). *Staat, Regierung, Politik [State, government, politics]*. Freiburg, Germany: Rombach.

Duit, A., Feindt, P. H., & Meadowcroft, J. (2016). Greening the Leviathan: The rise of the environmental state? *Environmental Politics, 25*(1), 1–23. https://doi.org/10.1080/09644016.2015.1085218

Elgie, R. (1995). *Political leadership in liberal democracies.* Hampshire: Palgrave Macmillan.

Elgie, R. (2015). *Studying political leadership.* Hampshire: Palgrave Macmillan.

Fischer, L.-B., & Newig, J. (2016). Importance of actors and agency in sustainability transitions: A systematic exploration of the literature. *Sustainability, 8*(476), 1–21. https://doi.org/10.3390/su8050476

Fukuyama, F. (2004). *State-building: Governance and world order in the twenty-first century.* Ithaca, NY: Cornell University Press.

Giddens, A. (1979). *Contemporary social theory.* London: Macmillan Education.

Göpel, M. (2016). *The great mindshift.* Wiesbaden, Germany: Springer.

Gough, I., & Meadowcroft, J. (2011). Decarbonizing the welfare state. In Dryzek, J. S., Norgaard, R. B., & Schlosberg, D. (Eds.), *Oxford Handbook of climate change and society.* Oxford: Oxford University Press.

Habermas, J. (1988). *Legitimation crisis.* Cambridge: Polity Press.

Heifetz, R. (2010). Leadership. In Couto, R. A., *Political and civic leadership: A reference handbook* (Eds.), (pp. 12–22). Thousand Oaks, CA: SAGE Publications.

Heinrichs, H. (2017). *Der gestaltende Staat im Kontext gesellschaftlichen Wandels [The formative State in context of societal change].* Umweltbundesamt. https://www.umweltbundesamt.de/sites/default/files/medien/1410/publikationen/2017-11-29-texte_107-2017_gestaltender-staat_0.pdf

Heinrichs, H. (2022). Sustainable statehood: Reflections on critical (pre-)conditions and design options. *Sustainability, 14*(15), 9461. https://doi.org/10.3390/su14159461

Heinrichs, H., & Laws, N. (2014). "Sustainability State" in the Making? Institutionalization of Sustainability in German Federal Policy Making. *Sustainability, 6*(5), 2623–2641. https://doi.org/10.3390/su6052623

Helms, L. (2012). *Poor leadership and bad governance.* Cheltenham: Edward Elgar Publishing.

Höfgen, M. (2020). *Mythos Geldknappheit. Modern Monetary Theory oder warum es am Geld nicht scheitern muss [Myth shortage of money. Modern monetary theory or why it does not have to fail because of money].* Stuttgart, Germany: Schäfer-Poeschel.

Jessop, B. (1990). *State theory: Putting the Capitalist State in its place.* University Park, PA: Penn State University Press.

Jessop, B. (2016). *The State: Past, present, future.* Cambridge: Polity Press.

Komives, S. R., & Dugan, J. P. (2010). Contemporary leadership theories. In Couto, R. A. (Ed.), *Political and civic leadership: A reference handbook* (pp. 111–120). Thousand Oaks, CA: SAGE Publications.

Körösényi, A. (2005). Political representation in leader democracy. *Government and Opposition, 40*(3), 358–378. https://doi.org/10.1111/j.1477-7053.2005.00155.x

Lange, S. (2003). *Niklas Luhmanns Theorie der Politik [Niklas Luhmann's political theory].* Wiesbaden, Germany: Westdeutscher Verlag/GWV Fachverlage GmbH.

Leggewie, C., & Nanz, P. (2016). Stärkung der Demokratie durch Institutionalisierung von Bürgerbeteiligung? [Strengthening of democracy through the institutionalisation of citizen participation?]. *Zeitschrift für Politikwissenschaft*

[Journal for political sciences], 26(3), 335–341. https://doi.org/10.1007/s41358-016-0060-1

Loorbach, D., Frantzeskaki, N., & Avelino, F. (2017). Sustainability transitions research: Transforming science and practice for societal change. *Annual Review of Environmental Resources*, 42(1), 599–626. https://doi.org/10.1146/annurev-cnviron-102014-021340

Mazzucato, M. (2018). *The entrepreneurial State. Debunking public vs. private sector myths*. London: Penguin Randomhouse.

Meadowcroft, J. (2006). Greening the State. *Politics and Ethics*, 2(2), 109–118. https://doi.org/10.1177/1743453X0600200203

Meadowcroft, J. (2011). Engaging with the politics of sustainability transitions. *Environmental Innovation and Societal Transitions*, 1(1), 70–75. https://doi.org/10.1016/j.eist.2011.02.003

Mohamad-Klotzbach, C., & Schlenkrich, O. (2017). Die wiederentdeckte Relevanz von Staat und Staatlichkeit [The rediscovered relevance of state and statehood]. *Journal for comparattive political sciences/Zeitschrift für vergleichende Politikwissenschaft*, 11, 479–487. https://doi.org/10.1007/s12286-017-0353-x

Moore, J. (2015). *Capitalism in the web of life*. London: Verso.

Osborne, S. P., & Brown, K. (2005). *Managing change and innovation in public service organizations*. London: Routledge.

Ospina, S. M., & Foldy, E. G. (2016). Collective dimensions of leadership. In Farazmand, A. (Ed.), *Global encyclopedia of public administration, public policy, and Governance* (pp. 838–844). https://doi.org/10.1007/978-3-319-20928-9_2202

Ottens, M., & Edelenbos, J. (2018). Political leadership as meta-governance in sustainability transitions: A case study analysis of meta-governance in the case of the Dutch National Agreement on Climate. *Sustainability*, 11(1), 110. https://doi.org/10.3390/su11010110

Page, M. B. (2016). Public leadership. Navigating leadership challenges and operating in service of the common good in an interconnected world. *International Journal of Public Leadership*, 12(2), 112–128.

Patterson, J., Schulz, K., Vervoort, J., van der Hel, S., Widerberg, O., Adler, C., Hurlbert, M., Anderton, K., Sethi, M., & Barau, A. (2017). Exploring the governance and politics of transformations towards sustainability. *Environmental Innovation and Societal Transitions*, 24, 1–16. https://doi.org/10.1016/j.eist.2016.09.001

Peters, B. G., & Pierre, J. (2006). Governance, government and the State. In Hay, C., Lister, M., & Marsh, D. (Eds.), *The State. Theories and issues* (pp. 209–222). New York, NY: Palgrave McMillan.

Rotmans, J., Kemp, R., & van Asselt, M. (2001). More evolution than revolution: Transition management in public policy. *Foresight*, 3(1), 15–31. https://doi.org/10.1108/14636680110803003

Selman, J. (2002). Leadership and innovation: Relating to circumstances and change. *The Public Sector Innovation Journal*, 7(3), 1–9. https://innovation.cc/discussion-papers/2002_7_3_5_selman_leadership-innovation.pdf

Sørensen, E. (2020). *Interactive political leadership. The role of politicians in the age of governance*. Oxford: Oxford University Press.

Sørensen, E. (2021). Political innovations: Innovations in political institutions, processes and outputs. In Sørensen, E. (Ed.), *Political innovations. Creative transformations in polity, politics and policy* (pp. 1–19). New York, NY: Routledge.

Sørensen, G. (2006). The transformation of the State. In Hay, C., Lister, M., & Marsh, D. (Eds.), *The State. Theories and issues* (pp. 190–208). New York, NY: Palgrave McMillan.

Tucker, R. C. (1995). *Politics as leadership*. Columbia, MO: University of Missouri Press.

Uhl-Bien, M. (2006). Relational leadership theory: Exploring the social processes of leadership and organizing. *The Leadership Quarterly, 17*(6), pp. 654–676. https://doi.org/10.1016/j.leaqua.2006.10.007

Virtanen, P., & Tammeaid, M. (2020). *Developing public sector leadership*. Cham, Switzerland: Springer Nature.

Volckmann, R. (2010). Integral leadership theory. In Couto, R. A. (Ed.), *Political and civic leadership: A reference handbook* (pp. 121–127). Thousand Oaks, CA: SAGE Publications.

WBGU. (2011). *World in transition. A social contract for sustainability*. https://www.wbgu.de/en/publications/publication/world-in-transition-a-social-contract-for-sustainability#section-downloads

PART II

How women leaders may drive political innovations for sustainable development

4

UNDERSTANDING HOW CONTEXT INFLUENCES POLITICAL LEADERSHIP

Navigating the parliamentary, administrative, and public arenas

For political leadership, context is critical because it can shape said leaders and present both barriers and opportunities to their efforts. Politicians act in three specific arenas: the parliamentary, administrative, and public arenas (Korte, 2019). In the parliamentary arena, political parties and their representatives bargain over policy decisions. The administrative arena includes the legislative, executive, and judicative where bargaining and non-public voting for consensus on political programs occur. The public arena involves public moods and opinions, publicity to gain power, and representative politics, where citizens stand in communication with politicians (Korte). To understand the structural factors influencing political leaders, it is paramount to briefly glimpse how these arenas may support or hinder them in their efforts, specifically regarding political innovations.

The public arena

Chapter 1 discussed the numerous past and current social, economic, and environmental factors that may influence the public's demands and opinions. The public can exert significant pressure on politicians to develop new innovative programs and policy agendas (Kingdon, 2011), thus creating pull factors for innovation. Policies then represent public opinion to some degree because policymakers depend on the public's support (Rasmussen et al., 2018). Indeed, social demands are critical for expanding State tasks and scope (Fukuyama, 2004) and, thus, potentially, sustainable statehood.

DOI: 10.4324/9781003507666-7

What drives innovation in the public arena is the evolution of followers from passive spectators with little interest in or capacity for contributing to governance to critical, empowered, and committed citoyens who want to be actively involved in shaping their living conditions (Nye, 2008). Citizens are becoming more confident and increasingly seek to solve their problems without political parties (Sørensen, 2020). This leads to more interactive forms of governance in which politicians explore and define policy problems, design policies and generate support for their implementation in dialogue with affected citizens, which may lead to more significant political innovation (Sørensen).

Citizens expect political leaders to justify their decisions and actively listen and respond to their ideas and demands (Rosanvallon, 2011) in "empowered participatory governance" processes (Fung & Wright, 2003). Respectively, public agencies, bureaucracies, and politicians are fostering engagement with citizens and other actors, increasing access and participation in governance and thus enabling more open and collaborative forms of innovation, e.g., via social media tools (Criado et al., 2013).

At the same time, the media's impact on politicians keeps increasing, and they take on an active role in the political process (Cohen et al., 2008). For one, in the age of "mediatisation," voters are unlikely to support politicians they do not know enough about. Thus, media affects how much and in what way the public perceives politicians. Media coverage has also become part of the policymaking process within legislative institutions, used by politicians to pressure their colleagues. Politicians may even adapt their behaviours to make them fit the media and actively shape public opinion (Cohen et al.). Because political innovations always include a risk, politicians may be sceptical about implementing them because they fear public blame for failure or the public perceiving government as gambling with public money (Mulgan & Albury, 2003). In turn, public and media resonance may negatively influence the implementation of innovations (Bommert, 2010).

Finally, culture, in terms of values, beliefs, and artifacts, also affects the innovation capacity of society and politics (Prim et al., 2017). It can be measured via the six dimensions of power distance, uncertainty avoidance, masculinity, individualism, long-term orientation, and indulgence. The lower the hierarchies are in a country, the greater the degree of innovation. The lower uncertainty avoidance the higher the promotion of innovations. Countries with low masculinity and high femininity also tend to produce more innovations because they tolerate errors and encourage experimentation. High individualism and long-term orientation may also lead to more innovations as independent countries favour innovations and plan them sustainably. High indulgence additionally causes individuals to long for new experiences and innovation. Finally, competitive cultures foster innovations in a race to the top (Prim et al.). A leader's cultural context thus may significantly influence their capacity to develop and implement political innovations.

The parliamentary arena

Considering the parliamentary arena, the type of democracy in a nation has a significant influence on innovation capacity. Majoritarian governments are more flexible in policymaking and therefore have potentially greater innovation capacity than consensus democracies (Lijphart, 2012). Executive power remains in the hands of one-party or bare-majority cabinets, which facilitates policy implementation considering veto player theory. In addition, majoritarian democracies tend to feature presidential systems where the head of government or president is not liable to the legislature and can make critical decisions without or even against advice from cabinets. Furthermore, majoritarian democracies feature a unitary and centralised government where local governments depend on the decisions and finances of the central government, binding them to centralised decisions. In consensus democracies, on the other hand, executive power is shared in broad coalition cabinets, and power is balanced between executive and legislative, making the implementation of new policies more complex. The head of State also depends on the legislature's confidence and may be dismissed from office, making them less flexible in their decision-making. Consensus democracies also feature federal and decentralised governments where central government and confederacies share power. Thus, the implementation of political innovations is complex on a national level but facilitated on a regional and local level (Lijphart).

Another critical factor is political parties, as they are key actors in modern democratic representation (Bischoff & Christiansen, 2021). They can organise legislative and oversight processes in parliament, realise policies and act as potential policy entrepreneurs for political innovations. Bischoff and Christiansen (2021) differentiate between innovations occurring at the party and the party system level and between the form, i.e., organisational and process aspects, and the content dimensions of representation, i.e., values, policies, decisions, and instruments. From this, they derive a typology of four areas where innovation can occur.

"Linkage" reflects the organisational traits and processes in political parties that link them to voters and other actors such as think tanks, unions, interest organisations, or the State itself (Bischoff & Christiansen, 2021). These actors typically play a role in the decision-making processes of political parties, their policymaking capacity, how they connect with other actors, and the extent to which they do so, e.g., how they recruit candidates, select leaders, collect resources, or adopt policy programmes (Bischoff & Christiansen).

A critical aspect is that political leaders must first come into office. The parties' electoral system determines this process (Rahat & Hazan, 2001). The first important aspect is how they select potential candidates: the nomination or proposal of names, approval of proposed candidates, decisions on the list, and the order of said candidates. The most inclusive form of candidacy selection is when all citizens can run for office, and the least inclusive is when only party members can do so along with further requirements (Rahat et al., 2008). In some systems, party leaders appoint candidates, representing enhanced representative control (Rahat & Hazan). In others, party members vote on candidate nominations, suggesting reduced representation control and greater inclusiveness (Rahat & Hazan). The party selectorate is thus most inclusive when an electorate of all party members can vote on a potential candidate and least inclusive when a party leader decides. In their paper on democracy and political parties, Rahat et al. (2008) suggest that these selectorates influence competition between incumbents and non-incumbents. Accordingly, the less inclusive a voting system is, e.g., via a nomination committee, the lower the competition will be between potential candidates. Competition is highest when candidates compete for the delegates' votes and medium when party members decide (Rahat et al.). These party systems determine whether an individual may even get the chance to become a political leader.

The second dimension, "program," refers to the political identity of parties, their ideology or vision, and the policy proposals connected to them (Bischoff & Christiansen, 2021). Different variables may thereby influence political parties' innovation capacity: whether they position themselves closer to the State or civil society, whether they draw on individual or collective resources, whether internal decision-making processes are hierarchical with top-down, centralised control or horizontal, open and democratic, and whether their organisational characteristics are professional and capital-intensive or amateur and volunteer-based (Krouwel, 2006). The party organisation may constrain party leadership, allow for room to manoeuvre on questions of policy and resources, or may make them independent from or dependent on powerful interests (Krouwel). Bischoff and Christiansen hypothesise that parties with top-down decision-making that draw on collective rather than individual resources may be better positioned for policy innovations than parties whose leadership is constrained by internal democracy or external actors. However, this may only be the case if leadership is motivated to drive an agenda of innovation (Bischoff & Christiansen). Ludger Helms (2016), on the other hand, argues that wicked problems require collective or shared leadership because information sharing and active deliberation among different actors are essential for respective policy proposals. These insights suggest that parties with horizontal, open, and democratic decision-making can foster more innovative policy agendas (Helms). Bischoff and Christiansen additionally suggest that parties with distinct ideologies may be less likely to adopt pragmatic policy changes. In contrast, parties with broad, vague, and more centred ideologies may be more likely to change and adopt new proposals. Still, they attest to an innovative role for radical parties, which may affect the position of mainstream parties with their proposals (Bischoff & Christiansen).

The third dimension, "interactions", concerns competition and cooperation in party systems (Bischoff & Christiansen, 2021). Based on veto-player theory, Bischoff and Christiansen hypothesise that systems with fewer parties in a governing coalition should create better conditions for passing innovative legislation that breaks with the status quo. The higher the number of actors, the more likely they can block legislation and prevent policy changes. On the other hand, more actors representing more diverse interests can also help create innovative solutions. Therefore, they conclude that more players may lead to lower legislative output but potentially more innovative solutions. In addition, they suggest that coalition agreements can aid the creation of innovative policies that might otherwise be difficult to pass. Thus, coalition governance arrangements may promote political innovation (Bischoff & Christiansen).

Furthermore, alternation influences innovation capacity because if a potential replacement does not threaten party players, they may have fewer incentives to innovate (Bischoff & Christiansen, 2021). However, parties need a certain time frame to develop and pass bills in parliament, and thus concise time horizons hamper the willingness to innovate and depart from the status quo. Finally, new configurations of governing coalitions and the new entry of parties into the system hold the most significant potential for introducing policy changes (Bischoff & Christiansen). However, governments, tend to innovate in one-time big shots, rather than ongoing and incrementally, to minimise risks in fear of the media's and opposition parties' exposure of public failures and creating an image of governments gambling with public money (Bommert, 2010).

The final dimension of the parliamentary arena is "policy" (Bischoff & Christiansen, 2021). Bischoff and Christiansen describe the policy space in terms of its degree of polarisation, i.e., how much party programmes differ and their types and number of policy dimensions. The degree of polarisation determines whether parties can find common ground and negotiate compromises regarding policy proposals. The stronger polarisation, the less likely compromises, and the more significant conflicts may be. But even if there is common ground among a majority, the government formation process may constrain them from turning innovations into reality. New policy types may also arise from new majority constellations and existing coalitions responding to outside pressures. On the other hand, party actors with similar views will tend to collaborate, and changes will likely be incremental rather than innovative. In contrast, when opinions differ, more diverse combinations of policy packages may win over the majority (Bischoff & Christiansen).

In summary, we can expect the most significant potential for party-induced innovations from political leaders in parties with strong organisational ties to civil society and richly developed programs. Furthermore, recent alternation, a coalition with a new constellation of parties, and parties representing different but not polar positions enable innovation. Political innovations and significant policy changes are also more likely the longer the government stays in office and the more significant the ideological difference between current and past governments.

Finally, we must also consider political actors' position in multi-level governance networks. According to transition research, local actors may only make modest progress regarding the broader market and political control mechanisms (Fischer & Newig, 2016). However, political consent often depends on local consensus and municipal action, and thus this finding cannot be generalised. The influence of the local level instead relies on the role of local policymakers, their framing and experimentation efforts, social capital, a sense of shared ownership and trust. Nonetheless, the literature suggests relatively weak agency for local actors (Fischer & Newig).

Transition literature has not yet researched political actors on regional levels enough to state whether they can successfully transform higher governance levels (Fischer & Newig, 2016). Thus far, they, however, assume that these actors often face limited opportunities. Reasons include that they may not be able to change laws, their administrative capacities are limited, and they require core actors and factors for change that appear out of reach. Therefore, actors on this level must cooperate with national or global actors to increase their legitimacy and access to funding. However, national actors rely on the support of regional planning and policies to implement their agendas. Therefore, linkages with policy arenas between higher and lower levels may provide regional actors with the agency to drive transformations (Fischer & Newig).

Most case studies in transition literature are set on the national level and, specifically, governments as collective actors (Fischer & Newig, 2016). The cases reveal that transitions indeed depend on national actors such as ministries because they have access to considerable resources and the potential to make quick changes in policies and fiscal measures. Some cases even suggest that corresponding innovations are often started on the national level and distributed to a local, regional, or even global scale (Fischer & Newig). To conclude, we may expect the greatest leeway for political innovations from national actors, followed by regional and local ones.

The administrative arena

Conventional wisdom states that public sector innovation is an oxymoron (Borins, 2002). According to public choice theory, this is the case because public sector agencies are monopolies with no competitive pressure to innovate. Furthermore, public sector culture seeks to organise corruption and ensure due diligence, thus hampering risk-taking associated with innovations. Corresponding organisations are often large bureaucracies structured for stable and consistent performance rather than ambitious public servants pushing for innovations (Borins). Finally, hierarchies, silo structures, and closed top-down bureaucratic processes often hamper innovation cycles (Bommert, 2010).

There is, however, evidence that the public sector creates innovations (Borins, 2002). Politicians play a central role in driving these innovations themselves or through their staff, depending on the political system (Borins). A study on the US and Commonwealth found that politicians developed between 11 and 21 percent of public sector innovations (Borins, 2001, pp. 468–469). Heads of agencies generated another 25 percent, and middle managers and front-line staff, 50–82 percent. Since public sector organisations are pyramidal, there are, however, fewer politicians and agency heads than front-line staff and managers. Therefore, politicians' propensity to innovate is more significant than all other actors. They typically initiate innovations in response to crises, defined as publicly visible failures, whilst agency heads initiate innovations when they take over as new leaders, and middle managers and front-line staff respond to internal problems or new technology opportunities. This shows the immense importance of political leaders in initiating innovations through their appointed agency heads or with the help of the bureaucratic staff. The study also revealed that it is up to executive politicians and senior public servants to foster organisational climates that support innovation from below. The greater the trust between political leadership and bureaucracy, the more bottom-up innovation will occur. In addition, innovations will have to be implemented by the bureaucratic staff, and thus the relationship between political leaders and the administrative staff is even more critical (Borins, 2001). This leads us to the next success factor: collaborative problem-solving efforts.

An essential suggestion by researchers involved with public sector innovation is that the innovation process needs to be open and collaborative (Bommert, 2010). Especially when aiming to solve the most pressing large-scale social, economic, and environmental challenges of our time, namely emergent challenges such as climate change or persistent problems such as mental health issues (Harris & Albury, 2009). This is a significant obstacle but also a chance because only around 15 percent of public sector innovations focus on involving citizens and six percent on involving private partners (De Vries et al., 2015, p. 154). The public sector, however, needs to harness these resources and the creativity of external networks and communities to create better outcomes and, open the innovation process to increase innovation quantity and quality (Bommert).

Grasping the decisiveness of structure and agency

Whereas the previous sections focused on structural barriers and opportunities, it is also paramount to explore existing analyses of the interplay of structure and agency and its influence on political leadership outcomes.

Institutional context and political will

Political scientist Fritz Scharpf (2000) takes an interaction-oriented approach to comparatively analyse the interactions among policymakers and the conditions enabling or impeding their ability to adopt and implement problem-driven policy responses. Scharpf treats institutions as a set of factors affecting the interactions among policy actors and, therefore, the capacity of policymaking systems to adopt and implement effective responses. In this perspective, he assumes that actors and their interaction choices, rather than institutions, are the proximate causes of policy responses, whereas institutional conditions are remote causes (Scharpf).

Scharpf (2000) suggests three dimensions of analysis for this structure-agency relation. Policy challenges may derive from changes in the policy environment, socioeconomic structures, or policy legacies. Actor orientations may stem from actor preferences or cognitive orientations. In contrast, institutional effects may arise from constraints to permissible policy options, actor constellations, modes of interaction, institutionally structured incentives, accountability incentives, and incentives to collaborate (Scharpf).

To analyse these factors, Scharpf (2000) suggests working with two different sets of theory-based hypotheses. The first is problem-oriented policy analyses which predict the choices one can expect if all policy actors had complete information and were exclusively motivated to realise public-interest maximising outcomes without institutional constraints. The second is rational-choice institutionalist analyses that predict the choices one should expect if all actors had full knowledge and were solely motivated to realise public-interest maximising results but remained embedded in their specific institutional setup. If both predictions match, one can conclude that institutional incentives favour the adoption of effective policy responses by agents, and if they do not, institutional obstacles represent the central barrier (Scharpf). Understanding institutional barriers is vital when analysing political leadership for sustainable development as path dependencies can prevent said leaders from implementing respective innovations.

Political time

Political scientist Stephen Skowronek (2011) sought out commonalities between specific contexts and similarities in presidential leadership across political time. In his original work from 1997, Skowronek tries to explain why some US presidents have been able to act as agents of change more successfully than others. Skowronek references three decisive factors: institutions, personality, and context. He emphasises the importance of context, rejects the idea that institutional resources are the most critical determinant of presidential leadership, and dismisses the idea that personality should be the focus of explanatory attention (Skowronek).

Skowronek (2011) argues that the extent to which a president can successfully reconcile the conflicting demands of disrupting and affirming the fundamental order of things determines their political outcome. Thereby he contrasts whether a president is opposed to or affiliated with the established order of ideas and interests, which he calls commitments, and whether these commitments were vulnerable or resilient at the time. He generalises these contexts implying that presidents do not face unique sets of circumstances but that there are similarities between different types of political situations. However, the expectations surrounding the exercise of power at particular moments in time and the respective perception of what is appropriate for a given president to do, vary. As these situations change, the dominant pattern of leadership changes. Skowronek calls these the cycles of political time, which recur across presidencies (Skowronek).

From these expectations and the identity of the incumbent president, Skowronek derives four types of politics (Skowronek, 2011). Politics of disjunction occurs when the incumbent president's political identity is affiliated with the current regime, but the regime is vulnerable (Skowronek, 2011). Politics of articulation occurs when the political identity is affiliated with the current regime, but the regime is resilient. Politics of pre-emption describes a time when the president's political identity is opposed to the regime, but the regime is resilient, making the president come across as too disruptive. Last, politics of reconstruction occurs when the president is opposed to the current regime, and the regime is vulnerable. Skowronek suggests that presidents may only succeed if regime expectations and political identity add up. In this line of argument, political leaders may only promote disruptive change in times of politics of reconstruction (Skowronek).

According to Skowronek (2011), these cycles repeat over time. The pattern goes from politics of reconstruction to politics of articulation, politics of pre-emption, politics of disjunction and back to politics of reconstruction. In line with this argument, Skowronek analysed American presidents. He concludes that Franklin D. Roosevelt followed politics of reconstruction, after which Lyndon B. Johnson followed politics of articulation, Jimmy Carter politics of disjunction, Ronald Reagan politics of reconstruction, Bill Clinton politics of pre-emption, George W. Bush, politics of articulation, and Barack Obama politics of pre-emption (Skowronek).

This research is significant because it demonstrates the immense influence of context, timing, and political identity on the outcome of political leaders striving to transform their political systems.

Skills in context

Bell et al. (2003) developed a framework that allows for comparing personal political skills in relation to contextual factors to find out which are decisive. They examine political skills in the sense of bargaining and coalitions, heresthetics, rhetoric, character as a skill, psychological health, moral purpose, and personal integrity. Skills in context refers to the historical situation, electoral politics, the dynamics of government, policy problems and achievements, and an assessment of skills in context. Strategic leadership is evaluated along purpose, discernment, and prudence and finally, teaching reality refers to leaders engaging in teaching, preaching, demagogy, cultural traps, and short-run or long-run politics and policy (Bell et al., p. 530).

The authors explore the cases of George Bush, John Major, and Jacques Chirac (Bell et al., 2003). Their findings include that all three men were transactional leaders, weak public speakers, lacked visions for the future, and each faced economic issues, requiring them to practice short-term politics for political survival. In this respect, their skills matched their contexts, and they were in the right position at the right time. The authors thus conclude that the effectiveness of political leadership depends on a favourable match of skills and historical context (Bell et al.). The account thereby sheds light on the interrelation of structure and agency rather than attributing a more significant influence to one or the other.

Leadership resources and external pressures

Alastair Cole (1994) offers a more exhaustive framework identifying 31 variables influencing political leadership in liberal democracies. He organises these variables under the two groupings of leadership resources and environmental pressures and six general headings of personal characteristics (e.g., political skills, personal attributes, political style), positional context (e.g., constitution, configuration of the party system, mode of election), internal constraints (e.g., public opinion, judicial constraints, cultural traditions), internal opportunities (e.g., strength from positional context, ability to define constraints as opportunities), external constraints (e.g., prestige of nation in the international system, role of supranational bodies, past policy choices), and external opportunities (e.g., personalising tendencies in foreign policy making, crisis in foreign policymaking, ability to define constraints as opportunities) (Cole, 1994, p. 456).

Cole (1994, pp. 467–468) derives significant hypotheses about political leadership from his in-depth analysis of former French President Francois Mitterrand. Personal characteristics underpin the exercise of political leadership but are usually incapable of moulding the leaders' environment following their wishes. This is true even in highly "personalist" regimes because personal power is restricted by crucial political, economic, and judicial institutions. Political leaders derive their authority from key political offices or positions, not personal qualities. Their resources and opportunities vary according to the type of executive structure involved and the interaction of the political executive with other variables outlined in the framework. Systems, where the chief executive has strong personal legitimacy, increase the resources at the leader's disposal. This would be different in political systems where power is more diffused and fragmented (Italy), where collegial government structures make decision-making a genuinely collective enterprise (Switzerland, Austria), or where there are permanent coalitions (Belgium, Netherlands, Denmark). External constraints imposed upon a country are more important in most respects than the formal structure of government for appraising the power of political leadership. Political, economic, social, and international constraints are imposing factors limiting the autonomy of national political leadership. The country or entity involved will also significantly affect the resources at the leader's disposal as the leaders of more powerful countries will possess more powerful bargaining positions than those of less influential nations (Cole).

Cole (1994) concludes that personal characteristics are not highly relevant to political leadership but that the resources leaders can access, and external constraints are specifically critical because they impose on their actions and outcomes. In a similar approach, political scientist Bert Rockman (1984) found that personal factors are not critically important for political leaders. Instead, external constraints such as political parties, elections, the media, public opinion, constitutional and historical factors, and political culture are key influences on leadership. Again, this is interesting because, similar to Skowronek's (2011) account, both Cole (1994) and Rockman (1984) stress the importance of structures and their influences rather than agency.

Context, skills, and individual capabilities

Of all the reviewed accounts, the management-based Sustainability Leadership model by the Cambridge Institute for Sustainability Leadership (Visser & Courtice, 2011) stresses the interrelation of structure and agency the most. The holistic leadership framework builds on the three categories of leadership context, individual leader, and leadership actions, which are required to bring about profound change. Context refers to the conditions or environment in which leaders operate and which directly or indirectly influence their decision-making. Individual leadership refers to the combination of traits, styles, skills, and knowledge that make the leader uniquely suited to address sustainability challenges effectively. Leadership actions finally refer to internal and external strategic actions necessary to address these challenges (Visser & Courtice).

Australian leadership expert André Taylor (2007, 2008, 2009) conducted a study on champions of change in sustainable urban water management, extending the Cambridge Institute for Sustainability Leadership model for his leadership analysis. The main variables include contextual factors within the champion's organization such as crises, the need for new strategies, organisational tasks, value congruence, technologies, structures, culture, person-organisation fit, change programs, life cycle stage and history, organisational level, the formality of the champion's role and nature of his colleagues (Taylor, 2007, p. 6). It also considers contextual factors outside the champion's organization such as crises and the need for new strategies, value congruence, and national culture. Most factors revolve around the champion her-/himself. These include personal characteristics such as persistence, vision, and strategic perspective, risk-taking, or extraversion. They further revolve around values such as strong environmental values, emotional intelligence, and congruence, as well as core skills such as communication, interpersonal and transformational leadership skills, strategic knowledge, generation, gender, work, and life experience. Taylor further analyses their behaviours, such as articulating an inspiring vision for the future, building and sustaining networks, establishing pilot projects, and a transformational leadership style. Regarding power, he explores their major power source and personal vs. positional power, as well as tactics, such as working in tandem with other executive champions or strong ties to stakeholders. Finally, leadership outcomes play an essential role (Taylor).

Taylor (2008) conducted multiple case studies involving six Australian water agencies to apply the model in practice. He found ten factors to be determining for SUWM champions: (1) openness to experience, as part of the Five-Factor Model of Personality, (2) high career mobility, (3) use of personal rather than positional power, (4) involvement in strategic, rather than operational and social networking, (5) articulation of an inspiring vision, (6) expression of enthusiasm and confidence, (7) persistence under adversity, (8) questioning the status quo, (9) gathering political and managerial support, and (10) strong collaborative organisational cultures that encouraged distributed forms of leadership, continual learning, responsible risk-taking, innovation, and environmental sustainability (Taylor, 2009).

What differs from the previously reviewed accounts is that the model acknowledges distinctive personality characteristics and focuses on personal forms of power that leaders derive from the social networks they are central to (Taylor, 2009). It further focuses on the distribution of leadership within groups and influence tactics such as persuasion, which help leaders become champions of their networks. Last, the study also found contextual factors assist championship (Taylor).

To conclude, the existing literature is inconclusive about whether agency or structure variables are more decisive for political leadership and rather stress the interrelation of both. The following chapter will dive deeper into agency variables so that we may better understand their influence on political leadership.

References

Bell, D. S., Hargrove, E. C., & Theakston, K. (2003). Skill in context: A comparison of politicians. *Presidential Studies Quarterly*, 29(3), 528–548. https://doi.org/10.1111/j.0268-2141.2003.00048.x

Bischoff, C. S., & Christiansen, F. J. (2021). Political parties and innovation. In Sørensen, E. (Ed.), *Political innovations. Creative transformations in polity, politics and policy* (pp. 74–89). New York, NY: Routledge.

Bommert, B. (2010). Collaborative innovation in the public sector. *International Public Management Review*, 11(1), 15–33. https://doi.org/10.4337/978184 9809757.00032

Borins, S. (2001). *The challenge of innovating in government*. Arlington, VA: PricewaterhouseCoopers Endowment for the Business of Government.

Borins, S. (2002). Leadership and innovation in the public sector. *Leadership & Organization Development Journal*, 23(8), 467–476. https://doi.org/10.1108/01437730210449357

Cohen, J., Tsfati, Y., & Sheafer, T. (2008). The influence of presumed media influence in politics. *Public Opinion Quarterly*, 72(2), 331–344. https://doi.org/10.1093/poq/nfn014

Cole, A. (1994). Studying political leadership: The case of Francois Mitterand. *Political Studies*, XLII, 42(3), 453–468. https://doi.org/10.1111/j.1467-9248.1994.tb01688.x

Criado, J. I., Sandoval-Almazan, R., & Gil-Garcia, J. R. (2013). Government innovation through social media. *Government Information Quarterly*, 30(4), 319–326. https://doi.org/10.1016/j.giq.2013.10.003

De Vries, H., Bekkers, V., & Tummers, L. (2015). Innovation in the public sector: A systematic review and future research agenda. *Public Administration, 94*(1), 146–166. https://doi.org/10.1111/padm.12209

Fischer, L.-B., & Newig, J. (2016). Importance of actors and agency in sustainability transitions: A systematic exploration of the literature. *Sustainability, 8*(476), 1–21. https://doi.org/10.3390/su8050476

Fukuyama, F. (2004). *State-building: Governance and world order in the twenty-first century*. Ithaca, NY: Cornell University Press.

Fung, A., & Wright, E. O. (2003). *Deepening democracy: Institutional innovations in empowered participatory governance*. London: Verso.

Harris, M., & Albury, D. (2009). Why radical innovation is needed for the recession and beyond: The Innovation Imperative. NESTA. https://media.nesta.org.uk/documents/the_innovation_imperative.pdf

Helms, L. (2016). Democracy and innovation: From institutions to agency and leadership. *Democratization, 23*(3), 459–477. https://doi.org/10.1080/1351034 7.2014.981667

Kingdon, J. W. (2011). *Agendas, alternatives, and public policies* (2nd ed.). New York, NY: Longman.

Korte, K. (2019). Das politische System der Bundesrepublik Deutschland [The political system of the German federal republic]. In Lauth, H., & Wagner, C. (Eds.), *Politikwissenschaft: Eine Einführung* (9th ed.) *Political science: An introduction* (pp. 63–99). Paderborn, Germany: Verlag Ferdinand Schöningh.

Krouwel, A. (2006). Party models. In Katz, R. S., & Crotty, W. J. (Eds.), *Handbook of party politics*. London: SAGE Publications.

Lijphart, A. (2012). *Patterns of democratic government forms and performance in thirty-six countries* (2nd ed.). Yale, CT: Yale University Press.

Mulgan, G., & Albury, D. (2003). *Innovation in the public sector*. Strategy Unit, Cabinet Office, London. http://www.sba.oakland.edu/faculty/mathieson/mis524/resources/readings/innovation/innovation_in_the_public_sector.pdf

Nye, J. (2008). *The power to lead*. Oxford: Oxford University Press.

Prim, A. L., Filho, L. S., Zamur, G. A. C., & di Serio, L. C. (2017). The relationship between national culture dimensions and degree of innovation. *International Journal of Innovation Management, 21*(1), 173001. https://doi.org/10.1142/s136391961730001x

Rahat, G., & Hazan, R. Y. (2001). Candidate selection methods. An analytical framework. *Party Politics, 7*(3), 297–322. https://doi.org/10.1177/135406 8801007003003

Rahat, G., Hazan, R. Y., & Katz, R. S. (2008). Democracy and political parties. On the uneasy relationships between participation, competition and representation. *Party Politics, 14*(6), 663–683. https://doi.org/10.1177/1354068808093405

Rasmussen, A., Mäder, L. K., & Reher, S. (2018). With a little help from the people? The role of public opinion in advocacy success. *Comparative Political Studies, 51*(2), 139–164. https://doi.org/10.1177/0010414017695334

Rockman, B. A. (1984). The leadership question: The presidency and the American system. New York, NY: Prager Publishers.

Rosanvallon, P. (2011). *Democratic legitimacy*. Princeton, NY: Princeton University Press.

Scharpf, F. W. (2000). Institutions in comparative policy research. *Comparative Political Studies, 33*(6–7). https://doi.org/10.1177/001041400003300604

Skowronek, S. (2011). *Presidential leadership in political time: Reprise and reappraisal* (2nd ed.). Lawrence, KS: University Press of Kansas.

Sørensen, E. (2020). *Interactive political leadership. The role of politicians in the age of governance*. Oxford: Oxford University Press.

Taylor, A. (2007). Sustainable urban water management champions: What do know about them? *13th International Rainwater Catchment Systems Conference*, Sydney, Australia. https://www.researchgate.net/publication/228623868_Sustainable_urban_water_management_champions_What_do_we_know_about_them

Taylor, A. (2008). Ten attributes of emergent leaders who promote sustainable urban water management in Australia. *11th International Conference on Urban Drainage*, Edinburgh, United Kingdom. https://doi.org/10.1201/9780203884102-9

Taylor, A. (2009). Sustainable urban water management: Understanding and fostering champions of change. *Water Science & Technology, 59*(5), 883–891. https://doi.org/10.2166/wst.2009.033

Visser, W., & Courtice, P. (2011). *Sustainability leadership: Linking theory and practice*. Cambridge: University of Cambridge Institute for Sustainability Leadership.

5
CULTIVATING CHANGE-DRIVEN LEADERSHIP STYLES AND SKILLS

Strategies and skills for social change and innovation

Developing and implementing political innovations for sustainable development calls for specific capabilities. However, theories of political leadership, collaborative governance, and political innovations have developed in isolation from each other (Sørensen & Torfing, 2019), and few have explored their interrelation, especially considering the challenge of sustainable development. To circumvent this research gap, the following sections explore leadership, governance, and innovation research relevant to exposing skills for driving said innovations.

Institutional Entrepreneurship

Researchers initially conceptualised *institutional entrepreneurship* (IE) regarding business organisations. It has the goal of institutional transformation, defined as the need to create a new system when ecological, political, social, or economic conditions make the existing system untenable (Walker et al., 2004). In these transformations, researchers attest that individual agents' visions and steering capacities are critical (Westley et al., 2013). At the same time, they stress the importance of systemic shifts in institutional underpinnings, such as mental models and resource flows, which are most often multi-level processes involving various actors with conflicting interests (Westley et al.). IE recognises the "paradox of embedded agency" as a core obstacle (Seo & Creed, 2002). In line with a distributed leadership

DOI: 10.4324/9781003507666-8

paradigm, Battilana et al. (2009, p. 68) suggest that institutional entrepreneurs are those "who leverage resources to create new or transform existing institutions. They can be organisations or groups of organisations, or individuals or groups of individuals...one variable, among a 'constellation' of others, that was relevant to the process of social change".

Two main conditions enable actors to become IEs: field characteristics and the actors' social position (Battilana et al., 2009, pp. 74–77). Field characteristics may include social upheaval, technological disruption, competitive discontinuity, and regulatory changes that disturb field-level consensus and create opportunities for introducing new ideas. The degree of heterogeneity in the field may also give rise to institutional incompatibilities that become a source of internal contradiction and may trigger actors to question existing institutional arrangements and diverge from them. The degree of institutionalisation further plays a role because it is associated with uncertainty levels and may provide strategic action opportunities. These enabling factors do not have to be exogenous, but IEs can deliberately create them. On the other hand, the actor's social position mediates their relationship with their environment. The entrepreneur's hierarchical and informal network position might affect their perception of a field and resource access (Batillana et al.).

IE theory further describes three critical steps of change implementation: developing a vision, mobilising people, and motivating others to achieve and sustain the vision (Battilana et al., 2009). A vision for divergent change that appeals to the actors needed to implement it is vital because changes built on existing institutions or changes breaking with existing institutions are subject to embeddedness and political opposition. Therefore, IEs ideally frame the change project in terms of the problem it helps to resolve (i.e., diagnostic framing), as preferred to existing arrangements (i.e., prognostic framing), and as motivated by compelling reasons (i.e., motivational framing). To carry out this type of framing, IEs need to understand other stakeholders' interests and have sufficient social skills, including the ability to secure cooperation and assess the configuration of their network so that they may act according to their position and the positions of other agents in the field. In addition, IEs need to be cognisant of and sensitive to their discursive and cultural contexts. They must cultivate alliances by defining protagonists, antagonists, and other actors who might be involved in the divergent change effort. The central aim is to reduce inherent contradictions in the coalition and simultaneously exacerbate contradictions among opponents by emphasising the failings of existing practices and norms that the new vision will forego. These strategies thus imply the necessity for a high level of empathy and Machiavellian strategic skills (Battilana et al.).

IEs also need to use discourse to convince others of the need for change and mobilise them (Battilana et al., 2009). This requires exceptional communication skills. IEs must communicate a vision that resonates with potential allies' values, employing framing and rhetorical strategies, connecting innovation to familiar templates, and simultaneously emphasise the need for change. This is associated with specific institutional structures of words, expressions, and meanings that enable IEs to articulate, manipulate, and recombine institutional logics. Successful IEs use analogies to legitimise their vision for change, develop stories, link past events to form a plot, define heroes and villains, gather and reemploy symbolic stories of past events or emphasise and relate single, local stories to more general issues. That makes their stories more attractive to various potential adopters (Battilana et al.).

Another necessary skill is resource mobilisation, including finances, formal authority and social capital (Battilana et al., 2009). Formal authority refers to the actors' legitimately recognised right to make decisions, e.g., the authority conferred by position. Social capital consists of the actor's informal network positions and web of social relations, which provide them with access to information and political support (Battilana et al.).

The influence of field characteristics is a final influential factor that refers to levels of institutionalisation and fragmentation (Battilana et al., 2009). When these characteristics are heterogenous, they appeal to the interests and values of dominant coalitions. Still, if they are heterogenous and fragmented, common ground needs to be established via discourse that resonates with the interests and values of these actors. Key barriers to breaking with institutions, thereby, are the "loosening" of institutional embeddedness by IEs aiming to mobilise political opposition from institutional defenders benefiting from the status quo (Battilana et al.).

Transition literature identifies nine key strategies necessary for institutional transformation (Westley et al., 2013). These only differ slightly from those previously suggested by Battilana et al. (2009) and include facilitating knowledge building and utilisation, building trust, legitimacy, and social capital, developing innovations, preparing and mobilising for change, recognising and seizing windows of opportunities, identifying and communicating opportunities for small wins, and facilitating conflict resolutions and negotiations (Westley et al.).

In a comparative analysis of three case studies in sustainable urban development, Klein Woolthuis et al. (2013) examined IE in practice. The study supports the theoretical proposition that IEs are essential to solving complex sustainability problems because they use concrete tactics to draw ways out of problem perceptions and initiate processes of collaborative problem-solving with multiple actors and institutions. In all three cases, sustainable urban development was an abstract concept none of the stake-holders could grasp and which therefore appeared wicked to them. IEs were critical to framing sustainable urban development as achievable via emotional visions and credible narratives to which all stakeholders could relate. Thereby IEs replaced old beliefs and enabled the initial project kick-offs. Already realised projects thereby represented a supportive contextual factor because they aided IEs in proving that their proposed theoretical solutions were feasible. Consequently, they could convince multiple stake-holders to support the underlying rationale of sustainable development. Moreover, collaboration was essential to realising the projects. All cases demonstrated how important the distribution of agency and the variety of skills and resources of actors from multiple domains were to creating inno-vative solutions to a perceived wicked problem. In line with collaboration efforts, lobbying tactics were omnipresent in all cases because IEs had to organise and manage supportive coalitions for their projects (Klein Woolthuis et al.). While the cases focused on individual IEs' roles, they equally demonstrated that collaborative efforts led to the final solutions.

Collective Leadership Compass

Another leadership model that focuses explicitly on collaborative leader-ship and sustainable transformations is the *Collective Leadership Compass* (CLC), which transformation expert Petra Künkel (2019) and the Club of Rome developed. It is a practical tool to advance transformative collective action for sustainability in complex multi-stakeholder initiatives, to bridge theory and practice, and to offer meta-level guidance for change agents. According to Künkel, collective leadership requires nested collaboration systems of actors aiming to change the status quo for the better. Collective leadership, in this sense, is "the capacity of a group of leaders to deliver their contribution to a more sustainable future...through assuming joint and flexible leadership in service of the common good" (Künkel, p. 21).

The tool facilitates these collaboration efforts and mainly applies to planning and reflection processes (Künkel, 2019). Accordingly, multi-stakeholder collaboration is a critical catalyst for creating new ways of collectively shaping the future. It represents a way of forming temporary, goal-oriented systems of human interaction. Thereby the CLC is based on six human competency dimensions that enhance actors' capacities for col-laboration and sustainability innovations: (1) Future possibilities refer to the ability to shape reality toward a sustainable future, (2) engagement refers to the creation of step-by-step engagement toward effective collabo-ration systems, (3) innovation refers to creating novelty and finding intel-ligent solutions to challenges, (4) humanity to reaching other's humanness to create a collective experience, (5) collective intelligence to harvesting differences and diversity through dialogue, and finally (6) wholeness to seeing the big picture and maintaining work towards it (Künkel, p. 23).

What is essential about the compass is that all dimensions must work in synch to lead to a project's success (Künkel, 2019). Future possibilities are worthless if not enough stakeholders commit to them. Thereby, sufficient engagement of diverse stakeholders is required, and these engagement processes, in turn, create trust and cohesion, invigorate network connections, and foster collective actions for tangible outcomes. Within this collaboration system, innovation is necessary to move forward. Still, innovation is only meaningful if it considers humanity and creates safe environments. Humanity, therefore, refers to the ability of all involved actors to connect to their human competency and respect the intrinsic value of all people. The dimension of collective intelligence builds on this humanity and the fact that the previous factors require an exchange about actions to be taken following meaning-making frameworks rooted in dialogue. All collective moves towards sustainability need to be embedded in people's ability to sense wholeness, which requires taking a step back, gaining perspective, and seeing a collaborative exchange effort from a larger context whilst simultaneously staying connected to the common good (Künkel).

Individual aspects, respective manifestations, and needed skills specify each dimension of the compass. In contrast to previously reviewed leadership models, the skills required of CLC are much more exhaustive and include more than 100 manifestations (Künkel, 2019). What is striking about them is that, in contrast to meta-governance and institutional entrepreneurship, they almost entirely stress soft skills such as self-awareness, empathy, optimism, inspiration, motivation, and drive in attempts to foster innovation and collaboration for the common good (Künkel).

Finally, Petra Künkel (2019) stresses that good process management is fundamental to providing a guiding structure to the involved actors and creating a functional and stable collaboration ecosystem. These processes comprise four phases. Phase 1 explores and engages in the issue by understanding the context, stakeholders, and viewpoints and raising energy for the cause (scoping and building). Phase 2 attends to building and formalising the collaboration ecosystem by clarifying goals and commitments, establishing resources, and planning the process (managing and maintaining). Phase 3 concerns implementing and evaluating the collaboration initiative by realising agreed-upon activities and evaluating progress and outcomes (reviewing and revising). Phase 4 then focuses on developing, replicating, or institutionalising these results by expanding dialogue activities and creating stable structures for change (sustaining outcomes).

This process is dialogic, iterative, and non-linear and thus may be repeated over again (Künkel).

Künkel (2019) and her team have applied the CLC in various international and local multi-stakeholder settings, such as the development of voluntary social and environmental standards for responsible supply chains in Southern Africa, water resource management in Tunisia, sustainable forestry in Laos, and economic development in Rwanda (Künkel). A brief review of the local example of the Nebhana Water Forum in Tunisia helps demonstrate the tool's application in practice (Künkel, pp. 186–192). In Tunisia, agriculture uses 82 percent of the country's water, and climate change, mismanagement, and overexploitation have led to a severely strained water supply that is also endangering cities. The government of Tunisia set out to develop a national strategy for Integrated Water Resource Management to improve water management and sustain ecosystems. They initiated a one-and-a-half-year process to shift dysfunctional patterns of interaction between farmers, government officials, citizens, and local NGOs, bringing together 300 stakeholders. There appeared to be a particular deadlock between farmers and local government. Still, through the CLC process, it was loosened and shifted towards a joint path towards the future-oriented management of water resources (Künkel).

The CLC inspired process designs and action planning and provided backbone support with a meta-guiding structure that enabled all stakeholders to better understand the dysfunctional situation (Künkel, 2019). The approach was further used as a process-monitoring tool in an unpredictable environment and helped keep sight of the interdependence of all challenges. The book only features how the team applied the compass for a situational analysis in the initial process design. The first phase involved engaging stakeholders for collaboration by understanding stakeholder groups' needs, perspectives, and concerns in listening sessions. They subsequently turned these sessions into dialogues between farmers and government officials. After six months, farmers realised the need to change their behaviour and engage in the process individually and collectively in a dialogue with government officials to find a joint solution. In the second phase, a water-related collaboration ecosystem was established through small cross-stakeholder dialogue forums, developing a water charter that entailed guiding principles for all stakeholders and an agreed-upon reference framework for integrated water resource management. The process had many iterative learning curves, bringing together two seemingly irreconcilable stakeholder groups. It shifted patterns of mistrust and malfunction towards collaborative and constructive interaction, and they jointly created innovative solutions for the common good (Künkel).

The CLC represents an impactful tool for multi-governance sustainability challenges and simultaneously comes true to the need for innovations for sustainable development. It is the most exhaustive leadership skill model reviewed and enhances the findings from IE theories.

Meta-governance

Several scholars suggest a new form of administrative or public sector leadership, as today's public sector institutions have become complex adaptive systems in multi-level governance networks (Ottens & Edelenbos, 2018; Sørensen & Torfing, 2019; Virtanen & Tammeaid, 2020). These networks comprise State, market, and civil society actors who contribute to producing public value via policy-making (Sørensen & Torfing, 2009). Actors within these networks interact through negotiations that may combine bargaining and consensus-seeking deliberation. Typically, no agreed-upon norms and procedures predetermine where and how legitimate actions are taken. These networks may include partnerships, joined-up government, co-governance mechanisms, strategic alliances, deliberative forums, advisory boards, or policy task forces (Sørensen & Torfing).

Public sector or political leaders are thereby ascribed the potential role of *meta-governors* (MG) or governors of governance (Ottens & Edelenbos; cf. Sørensen & Torfing, 2009). Meta-governance "enables politicians and public managers to exercise state power in a decentred polity in which power is dispersed within complex networks, bringing together public and private actors from different levels and polity areas" (Ottens & Edelenbos, 2018, p. 5). We may describe the role of meta-governors as involving: (1) the production and dissemination of hegemonic norms and ideas about how to govern and be governed, (2) political, normative, and context-dependent choices among different mechanisms of governance, or different combinations thereof, and (3) the strategic development of particular institutional forms of governance to prevent dysfunctions and advance particular political goals (Sørensen & Torfing, p. 246).

Sørensen and Torfing (2009, pp. 246–247) thereby differentiate between the importance of political leaders engaging in hands-off meta-governance, which they deploy distanced from the governance network itself, and hands-on meta-governance, which shows direct interference within the operations of the governance network. The former involves network design and framing. Network design aims to influence the scope of governance networks, their participants, and the design of internal processes and is vital when governance networks are first formed. It involves setting policy goals and deadlines, choosing actors to contribute, designing procedures for cooperation and negotiation, and ensuring the strong democratic performance of the network by creating public awareness (Sørensen & Torfing).

Network framing includes the formation of overall goals, the specification of fiscal and legal conditions, storytelling regarding the joint mission of the governance network, and framing policy objectives to align all actors' goals and convince them of the need to take action (Sørensen & Torfing, 2009). For multi-governance networks to be effective they need to:

1. produce a clear and well-informed understanding of the often complex and cross-cutting policy problems and policy opportunities at hand,
2. generate innovative, proactive, and yet feasible policy options that match the joint perception of the problems and challenges facing the network actors,
3. reach joint policy decisions that go beyond the least common denominator while avoiding high costs and unwarranted cost shifting,
4. ensure a smooth policy implementation based on continuous coordination, a high degree of legitimacy, and program responsibility among all the relevant and affected actors,
5. provide a flexible adjustment of policy solutions and public services in the face of changing demands, conditions, and preferences,
6. create favourable conditions for future cooperation through cognitive, strategic, and institutional learning that construct common frameworks, spur the development of interdependency, and build mutual trust (Sørensen & Torfing, p. 242).

Hands-on meta-governance includes network management and participation (Sørensen & Torfing, 2009). Network management revolves around interactions and dialogues within the network. Meta-governors can increase the effectiveness of networks by empowering network actors through funding or learning processes, whilst they can reduce tensions through agenda-setting and the facilitation of cross-frame learning. They may further empower weak and marginalised actors with knowledge, resources, or veto powers and increase transparency by ensuring all information is circulated and accessible. Finally, network participation aims to facilitate cooperation among actors, create a sense of ownership for small victories and trust among actors, foster commitment and willingness to share resources and risks, and develop broad and inclusive policy agendas, so no actor feels marginalised (Sørensen & Torfing).

Overall, political leaders are specifically qualified for the role and tasks of meta-governance because they are formally in charge of defending the public interest and actors with the knowledge, resources, and capacities for strategic leadership (Ottens & Edelenbos, 2018). Still, research reveals that they thus far play a limited role in meta-governance networks, and administrative public managers take on the role instead (Koppenjan et al., 2011). This is partially because the notion that meta-governance involves political decisions, that only elected politicians have sufficient democratic legitimacy to make, is still widely ignored (Sørensen & Torfing, 2019).

In her latest research, Eva Sørensen (2020) advanced the concept of meta-governance, suggesting that it overlooks the relational character of leadership and management, discussed previously in terms of shared leadership. She thus suggests the model of *interactive political leadership* (IPL) as a "strategic effort to engage relevant and affected members of the political community in the formulation and implementation of political visions, strategies, and policy solutions" in a context of dispersed public leadership (Sørensen, 2020, p. 35). IPL thus involves more collaborative methods, which include the strategic design and framing of arenas through collaboration, policies reflecting multiple needs, concerns, and aspirations, and collaborative policymaking and implementation (Sørensen). The proposition of IPL goes hand in hand with other new leadership proposals, such as that of Jennifer Lees-Marshment (2015), who calls for *deliberative political leadership*, in which political leaders actively seek to integrate inputs from actors inside and outside of government into their policy solutions. Governance experts Kane et al. (2009) refer to *dispersed democratic leadership*, where leadership diffuses throughout the political, administrative, judicial, social, and economic spheres, and political leaders collaborate with actors outside the formal political system.

The Danish Municipality of Gentoffe implemented the concept of meta-governance and interactive political leadership when reforming its City Council (Sørensen & Torfing, 2019). Dedicated Task Committees solved local challenges via new policies to strengthen local political leadership. They consisted of elected politicians, local citizens, and other stakeholders working together for 3 to 9 months. External participants could apply via the Council's website. The focus was set on participants who bring new experiences, ideas, and resources to co-create innovative solutions to wicked problems. A mandate selected by the City Council regulated the Committees. They defined the policy problem, described the background and existing policies, and suggested the specific aim of the committee, such as a vision, policy proposals, or initiatives. Finally, the Task Committees' outcomes were discussed, amended, and endorsed by the City Council (Sørensen & Torfing).

One of the first Task Committees developed a new youth policy for Gentoffe (Sørensen & Torfing, 2019). Local youths from different high schools with diverse backgrounds and life experiences worked with politicians for almost one year. The involved politicians quickly realised that the youths' problems differed significantly from their knowledge and expectations. Through the Task Committee, the politicians developed a new understanding of the actual problems and an innovative policy solution. The collaborative effort increased the city's innovation capacity whilst, simultaneously, the youth was intrigued by local politics and considered becoming involved permanently (Sørensen & Torfing). What the case of Gentoffe shows is that collaborative efforts and citizen participation can heighten innovative capacity and simultaneously strengthen democracy if models, processes, and responsibilities are well laid out.

Embracing transformative leadership styles

Aside from leadership skills, leadership styles are crucial for leaders trying to drive change and implement political innovations in complex multi-governance networks. The following sections will thus dive into three prominent leadership styles that inspire change in people and organisations and their associated traits.

Authentic Leadership

The *Authentic Leadership* (AL) model stems from organisational development in a business context. A fundamental premise is that AL has the potential to make a real difference in organisations by helping individuals find meaning and connection at work, promoting transparency, building trust and commitment, and fostering inclusive structures and positive ethical climates (Avolio & Gardner, 2005). According to empirical evidence, AL is a predictor of job satisfaction, leads to better relationships with colleagues, higher levels of trust, greater productivity, and a more positive work environment, and is key for transforming visions into reality (Jensen & Luthans, 2005).

Avolio and Gardner (2005) distinguish between specific factors that determine AL. For one, ALs have positive psychological capacities vital to change and play a significant role in developing followers, teams, organisations, and communities. These capacities include confidence, optimism, hope, and resilience and heighten the self-awareness and self-regulatory behaviours of the leader in a process of positive self-development. ALs also take on a positive moral perspective. This refers to ethical and transparent decision-making processes based on moral capacity, efficacy, courage, and resilience in addressing ethical issues and achieving authentic and sustained moral actions. Another premise of AL is the leaders' self-awareness. It encompasses the leaders' consciousness of their own existence and what this constitutes within the context they operate in. Self-awareness is a process of understanding one's talents, strengths, sense of purpose, beliefs, and core values. The fourth and final capacity is self-regulation and self-control, which involves setting internal standards for oneself, assessing discrepancies between one's standards and actual outcomes, and identifying intended actions to reconcile said discrepancies. Through this process of self-regulation, leaders align their values with their intentions and efforts, presenting themselves as transparent and authentic to their followers (Avolio & Gardner).

Other factors directly relate to leadership processes and behaviours, such as personal and social identification processes through which followers identify with ALs and their values (Avolio & Gardner, 2005). Said leaders influence their followers through positive moral perspectives, self-regulatory processes, or displaying self-awareness. This goes hand in hand with the notion of leaders "leading by example" through transparent decision-making, confidence, optimism, hope, resilience, and consistency between their words and actions. Lastly, ALs also develop their followers by offering support in self-determination and influencing them through emotional contagion and positive social exchanges. They create upward learning and transformation spirals and establish respectful and trusting relationships. Furthermore, as they do for themselves, ALs also heighten the self-awareness and shape the self-regulatory processes of their followers, helping them to develop clarity about their values and identity, resulting in transparent relations with associates and authentic behaviour. Shared and complementary goals, which reflect the leaders' and followers' values, further facilitate these relations. After all, leaders and followers stand in a reciprocal relationship, helping each other become more authentic and learning from each other. ALs may not explicitly set out to transform their followers but do so by being role models (Avolio & Gardner).

ALs are typically active in dynamic and emergent contexts which shape their leadership. Avolio and Gardner (2005) suggest that uncertainty and an inclusive, ethical, positive, and strength-based culture contribute to leaders' and followers' self-awareness. Environments that provide open access to information, resources, support, and equal opportunity for everyone to learn and thrive, will empower leaders and make them more effective. High uncertainty simultaneously characterises their context (Avolio & Gardner) and therefore the leadership style suits MG, IE, and CLC challenges.

The last factor defining AL is veritable and sustained performance beyond expectations (Avolio & Gardner, 2005). Sustained performance represents the organisation's ability to achieve persistently high performance over a long period, whilst veritable performance addresses the genuine and ethical values used to attain this performance. Non-financial tangibles and tacit knowledge, including human, social, and psychological capital, are central to this factor and stimulated by ALs (Avolio & Gardner).

The Authentic Leadership Questionnaire developed by Avolio et al. (2017) allows for the practical analysis of this leadership style. In the questionnaire, the four critical variables, self-awareness, transparency, ethical/moral, and balanced processing, are inquired along 32 items. Authentic leadership then forms the basis of transformational leadership (Avolio et al.).

Transformational Leadership

Transformational Leadership (TL) dates to leadership expert James Burns (1978). Burns advised leaders to develop their followers to become leaders by engaging them toward positive moral outcomes via trust and honourable relationships. Respectively, TL stimulates and inspires followers to achieve extraordinary results and, in the process, develop their own leadership capacity (Burns). TLs respond to followers' needs, empower them, and align the objectives and goals of individual followers, the leader, and the group (Bass & Riggio, 2006). Bass and Riggio (2006) further add that TL must be uplifting and authentic and transcend the leaders' self-interests for practical or moral reasons.

As previously mentioned, TL builds on AL and thus many of its facets overlap, including building trust, acting with integrity, encouraging others, encouraging innovative thinking, and coaching and developing people (Bass & Riggio, 2006). In addition, it integrates two facets of transactional leadership, namely rewarding achievement and monitoring deviations and mistakes. Another dimension refers to passive and avoidant behaviours, including fighting fires, i.e., whether leaders wait for a problem to appear before they take corrective actions, and avoiding involvement, i.e., refusing to assume responsibilities that are part of their leadership position. Finally, TL also specifies leadership outcomes similar to AL, relating to generating extra effort, productivity, and satisfaction. Bass and Riggio developed the Multifactor Leadership Questionnaire (MLQ) with 73 items to test TL (Bass & Riggio).

In an empirical study, Judge and Bono (2000) combine the TL theory with the Five-factor Personality Model. The model includes the dimensions of Extraversion, Agreeableness, Conscientiousness, Emotional Adjustment, and Openness to experience. Extraversion refers to an individual's tendency to be outgoing, assertive, active, and excitement-seeking, as extraverted individuals are strongly predisposed to experience positive emotions. Agreeableness is the tendency to be kind, gentle, trustworthy, and warm. Achievements and dependability indicate Conscientiousness and correlate most with performance. Emotional Adjustment is the trait that leads to life satisfaction, freedom from depression, and other mental ailments, presenting the opposite of Neuroticism, namely the tendency to be anxious, fearful, depressed, and moody. Finally, Openness to experience is the tendency to be creative, imaginative, perceptive, and thoughtful and correlates highly with intelligence (Judge & Bono).

Judge and Bono (2000) find Extraversion and Agreeableness to be predictors of TL, testing their hypothesis with samples of leaders across 200 organisations along the questionnaire. The approach of linking TL and the Five-factor model advances the MLQ by breaking the model down to individual leaders' personality traits.

Social Change Model of Leadership

Another useful leadership model is the *Social Change Model of Leadership* (SCM), which comes true to the challenges of sustainable development, MG, CLC, and emergent leadership perceptions. SCM explores positive social change to improve humanity's conditions and care for the environment (Komives et al., 2017). According to SCM, leadership is concerned with responsibly choosing courses of action toward a desirable future and social change, thereby stressing that leadership and change are intertwined (Komives et al.). This stands in contrast to the notion of management, which revolves around preservation or maintenance (Astin & Astin, 2000). Leadership thereby also implies intentionality, in that change is not random but instead directed toward some desired and valued future end or condition. Finally, the concept sees leadership as collaborative rather than an effort of a single individual and a process rather than a position (Astin & Astin).

The SCM builds on seven fundamental values that individuals, groups, and communities should strive for to bring about social change (Komives et al., 2017). They are grouped into the dimensions of individual values, group values, social/community values, and change (Komives et al.). The individual values involved in the model include consciousness of self, congruence, and commitment (Roberts, 2017, pp. 50–51). Consciousness of self refers to the necessity to be aware of one's personal beliefs, values, attitudes, and emotions, i.e., having self-awareness, being consciously mindful, introspecting, and continually reflecting on oneself. Congruence refers to identifying personal values, beliefs, attitudes, and emotions and acting along them. This value relates to facets of AL, including authenticity and conformity of values and actions. The third individual value, commitment, is based on intrinsic passion, energy, and purposeful investments toward action. Respective leaders are willing to get involved and follow through on this commitment (Roberts).

Group values entail collaboration, which is necessary to multiply group efforts by capitalising on diversity, strengths of relationships, and interconnections of individuals involved in the process (Roberts, 2017). Groups work toward a common purpose with mutually beneficial goals and generate creative solutions by sharing authority, responsibility, and accountability. The second value, common purpose, revolves around a shared vision, values, and collective aims. Controversy with civility refers to the fact that groups always have differing viewpoints. To create change and generate innovative solutions, civil, open, and critical discourse must integrate these multiple perspectives. Finally, society/community values refer to citizenship and the concept of the citoyen explored in Chapter 3. Citizens become citoyens when individuals are connected to society and actively work toward change to benefit others through community involvement, care, or other services. In the model's centre stands change as the SCM's ultimate goal (Roberts).

The Socially Responsible Leadership Scale helps assess the SCM's core values along 34 items (SLRS, 2019). The questionnaire integrates personal qualities that leaders require to be transformational while including group values and how groups need to interact to drive change (SLRS). Leaders cannot learn the values of the SCM at one point since it is an ongoing learning process best applied in real-life situations (Roberts, 2017). Thereby the learning process is described as the knowing-being-doing framework, as individuals move from knowing and understanding the values to being and having them, and ultimately to doing and demonstrating them (Roberts).

The SCM leadership style appears to come closest to the requirements of collaborative innovation processes and the CLC. However, it presumes the willingness of all involved actors to work towards the same vision rather than creating it in a process as AL and TL do.

The addressed leadership styles demonstrate that successful leadership depends both on individual qualities and traits that are part of our personality as well as strategies and skills that can be learned to drive change processes. Both equally demonstrate the importance of individual agency for the implementation of political innovations and a transformation to sustainable development.

References

Astin, A. W., & Astin, H. S. (2000). *Leadership reconsidered: Engaging higher education in social change*. Battle Creek, MI: W. K. Kellog Foundation.

Avolio, B. J., & Gardner, W. L. (2005). Authentic leadership development: Getting to the root of positive forms of leadership. *The Leadership Quarterly*, 16(3), 315–338. https://doi.org/10.1016/j.leaqua.2005.03.001

Avolio, B. J., Gardner, W. L., & Walumbwa, F. O. (2017). *Authentic leadership questionnaire*. Mindgarden. https://www.mindgarden.com/69-authentic-leadership-questionnaire

Bass, B. M., & Riggio, R. E. (2006). *Transformational leadership* (2nd ed.). Brighton: Psychology Press.

Battilana, J., Leca, B., & Boxenbaum, E. (2009). How actors change institutions: Towards a theory of Institutional Entrepreneurship. *Academy of Management Annals, 3*(1), 65–107. https://doi.org/10.5465/19416520903053598

Burns, J. M. (1978). *Leadership*. New York, NY: Harper Row.

Jensen, S. M., & Luthans, F. (2005). Entrepreneurs as authentic leaders: Impact on employees' attitudes. *Leadership & Organization Development Journal, 27*(8), 646–666. https://doi.org/10.1108/01437730610709273

Judge, T. A., & Bono, J. E. (2000). Five-factor model of personality and transformational leadership. *Journal of Applied Psychology, 85*(5), 751–765. https://doi.org/10.1037/0021-9010.85.5.751

Kane, J., Papatan, H., & t' Hart, P. (2009). Dispersed democratic leadership revisited. In Kane, J., Patapan, H., & t' Hart, P. (Eds.), *Dispersed democratic leadership: origins, dynamics, and implications* (pp. 299–321). Oxford: Oxford University Press.

Klein Woolthuis, R., Hooimeijer, F., Bossink, B., Mulder, G., & Brouwer, J. (2013). Institutional entrepreneurship in sustainable urban development: Dutch successes as inspiration for transformation. *Journal of Cleaner Production, 50*, 91–100. https://doi.org/10.1016/j.jclepro.2012.11.031

Komives, S. R., Wagner, W., & Associates. (2017). *Leadership for a better world: Understanding the social change model of leadership development*. San Francisco, CA: Jossey-Bass.

Koppenjan, J. F. M., Kars, M., & van der Voort, H. G. (2011). Politicians as metagovernors. Can metagovernance reconcile representative democracy and network reality? In Torfing, J., & Triantafillou, P. (Eds.), *Interactive policy making, metagovernance and democracy* (pp. 129–148). Colchester: ECPR Press.

Künkel, P. (2019). *Stewarding sustainability transformations*. Cham, Switzerland: Springer Nature

Lees-Marshment, J. (2015). *The Ministry of public input*. Basingstoke: Palgrave-Macmillan.

Ottens, M., & Edelenbos, J. (2018). Political leadership as meta-governance in sustainability transitions: A case study analysis of meta-governance in the case of the Dutch National Agreement on Climate. *Sustainability, 11*(1), 110. https://doi.org/10.3390/su11010110

Roberts, D. C. (2017). Understanding the social change model of leadership development. In Komives, S. R., & Wagner, W. (Eds.), *Leadership for a better world* (pp. 35–37). San Francisco, CA: John Wiley & Sons.

Seo, M. G., & Creed, W. E. (2002). Institutional contradictions, praxis, and institutional change: A dialectic perspective. *The Academy of Management Review, 27*(2), 222–247. https://doi.org/10.2307/4134353

SLRS. (2019). *Socially responsible leadership scale*. National Clearinghouse for Leadership Programs. https://srls.umd.edu

Sørensen, E. (2020). *Interactive political leadership. The role of politicians in the age of governance*. Oxford: Oxford University Press.

Sørensen, E., & Torfing, J. (2009). Making governance networks effective and democratic through metagovernance. *Public Administration, 87*(2), 234–258. https://doi.org/10.1111/j.1467-9299.2009.01753.x

Sørensen, E., & Torfing, J. (2019). Designing institutional platforms and arenas for interactive political leadership. *Public Management Review, 21*(10), 1443–1463. https://doi.org/10.1080/14719037.2018.1559342

Virtanen, P., & Tammeaid, M. (2020). *Developing public sector leadership*. Cham, Switzerland: Springer Nature.

Walker, B. H., Holling, S. R., Carpenter, S. R., & Kinzig, A. (2004). Resilience, adaptability and transformability in social-ecological systems. *Ecology and Society, 9*(2), 5. https://doi.org/10.5751/es-00650-090205

Westley, F. R., Tjornbo, O., Schultz, L., Olsson, P., Folke, C., Crona, B., & Bodin, Ö. (2013). A theory of transformative agency in linked social-ecological systems. *Ecology and Society, 18*(3), 27. https://doi.org/10.5751/es-05072-180327

6

EXPLORING WOMEN'S POLITICAL LEADERSHIP FOR SUSTAINABLE DEVELOPMENT

Female, feminist, and women's leadership

In the 1930s psychologists started differentiating between men and women as well as masculinity and femininity (Hyde et al., 2019). From this developed the gender binary, i.e., the belief, that all individuals can be sorted into these two biologically determined categories. This is based on the concept of sexes, which differentiates males and females along biological features (Hyde et al.). As previously discussed in Chapter 1, women have been particularly disadvantaged along the gender binary by the patriarchal structures that shaped capitalism as an institutionalised social order. Feminist movements have thus long fought to end the oppression that women face as a group based on their sex and gender (Mikkola, 2022, January 18). The latter is socially constructed and shapes norms and expectations of women and men along specific traits (Mikkola).

Executive leadership research has primarily focused on men (Jalalzai, 2008) and women leaders are still systemically discriminated against both in theory and practice (Pullen & Vacchani, 2020). However, research on women political leaders suggests that they may take on a particular role in driving political innovations because women, "often being outsiders... or among the first, to apply for higher political offices,... are still seen as novelty. In this way, they may respond to the increasing demand for change coming from citizens tired of the old politics" (Campus, 2013, p. 114). Political leadership expert Ludger Helms (2016) further suggests that there may be a nexus between women political leaders and transformational leadership, while Michael Genovese and Janie Steckenrider (2013) suggest

DOI: 10.4324/9781003507666-9

that the emergence of women political executives may be both an effect and cause of social change. Therefore, understanding women's political leadership is of particular relevance to driving the necessary sustainability transformation explored in Chapters 2 and 3.

Still, this research does not seek to reinforce gendered stereotypes, understand women only in relation to men (Pullen & Vacchani, 2020), or discriminate against non-binary gender identities (Mikkola, 2022, January 18). The type of leadership explored in this book can be practised by any-one regardless of sex and gender because all humans possess both tradi-tionally assigned feminine and masculine psychological characteristics (Hyde et al., 2019). At the same time, the research recognises that there is a lack of research on women leaders and that women remain a political minority, under pressure to comply with gender expectations. Thus, there is still a need to expand this research perspective by contributing to wom-en's approaches to political leadership. Accordingly, the following sections explore which structure and agency variables may be particularly enabling or hindering women in executive political leadership positions.

The influence of structures on women leaders

Whilst women political leaders may be effective at developing and imple-menting political innovations, specific contextual factors are hindering them due to their gender. Women's leadership expert Karin Klenke (2017, p. 78) refers to a Gallup poll from 1937, which asked respondents in the United States if they would vote for a woman as president if she were as qualified as a male candidate in every respect. The predominant response was "no". Since then, attitudes have evolved, and women have become more accepted in politics. In 1953, 33 percent of respondents were already willing to vote for a woman president, and in 2006, it was 92 percent (Klenke). Attitudes and institutions have changed significantly, and a his-torically unprecedented number of women have served as presidents and prime ministers in many countries worldwide (Montecinos, 2017). The 1979 Convention on the Elimination of All Forms of Discrimination against Women, the Beijing Platform for Action, the 1985 UN Decade for Women, the 2000 Millennium Summit, and the 2015 UN Sustainable Development Summit, amongst others, contributed to gender balance in political decision-making (Montecinos). Furthermore, gender quotas were introduced, strengthening the pool of qualified women eligible for leader-ship roles and promoting women's access to leadership roles in the politi-cal system (Klenke). Still, in 2024, only 17 women were heads of govern-ment and 19 heads of State (UN Women, 2024). Women only represented 23.3. percent of Cabinet members heading Ministries and the most commonly held portfolios were Women and gender equality, Family and children affairs, Social inclusion and development, Social protection and social security, and Indigenous and minority affairs. Finally, only 26.9 percent of parliamentarians were women, and 35.5 percent of elected members in local deliberative bodies (UN Women). Whilst this represents a continuous increase, the representation of women in politics is still far from equal.

Karin Klenke (2017) presents several reasons for the underrepresentation of women in American politics, which may also apply to other countries: women's responsibility for the family, gender differences in political ambition, biases in the recruitment of political elites, the inability to raise money for political campaigns, voter attitudes toward women politicians, and women being less likely to find themselves qualified for office as well as more risk averse than their male counterparts. Indeed, studies reveal that women are 16 percent less likely than men to have thought of running for office (Lawless & Fox, 2012). Nonetheless, they also show that once women achieve a nomination, they are as successful as men in winning elections (Fox & Lawless, 2004).

Women still face substantial hurdles because they must satisfy gender expectations (Montecinos, 2017). The cultural establishment of female stereotypes is a critical factor that hampers women's political representation (Montecinos), and politically ambitious women cannot escape the consequences (Genovese & Steckenrider, 2013). Society still expects and prefers women to be communal, kind, warm, gentle (Klenke, 2017), affectionate, sensitive, nurturing (Eagly & Karau, 2002), and compassionate (Brooks, 2011). Conversely, men are expected to portray confidence, aggressiveness, and self-direction (Klenke). Leadership has thereby been most typically associated with male qualities. Women's femineity is often deemed offensive in political offices, where they are perceived to lack the fortitude related to male leadership (Montecinos). If women leaders embrace more masculine leadership styles and fail to be congruent with female stereotypes, they find themselves disadvantaged in hiring decisions and performance evaluations (Klenke). Still, women are expected to perform masculine, rational leadership while simultaneously subjecting themselves to feminine ideals (Fletcher, 2004). If they fail to do so, they are evaluated negatively and less likely to be selected for top leadership positions (Heilman & Okimoto, 2007). This is particularly true for politics, which is still considered a "man's world" (Genovese & Steckenrider, 2013), and executive positions which remain the most gendered of all political offices (Bauer & Tremblay, 2011).

An enabling factor for women executive leaders is that of family (Genovese & Steckenrider, 2013). They often have strong bonds to their fathers and come from families where they were granted opportunities for personal development, much was expected of them, and they were pushed beyond stereotypes and role limitations (Genovese & Steckenrider). Family connections also help women achieve executive positions (Wiltse & Hager, 2021). If a male family member holds a political office or serves as a high-ranking government official, women are more likely to become executives. Still, political activism and a political career are also paths to executive positions. Across these paths, women are typically relatively highly educated (Wiltse & Hager).

The media have long portrayed women and men as psychologically different and subconsciously shaped public convictions and attitudes (Belasen & Frank, 2012). Since the TV era, the media often portrayed male executive politicians such as presidents as attractive, popular, and entertaining stars. At the same time, women are still most often stereotyped as housewives, mothers, or objects of aesthetic pleasure. Depending on how frequently the media address these stereotypical images, they can act as perpetrators (Belasen & Frank). These stereotypes not only influence public perception but can also damage women's sense of self-worth and self-efficacy (Simon & Hoyt, 2013). Research shows that women exposed to female stereotypes reported lower beliefs in their leadership abilities and aspirations (Simon & Hoyt). In addition, the role model hypothesis suggests that since only a few women are in highly visible political offices, young girls see few reasons for becoming active in politics (Klenke, 2017). Conversely, the presence of women in the highest political offices can increase women's political agency, send a message about women belonging in the political sphere, shape attitudinal and behavioural responses of the public and even enhance political engagement among the public (Jalalzai, 2018). Furthermore, the political empowerment of women leaders directly decreases the role of gender inequality as an obstacle to political incorporation (Alexander et al., 2018).

Aside from the media, women have long faced systemic discrimination in theory and practice due to decades of research investigating the gendered nature of leadership (Pullen & Vacchani, 2020). Traditional leadership theories of the "great man" were associated with masculinity, even though both men and women can practice it. On the other hand, traits related to post-heroic leadership are portrayed as feminine because they include values and capabilities such as empathy, vulnerability, and collaboration. These associations pressure women and men to "to gender" and thereby define themselves along stereotypes. In the course of the transformation of leadership paradigms and a greater focus on seemingly feminine traits, a body of literature on the "female advantage" has even emerged. It portrays leadership attributes that give women an advantage in the workplace and focuses on what differences women leaders can bring to organisations

(Pullen & Vacchani). Studies found that organisational contexts are uncongenial for women leaders if they are male-dominated, the woman is solo, tasks are stereotypically masculine, and if the organisation favours hierarchy and power over egalitarianism and influence (Eagly & Johnson, 1990). Thus, the apparent "female advantage" only applies to organisations that are not "typically male," which does not apply to political systems. Accordingly, juxtaposing emotion and rationality reinforces the gender bind in leadership (Pullen & Vacchani). Women who show decisive behaviour and forceful communication associated with male leadership are often labelled selfish and hysterical (Vroman & Danko, 2020).

The concept of the "glass ceiling" reveals more of this gender-culture interrelation in a more general career context (Klenke, 2017). It refers to an invisible barrier to the advancement of women and minorities in management. This ceiling appears strong enough to hold women back from top-level jobs due to gender rather than a lack of skills, education, or experience (Hymowitz & Schelhardt, 1986). The "glass wall", a barrier surrounding influential senior male executives, follows the glass ceiling. It implies that even when women break through the glass ceiling and get promoted to senior management levels, they will face an even more significant challenge rising to top-level positions (Hymowitz & Schelhardt). Haslam and Ryan (2008) further add that women will likely find themselves on a "glass cliff". The metaphor refers to organisations often promoting women to executive roles in times of crisis. This makes their positions risky because the organisations are likely to attract bad performance, thus potentially leading to the association of women leaders with failure (Haslam & Ryan). In fact, political transition and instability have coincided with women's ascension to executive offices all over the world (Jalalzai, 2008). At the same time, major electoral defeats or scandals may also present an opportunity for women leaders to use gender stereotypes of being healers, unifiers, or reformers (Jalalzai, 2018).

The brief review shows that women in political leadership positions, striving to implement political innovations for sustainable development, face many culturally and institutionally grounded gender-biased barriers that may hinder their accession to office and their perception once they reach a leadership position.

Women's leadership capabilities

Just as contextual variables influence women leaders specifically, women's leadership research highlights capabilities that they may employ or excel at. Indeed, these may be particularly relevant to leaders having to challenge these gender roles (Genovese & Steckenrider, 2013). Said leaders will have to develop strategies to learn to effectively cope with and even turn gender biases to their advantage (Genovese & Steckenrider).

Leadership expert Karin Klenke (2017) states that women political leaders need to be savvy, use power bases, resources, and information effectively, and have the ability to deploy knowledge to exercise formal power. Political savvy relates to practicality and knowledge in politics based on experience, the ability to manage multiple agendas simultaneously, and, most importantly, act ethically. Politically savvy leaders live by a code of ethics, do not follow self-serving goals and agendas, and have low ego needs. According to Klenke, women are somewhat predestined for this skill because socialisation practices often condition them to put their needs behind those of others and to establish deep connections and relationships. Furthermore, politically savvy leaders take responsibility for their actions and choices, believe in and care about the issues at hand, and play above the board to legitimise their tasks to build credibility and momentum for change. Finally, politically savvy leaders know the importance of forming coalitions and alliances, are skilled in interpersonal diplomacy, give credit, strive for win-win situations, and work to minimise the experience of loss for others. Thereby they ensure that all involved parties get something positive out of the experience. A survey on women's leadership revealed that politically savvy leaders also had better career prospects and trajectories. To build political savvy, women can develop networking strategies and skills, including seeking mentoring relationships, scanning their environments to adapt behaviours to changing circumstances, thinking before acting, and inspiring trust by behaving genuinely and exhibiting honesty, integrity, and trustworthiness (Klenke). These skills resemble those addressed in IE, MG, and CLC theories.

Another skill Klenke (2017 cf. Gardner & Clevenger, 1998) addresses is impression management, which she finds particularly important for women politicians. Impression management is how individuals try to control or steer the impressions other people have of them. It includes four strategies to create a trustworthy, moral, attractive, esteemed, and influential image associated with desirable leaders. Exemplification refers to "leading by example" and behaviours that present leaders as morally worthy, integer, and honest, resulting in extraordinary levels of trust and commitment to their causes. Ingratiation is a strategy to make an audience like the leader and attribute desirable qualities such as warmth, attractiveness, charm, and humour to them. Intimidation is a strategy that refers to aggressively showing anger to get voters' attention, which can have positive consequences for women leaders, such as higher performance ratings and a perceived ability to get the job done. Nonetheless, it can also have adverse effects because leaders may appear too forceful, aggressive, bossy, pushy, and thus less likeable. Finally, supplication occurs when individuals present themselves as vulnerable and weak to secure empathy and help from others. Leaders can employ this strategy to excuse poor performance or avoid obligations and criticism. Still, they may risk creating the impression of being weak, lazy, insecure, or emotionally unstable (Klenke).

Another set of skills relates to those evaluated in IE and the CLC. One is contextual intelligence, e.g., the leaders' ability to interpret the social, political, technological, and demographic fabric of their time, place, and respective reactions (Ambler, 2005). Women are particularly prone to this skill due to their heightened empathy and sensitivity. Another skill is visioning (Klenke, 2017). Research on gender differences shows that visioning is essential for executive roles, but women are perceived as lower in this skill than their male peers (Klenke). However, this perception may be due to gender stereotypes, and no further research could be found to reveal whether this was actual or perceived.

Finally, the culture of power influences women leaders because leadership and power are inextricably linked (Klenke, 2017). Power describes the relationships among actors in the political arena and can derive from knowledge, expertise, or resources. One significant influence on women's low representation in executive political offices is how they perceive power in contrast to men. The effectiveness of leaders partially depends on their ability to share rather than hoard power. Still, power is a gendered concept, and the stereotypic notion that women and power are mutually exclusive hard to overcome. Leaders can thereby exercise power in three different ways. "Power over" relates to dominance and top-down decisions. Research on leadership reveals that women are typically reluctant to exercise "power over" because it implies dominating others (Klenke). The second definition is "power to" or empowerment, which suggests that an effective leader shares power with others (French & Raven, 1959). Women leaders in executive positions stress that exercising "power with" rather than "power over" significantly contributed to their success (Coleman, 2011). This may be because women leaders typically do not want power for power's sake but to improve the lives of others (Klenke). This exercise of power is particularly relevant to the collaborative MG, IE, and CLC models.

The brief review highlights that women leaders may be specially cut out for employing the skills necessary for MG, IE, and CLC, which are essential for developing and implementing political innovations.

Women's leadership styles and qualities

The previously discussed leadership models are all described as gender-neutral. Nonetheless, some types of leadership are more suitable to or favoured by women. A study by Stempel et al. (2015) explores the relationship between Transformational Leadership (TL) and women's leadership. They find that this type of leadership is more typical of women than male leaders. Even charisma and contingent rewards are more typical of women's leadership behaviour. Only the two sub-dimensions inspirational motivation and idealised influence had no gender-specific estimations, and transactional facets were perceived as gender-neutral (Stempel et al.). Eagly and Karau (2002) further suggest that TL may be particularly advantageous for women because it encompasses behaviours consistent with female gender role demands, supportive and considerate behaviours, and interpersonally oriented and democratic leadership styles.

Ruderman et al. (2002) further found that the success of women in leadership depended on variables similar to Authentic Leadership (AL): (1) authenticity: a fit between inner values and beliefs and outer behaviours, (2) connection: the need to be close and intimate with others, (3) controlling your destiny: being active in achieving one's life and career goals, (4) wholeness: integrating one's varied life roles and having time to pursue them, and (5) self-clarity: reflecting an understanding of one's motives, values, behaviours, and experiences (Ruderman et al.).

Marianne Coleman (2011, pp. 47–50), on the other hand, did not research a specific leadership style but conducted a study with 60 women in executive positions to explore which factors they identified as contributing to their career success. What these women stressed was, first and foremost, their agency. The women proactively shaped their careers and referred to similar qualities central to their success: drive, determination, ambition, single-mindedness, persistence, proactiveness, a positive mindset, confidence, determination, and a strong conviction. Furthermore, they stressed factors such as enthusiasm, passion, enjoyment, and love for work (Coleman).

Finally, consultant and women's rights advocate Shawna Wakefield (2017, p. 64) defines women's transformative leadership based on interviews with leaders in women's movement-building. According to her, these transformative leaders:

- Model female purpose and principles, e.g., by engaging in ongoing processes of self and interpersonal reflection, signalling their purpose, creating opportunities for leaders to emerge, and engaging in intersectional analyses and approaches.
- Inspire a shared vision based on personal and collective reflexivity, e.g., by providing reflection spaces for people to contribute to the vision, engage in collective practices, cultivate new qualities, and by sharing knowledge about just organisational cultures.

- Empower and enable others to act, e.g., by recognising and valuing all contributions people make, practicing collective leadership, fostering openness and trust, clarifying expectations for responsibilities and conflict resolution, prioritising skill development, facilitating connections, and developing trust by linking personal struggles to political actions.
- Challenge patriarchal norms and oppressive power, e.g., by using tools and processes to surface harmful power embedded in institutions, identifying positive forms of power, promoting structures, processes, and collective practices that disable patriarchal norms, driving values-based organising principles, and enabling team members to better establish and hold each other accountable for new norms.
- Encourage the integration of heart, mind, and body, e.g., by encouraging interpersonal relationships, reducing stress and burnout, coaching and mentoring to help others through ongoing challenges, recognising the trauma women experience, and valuing and promoting self- and collective-care strategies.

Wakefield's findings on the strategies and practices these women use also highly reflect and match the change-driven leadership styles discussed in Chapter 5 such as Authentic Leadership or the Social Change Model of Leadership.

Overall, the brief review of leadership styles reveals a significant match between women's qualities and transformative leadership styles necessary to unite actors in potentially driving and implementing a shared vision for sustainable development.

Grasping the emergent phenomenon

The exploration in Chapters 1–6 reveals that *women's political leadership for sustainable development* is a normative leadership concept that is feasible and necessary considering today's economic, social, and ecological crises.

What we appear to need are women political entrepreneurs who create new demands for their strong political visions of what ought to be – namely, sustainable development. These leaders deliberately create the circumstances for sustainable statehood as a prerequisite for driving sustainable development via the State. They thereby seek to relieve capitalism's pressure on its background conditions, e.g., social reproduction, non-human nature, polity, racism, imperialism, and expropriation. They can do so via sustaincentric approaches and taming the capitalist foreground conditions or socio-ecocentric approaches, transforming or even overcoming capitalist logics. Women leaders can succeed at this task by becoming orators for a new narrative and hegemonic project around sustainable development, shaping public opinion, and persuading them that this vision is good for society. Furthermore, they should become public opinion leaders, creating respective agendas and institutionalising their narrative within State institutions. Finally, they must enable greater leadership for sustainable development within the State and beyond.

In their pursuit, they face various potential structural barriers. Some are gender-neutral, such as path dependencies in the administrative sphere or society's general risk-aversiveness. Others are gender-specific, such as stereotypes or the glass ceiling. Still, the research suggests that women leaders possess unique skills and qualities, making them particularly suited for this task. Implementing a transformative vision requires skills and traits associated with the transformative leadership styles of Meta-governance, Institutional Entrepreneurship, and the Collective Leadership Compass, as well as Authentic, Transformational, and Social Change leadership models. Judging by the reviewed literature, women are predestined for these types of leadership, their behaviours and skills being consistent with the models. These include a range of analytical, personal, communication, positional, strategic, organisational, and follower-empowerment skills. To highlight a few, women are typically politically savvy. Due to socialisation practices, they tend to live by a code of ethics, do not follow self-serving goals, and have low ego needs. They take responsibility for their actions, know the importance of forming coalitions and alliances, are skilled in interpersonal diplomacy, and play above the board to build credibility and momentum for change. In addition, women are especially prone to soft skills and qualities associated with transformative leadership styles, including inspiring trust by behaving genuinely and exhibiting honesty. Women leaders also typically exercise "power with" rather than "power over" because they usually do not want power for power's sake but to drive social change and improve the lives of others. Finally, women leaders may act on typical "male qualities" required to convince risk-averse society to follow progressive agendas, including ambition and determination.

Figure 6.1 showcases a theoretical analytical framework of the phenomenon which builds on the variables derived from Chapters 1–6 (details in Appendix 1.0). It sheds light on the structure-agency duality and what may determine the successful outcome of women's political leadership for sustainable development.

Chapters 7–9 apply this analytical framework in practice to showcase women's political leadership for sustainable development on national, regional, and local governance levels and further explore the validity of the normative concept.

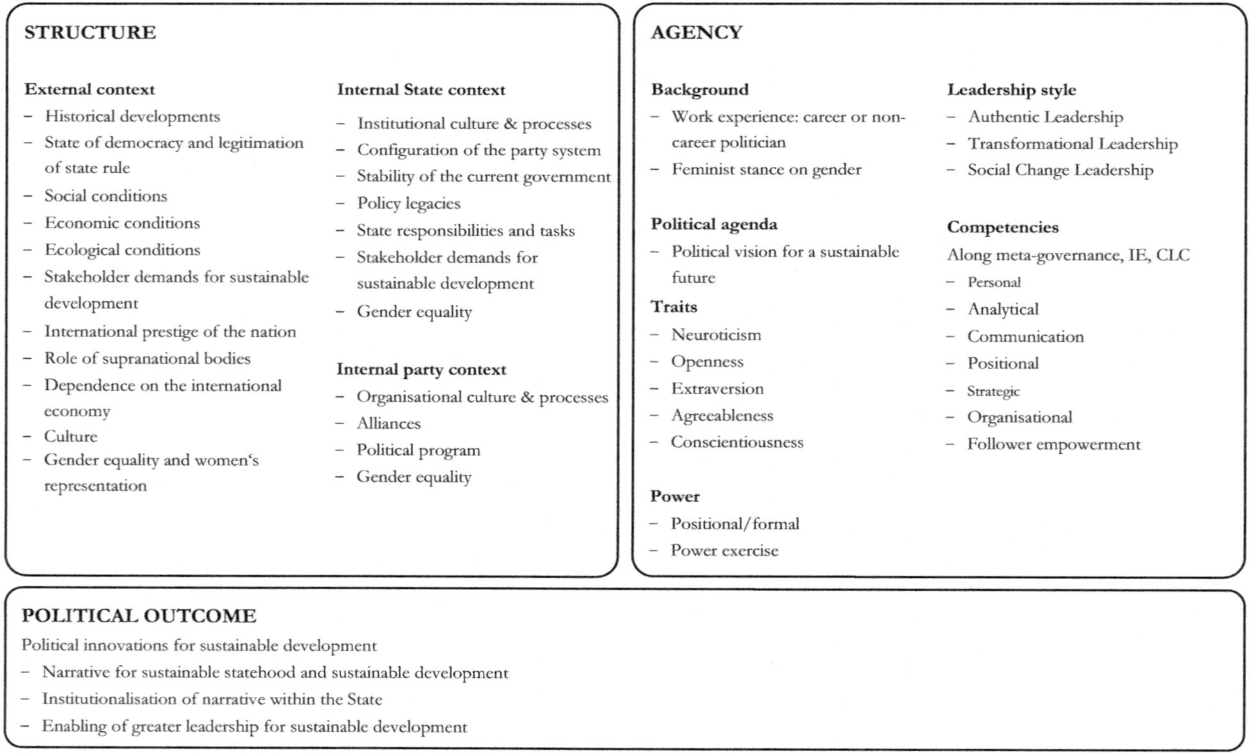

STRUCTURE

External context

- Historical developments
- State of democracy and legitimation of state rule
- Social conditions
- Economic conditions
- Ecological conditions
- Stakeholder demands for sustainable development
- International prestige of the nation
- Role of supranational bodies
- Dependence on the international economy
- Culture
- Gender equality and women's representation

Internal State context

- Institutional culture & processes
- Configuration of the party system
- Stability of the current government
- Policy legacies
- State responsibilities and tasks
- Stakeholder demands for sustainable development
- Gender equality

Internal party context

- Organisational culture & processes
- Alliances
- Political program
- Gender equality

AGENCY

Background

- Work experience: career or non-career politician
- Feminist stance on gender

Political agenda

- Political vision for a sustainable future

Traits

- Neuroticism
- Openness
- Extraversion
- Agreeableness
- Conscientiousness

Power

- Positional/formal
- Power exercise

Leadership style

- Authentic Leadership
- Transformational Leadership
- Social Change Leadership

Competencies

Along meta-governance, IF, CLC

- Personal
- Analytical
- Communication
- Positional
- Strategic
- Organisational
- Follower empowerment

POLITICAL OUTCOME

Political innovations for sustainable development

- Narrative for sustainable statehood and sustainable development
- Institutionalisation of narrative within the State
- Enabling of greater leadership for sustainable development

FIGURE 6.1   A framework of women's political leadership for sustainable development.

References

Alexander, A. C., Bolzendahl, C., & Jalalzai F. (2018). Introduction to measuring women's political empowerment across the globe: Strategies, challenges, and future research. In Alexander, A. C., Bolzendahl, C., & Jalalzai, F. (Eds.), *Measuring women's political empowerment across the globe* (pp. 1–25). Basingstoke: Palgrave-Macmillan.

Ambler, G. (2005). *Understanding leadership in context.* www.thepracticeofleadership. net/2005/12/08/understanding-leadership-context/

Bauer, G., & Tremblay, M. (2011). *Women in executive power: A global overview.* London: Routledge.

Belasen, A., & Frank, N. (2012). Women's leadership: Using the competing values framework to evaluate the interactive effects of gender and personality traits on leadership roles. *International Journal of Leadership Studies, 7*(2), 192–214. https://www.regent.edu/acad/global/publications/ijls/new/vol7iss2/IJLS_ Vol7Iss2_Belasen_pp192-215.pdf

Brooks, D. (2011). Testing the double standard for candidate emotionality: Voter reactions to the tears and anger of male and female politicians. *Journal of Politics, 73*(2), 597–615. https://doi.org/10.1017/s0022381611000053

Campus, D. (2013). *Women political leaders and the media.* Basingstoke: Palgrave Macmillan. https://doi.org/10.1057/9781137295545

Coleman, M. (2011). *Women at the top. Challenges, choices and change.* London: Palgrave Macmillan.

Eagly, A. H., & Johnson, B. T. (1990). Gender and leadership style: A meta-analysis. *Psychological Bulletin, 108*(2), 233–256. https://doi.org/10.1037/0033-2909.108. 2.233

Eagly, A. H., & Karau, S. J. (2002). Role congruity theory of prejudice toward female leaders. *Psychological Review, 109*(3), 573–598. https://doi.org/10. 1037//0033-295X.109.3.573

Fletcher, J. K. (2004). The paradox of postheroic leadership: An essay on gender, power, and transformational change. *The Leadership Quarterly, 15*(5), 647–661. https://doi.org/10.1016/j.leaqua.2004.07.004

Fox, R., & Lawless, J. (2004). Entering the arena? Gender and the decision to run for office. *American Journal of Political Science, 48*(2), 264–277. https://doi. org/10.1111/j.0092-5853.2004.00069.x

French, J., & Raven, B. (1959). The bases of social power. In D. Cartwright, & A. Zander (Eds.), *Studies in social power* (pp. 150–167). Ann Arbor, MI: University of Michigan Press.

Gardner, W., & Clevenger, D. (1998). Impression management techniques associated with transformational leadership leaders at the world class level. *Management Communication Quarterly, 12*(1), 237–251. https://doi.org/10.1177/ 0893318998121001

Genovese, M. A. & Steckenrider, J. S. (2013). *Women as political leaders. Studies in gender and governing.* London: Routledge.

Haslam, S. A., & Ryan, M. (2008). The road off the glass cliff: Differences in perceived suitability of men and women for leadership positions in succeeding and failing organizations. *The Leadership Quarterly, 19*(5), 530–546. https://doi. org/10.1016/j.leaqua.2008.07.011

Heilman, M. E., & Okimoto, T. G. (2007). Why are women penalized for success at male tasks? The implied community deficit. *Journal of Applied Psychology*, 92(1), 81–92. https://doi.org/10.1037/0021-9010.92.1.81

Helms, L. (2016). Democracy and innovation: From institutions to agency and leadership. *Democratization*, 23(3), 459–477. https://doi.org/10.1080/1351034 7.2014.981667

Hyde, J. S., Bigler, R. S., Joel, D., Tate, C. C., & van Anders, S. M. (2019). The future of sex and gender in psychology: Five challenges to the gender binary. *American Psychologist*, 74(2), 171–193. https://doi.org/10.1037/amp0000307

Hymowitz, C., & Schelhardt, T. (1986). The glass ceiling: Why women can't seem to break the invisible barrier that blocks them from top jobs. *Wall Street Journal*, 57, 4–5. https://www.proquest.com/docview/135185178

Jalalzai, F. (2008). Women rule: Shattering the executive glass ceiling. *Politics & Gender*, 4, 205–231.

Jalalzai, F. (2018). Women heads of state and government. In Alexander, A. C., Bolzendahl, C., & Jalalzai, F. (Eds.), *Measuring women's political empowerment across the globe* (pp. 257–282). Basingstoke: Palgrave-Macmillan.

Klenke, K. (2017). *Women in leadership* (2nd ed.). Bingley: Emerald Publishing.

Lawless, J., & Fox, R. (2012). *Men rule the continued under-representation of women in U.S. politics*. Washington, DC: Women & Politics Institute.

Mikkola, M. (2022, January 18). *Female Perspectives on Sex and Gender*. Stanford Encyclopedia of Philosophy. https://plato.stanford.edu/entries/feminism-gender/

Montecinos, V. (2017). Introduction. In Monetcinos, V. (Ed.), *Women presidents and prime ministers in post-transition democracies* (pp. 1–36). London: Palgrave Macmillan.

Pullen, A., & Vacchani, S. J. (2020). Female ethics and women leaders: From difference to intercorporeality. *Journal of Business Ethics*, 173(2), 1–11. https:// doi.org/10.1007/s10551-020-04526-0

Ruderman, M. N., Ohlott, P. J., Panzer, K., & King, S. N. (2002). Benefits of multiple roles for managerial women. *Academy of Management Journal*, 45(2), 369–386. https://doi.org/10.5465/3069352

Simon, S., & Hoyt, C. L. (2013). Exploring the effect of media images on women's leadership self-perceptions and aspirations. *Group Processes & Intergroup Relations*, 16(2), 232–245. https://doi.org/10.1177/1368430212451176

Stempel, C. R., Rigotti, T., & Mohr, G. (2015). Think transformational leadership – think female? *Leadership*, 11(3), 259–280. https://doi.org/10.1177/ 1742715015590468

Vroman, S. R., & Danko, T. (2020). Against what model? Evaluating women as leaders in the pandemic era. *Gender, Work and Organization*, 27, 860–867. https://doi.org/10.1111/gwao.12488

Wakefield, S. (2017). *Transformative and Female Leadership for Women's Rights*. Oxfam. https://s3.amazonaws.com/oxfam-us/www/static/media/files/ Transformative_and_Female_Leadership_for_Womens_Rights.pdf

Wiltse, E. C. & Hager, L. (2021). *Women's paths to power: Female presidents and prime ministers, 1960-2020*. Boulder, CO: Lynne Rienner.

UN Women. (2024). *Facts and figures: Women's leadership and political participation*. https://www.unwomen.org/en/what-we-do/leadership-and-political-participation/ facts-and-figures

PART III

Cases of women's political leadership for sustainable development

7

JACINDA ARDERN

Pioneering national political innovations

Understanding the context Jacinda Ardern faced

The chapter starts by providing background information on New Zealand to describe the context that Jacinda Ardern faced. New Zealand has a land area of 267.710 km² (World Data, 2022) and around 5 million inhabitants (Szöllösi-Circa, 2022, p. 93). It is a young nation since the first Māori arrived less than 1000 years ago and British settlers only two centuries ago (Vowles, 2020a, p. 46). It is one of the most ethically and culturally diverse countries worldwide (Barker & Vowles, 2020). In 2018, 70 percent of the inhabitants were European, 17 percent Māori, 15 percent Asian, 8 percent Pacific, and 1 percent Middle Eastern, Latin American, and African (Stats NZ, 2019, September 23). Eighty-seven percent of the population thereby lives in urban areas (World Data, 2022).

New Zealand was the prototype of a majoritarian democracy until 1996 when they introduced the mixed-member proportional (MMP) governing system via referendum (Lijphart, 2012, p. 74). In the MMP, voters cast an electoral vote for the candidate representing the electorate in parliament, and a party vote for their preferred political party (Chapman, 2020). One hundred twenty representative seats, seven of which are Māori electorate seats, currently make up parliament (Chapman). The power of the State is unitary and centralised, without a constitution and judicial review of legislation (Lijphart), parliament concentrates authority, and the government wields potentially limitless power (Barker & Vowles, 2020). The Prime Minister is the head of State and government and exercises the greatest executive power in the political system (Lijphart).

DOI: 10.4324/9781003507666-11

Since the 1930s, the centrist liberal National Party and left-leaning Labour Party traditionally dominated New Zealand politics (New Zealand Parliament, 2020a, March 3). With the introduction of the MMP in 1996, the first coalition government was formed (New Zealand Parliament). Since then, every election has seen around 120 members from five to eight parties elected to parliament, consequently becoming more representative of the population (New Zealand Parliament, 2021, June 29). In 2020, half of the parliament were women, one in five Members of Parliament was of Māori descent, one in 12 of Pacific ethnicity, and one in 15 of Asian descent (New Zealand Parliament).

It is vital to understand New Zealand's political course over the past fifty years to comprehend the economic, social, and ecological conditions Jacinda Ardern and her government faced. In the mid-1930s, the first Labour government developed a Welfare State to respond to the collapse of world markets during the Great Depression (McClintock, 1998, pp. 498–499). They extensively intervened in the market system. At the same time, they expanded the public provision of housing, education, health care, and universal security as a right for all. After 1949 the National Party governed and added to previous Labour policies, e.g., by introducing a universal national superannuation scheme and undertaking significant infrastructure investments in the energy sector. However, they failed to diversify New Zealand's economy and it reached a crisis in the early 1980s (McClintock).

In 1984, Labour governed again (McClintock, 1998). Under their leadership, the political program changed altogether, following the neoliberal agenda explored in Chapter 1. Radical liberalisation reforms and a neoliberal attitude towards the domestic economy hollowed out the manufacturing sector, tied it to a "monoculture of grass" and integrated economic prospects into the world market. This made the economy highly vulnerable to external shocks (McClintock, p. 500). At the same time, they sold government assets and abolished entire departments (Vani & Harte, 2021). Unemployment peaked at eleven percent in 1991 and coincided with the worst crime and homicide rates New Zealand had ever witnessed (Vani & Harte, p. 15). The public sanctioned the Labour Party and the National Party came to rule once more (Vani & Harte).

In the 1990s, the National Party's finance minister Ruth Richardson implemented even more significant neoliberal reforms (Marcetic, 2021, May 25). She extended Labour's free-market reforms and put in place the most extreme case of Welfare State retrenchment in the Western world. It included the mass sell-off of State assets, the dismantling of regulations and economic controls, and significant cuts to the welfare budget. The program dramatically increased hunger, poverty, and wealth inequality (Marcetic).

Today, New Zealand still boasts one of the most deregulated economies in the OECD and a minimised role for government (Rosenberg, 2021). There was some retreat from the neoliberal course under Helen Clark's Labour-led government between 2000 and 2008 (Barnett & Bagshaw, 2020, p. 81). They had declared that the market model mantra "individual success and personal responsibility" was not working and that the State had to provide "positive welfare" once again (Maharey, 2000, September 15). However, the National Party pushed these developments back to some extent whilst heading the government between 2009 and 2016 (Barnett & Bagshaw, p. 81).

In 2017, the year of Jacinda Ardern's election, economic growth stood at 3 percent, much higher than in comparator countries such as Australia, the United States, or Japan (Szöllösi-Circa, 2022, p. 45). However, they had seen no real wage growth in recent years, which was partially due to high immigration and respective competition in the labour market, leading to a lack of incentives for businesses to increase productivity (Szöllösi-Circa).

The economy still builds on natural resources, as New Zealand represents the second wealthiest nation in the world regarding natural resources per capita (Szöllösi-Circa, 2022, p. 122). This abundance is reflected in their exports, which stood at NZ$ 40.5 billion in 2019, compared to service exports of NZ$ 17.2 billion (OEC, 2022). New Zealand is the world's most significant exporter of concentrated milk, rough wood, butter, casein, and honey, whilst tourism is the most crucial export sector regarding services. In 2020, the size of New Zealand's economy was roughly NZ$ 300 billion (Szöllösi-Circa, 2022, p. 93).

However, recent economic growth did not benefit low- and middle-income earners (Vowles, 2020a), and overall, wellbeing in New Zealand is faltering (McClure, 2021, April 10). The country ranks in the top third of the OECD regarding the highest income inequality (MPISOC, 2019, pp. 4–5). In total, 9.8 percent of the population aged 15–64 received the main welfare benefit in 2018, and the number of Hardship Assistance grants rose to 385.000 in 2018. In 2017, a further 4.9 percent were unemployed, representing 12.1 percent of the working-age population. The same year, thirteen percent of children under 18 lived below the 50-percent-of-median-income poverty threshold (MPISOC, pp. 4–5), and youth suicide rates were the highest in the Global North (McClure, 2021, April 10). General suicide rates across the population are also among the highest in the OECD (MPISOC).

New Zealand faces an ongoing housing crisis (Chapman, 2020). Since 1990 housing costs have increased for all income quintiles and more than doubled for the lowest income quintile, making them the most unaffordable prices in the world (Stats NZ, 2021, February 16). Increasing immigration puts additional pressure on housing, homelessness, infrastructure, and social services (Vowles, 2020a).

Finally, the Indigenous Māori population falls victim to inequality. Māori comprise a disproportionately high share of incarceration, poverty, and health statistics and a vastly disproportionately low one in education and asset ownership (Mintrom, 2019, p. 894). Māori life expectancy rates are approximately 10 percent lower than non-Māori, the unemployment rate is twice as high, and they make up 50 percent of the nation's prison population (Mintrom).

In addition to social detriments, New Zealand faces a range of ecological challenges. Considering planetary boundaries, the nation has passed into a high-risk zone regarding biodiversity and climate change and is at an increased risk regarding water use, nitrogen and phosphorus levels (Globaia, 2022). Boasting one of the greatest biodiversity ranges in the world (Environment Guide, 2022), the expanding economy and increased production threaten this diversity due to habitat loss with many species being threatened or at risk of extinction (Ministry of the Environment, 2020). Indigenous forests were decimated due to extensive land clearance and logging, most lakes and rivers are in poor or very poor ecological health, and the majority of wetlands were lost due to grazing and drainage for urban development, weed invasion, or barriers to fish migration (Ministry for the Environment, 2022a). Across the country, nitrogen dioxide concentrations are higher than the WHO recommendations, and carbon dioxide emissions are skyrocketing due to transport and methane from agriculture (Ministry for the Environment, 2022b). Air quality is also dramatic and way above WHO recommendations. Finally, emissions rose by 57 percent between 1990 and 2018, and the consequences are felt in rising temperatures, rainfall, and sea levels (Ministry for the Environment, 2022b).

Social and ecological conditions are dire in New Zealand but still, there have been a range of advances regarding politics for sustainable development. Helen Clark, who was Prime Minister between 1999 and 2008 (New Zealand Parliament, 2020b, October 12), acted as a champion for sustainable development (Policy Commons, 2019, November 26). Under Clark, the government first adopted wellbeing (Weijers & Morrison, 2018) as an ethical concept that asks how we ought to live and the virtues of finding happiness and life satisfaction (La Placa et al., 2013). In 2011, New Zealand's Treasury published the Living Standards Framework, a public dashboard measuring wellbeing indicators, desiring to clarify the institution's vision of working for higher living standards for New Zealanders rather than merely measuring GDP (Weijers & Morrison). Between 2009 and 2016, the National Party also instated flagship programs, such as Better Public Services, to foster inter-agency collaboration and a social investment approach with evidence-based policy decision-making (Macaulay, 2021).

Finally, New Zealand champions women's rights and representations. In 1893, it became the first country in the world where women gained the right to vote (Ministry for Women, 2020, June 26). Today, it has a Ministry dedicated to women's development (Ministry for Women) and ranks 8th in the world regarding gender equality (UNDP, 2022). Women continue to outperform men in education, and the gap between men and women holding tertiary qualifications continues to decrease (Ministry for Women). In 2019, the gender pay gap remained among the lowest worldwide at 9.3 percent (Ministry for Women). In the political sphere, New Zealand is also a leader in equality. Women comprise more than 40 percent of parliament (UNDP, 2022), and to date, they have had three female prime ministers (New Zealand Parliament, 2020b, October 12).

Having set the scene with the most important key facts about the context Jacinda Ardern faced as a political leader, we can now delve into her leadership.

Examining Jacinda Ardern's leadership

Path to becoming Prime Minister

Jacinda Ardern was born in Hamilton, New Zealand on July 26th, 1980 (Vani & Harte, 2021, p. 10). She grew up in Murupara, a small settlement on the North Island. It has been one of the country's most deprived towns since New Zealand's neoliberal course in the 1980s when almost two-thirds of the town's population had become reliant on welfare (Vani & Harte, p. 15). Accordingly, Ardern states that her early childhood years shaped her as a politician. She developed a social conscience, seeing her schoolmates without proper clothes and food, many losing their jobs, and neighbours committing suicide out of desperation (Vani & Harte). When Ardern was eight, her family moved to Morrinsville, one of the country's most prosperous dairy farming regions, where many refugees settled (Chapman, 2020, p. 15). Thus, wealth and poverty were neighbours during Ardern's youth, further shaping her contact with social inequality (Chapman).

Ardern was a high achiever at school (Vani & Harte, 2021). She participated in debating, speech, science, and writing competitions, joined the student council, was the sole student representative on the Board of Trustees, and part of a Human Rights Group (Chapman, 2020). The most significant influence on her was her teacher Gregor Fountain, who taught both sides of New Zealand's colonial history, including the attempted genocide of Māori by Europeans (Chapman). Ardern states that Fountain taught her how to question everything, including her own beliefs and opinions, whilst encouraging her activism, promoting ideals of justice, and questioning humankind and its motivations (Vani & Harte).

Ardern's parents were hard-working, down-to-earth, and role models to her (Blackwell & Hobday, 2020). Her father's diplomatic approach to conflicts as a policeman shaped her leadership style (Chapman, 2020) because he tried to understand all perspectives and work through opposing views (Vani & Harte, 2021). At the same time, Ardern saw her father engage in various activities to relieve environmental disasters and human suffering (Vani & Harte). Ardern describes her mother as a compassionate and generous "epitome of kindness," always helping anyone in need (Blackwell & Hobday, 2020, p. 32). Both parents were Labour Party supporters but not overly political (Vani & Harte). Still, Ardern stems from a family of bold feminists (Vani & Harte, pp. 55–58). In 1872, her great-great-grandmother emigrated from London to New Zealand and later became New Zealand's first national female sports star. Her daughter, Ardern's great-grandmother, was one of the women who signed the 1893 Women's Suffrage Petition. Ardern's grandmother was also a feminist Labour supporter who campaigned with former Prime Minister Norman Kirk, one of Ardern's political idols (Vani & Harte). Ardern thus grew up with strong political women who inspired her to become a champion for women's rights and gender equality (Blackwell & Hobday, 2020). In 1996, Ardern's aunt, a long-time Labour Party supporter, got her in touch with MP Harry Duynhoven for volunteer work and inspired her to join the Labour Party at age seventeen (Vani & Harte, p. 54). Ardern states that she "wasn't looking for a career [but wanted] perhaps naively, to change the world" (Ardern, 2019a, September 25).

After college, Ardern moved to Hamilton to pursue a Bachelor of Communications with a minor in Politics at the University of Waikato (Vani & Harte, 2021). A former professor stressed how strong Ardern's humility, social consciousness, and communication skills were at the time (Vani & Harte). She started spending a lot of time with members of the gay community, promoting the Civil Union Act for equal rights for everyone (Chapman, 2020). After graduating in 2001, Ardern moved to Wellington to become MP Harry Duynhoven's private secretary, who was Associate Minister of Energy at the time (Chapman, p. 28). Two years later, in 2003, a friend introduced Ardern to the New Zealand Young Labour Committee, and she was elected Vice President shortly after (Vani & Harte, p. 74). At this point, there were not many women active in Young Labour and gender played a significant role in her obtaining the position. Ardern's reputation started preceding her and eventually, she successfully applied for a researcher and adviser position with Phil Goff, Minister of Justice and Foreign Affairs (Vani & Harte).

Soon after, Ardern was headhunted as policy advisor by Prime Minister Helen Clark's head of staff (Vani & Harte, 2021). Clark needed to appeal more to younger voters, facing a difficult election against National Party leader Don Brash. Ardern was only 24 years old and a novice at party politics (Vani & Harte, p. 35). During the election campaign, she formed strong bonds with colleagues and seniors in Labour and the unions. These connections would later be crucial to her ascent within the party. But most importantly, Helen Clark became Ardern's mentor and role model. Ardern admired Clark's iron will, dedication to objectives, commitment to gender equality, dignity, public debating skills, and despise for power politics (Vani & Harte).

In 2006, after the successful election campaign, Ardern moved to New York to work for worker's rights campaigns and volunteer at a soup kitchen (Chapman, 2020). Shortly after, she became an adviser in Tony Blair's Cabinet and was responsible for health and safety employment regulations (Ross, 2018). Later she liaised with small businesses, local authorities, and the police in the Department of Business and Industry (Ross). During her time in London, Ardern became the global President of the International Union of Socialist Youth (Chapman).

In 2008, Labour did not expect to win elections after three increasingly unpopular terms in government (Chapman, 2020, pp. 43–44). They also needed more female members since a 2006 campaign required a 50/50 gender balance for Labour Members of Parliament (MPs) and Senior Labour Party members. That year, Ardern was called by her former boss Phil Goff, asking her to run for MP. A representative of the unions, with whom Ardern had coordinated the relationships between Labour and the unions, had put her name forward. In addition, Ardern held Helen Clark's approval and was the right person at the right time because she was young, committed, and a woman (Chapman). She was placed on the 20th spot on the Labour Party list, returned from London shortly before Election Day, and lost against the incumbent National Party candidate (Vani & Harte, 2021, p. 111). Due to her high place on the list, she was nonetheless guaranteed a seat in parliament, and at 28, she became the youngest MP (Vani & Harte, p. 111), Labour Spokesperson for youth affairs, and Associate Spokesperson for justice (Chapman).

In 2011 and 2014, Ardern ran again in Central Auckland, lost the elections but retained her seat as MP due to her list placement (Chapman, 2020). During the same time, Labour had some of its worst polling in party history, mainly due to continuous internal fighting and bad leadership (Chapman). Two Labour leaders resigned, and Andrew Little eventually took over (Vani & Harte, 2021). All the while, Ardern's public profile started lifting, with the media framing her as the Labour Party's next star (Chapman).

In December 2016, National's Prime Minister John Key resigned, and three days later, a Senior Labour member resigned from his MP role, his seat in Mount Albert becoming vacant (Vani & Harte, 2021, pp. 148–152). Ardern stepped in and won her first election. As Prime Ministers are traditionally elected MPs, this was a significant step toward becoming Prime Minister (Vani & Harte). Eventually, the Deputy Leader of the Labour Party was asked to resign so that Ardern could replace her as a young and fresh face (Chapman, 2020). In 2017, the year of national elections, Labour had its worst internal polling result in party history. Five months into Ardern becoming Deputy Leader, Andrew Little resigned, with Ardern polling higher in preferred Prime Minister polls than him. Little's resignation would be considered one of New Zealand politics' most challenging and significant strategic moves (Chapman). On August 1, 2017, seven weeks before Election Day, Labour unanimously voted for Ardern to become the Labour Party leader and run for the office of Prime Minister (Vowles et al., 2020, p. 3).

Ardern rapidly gained public popularity (Chapman, 2020). Labour's polling increased from 9 percentage points to 33.1 within ten days of her election (Chapman, p. 94). The media quickly termed the widespread enthusiasm "Jacindamania" (Edwards, 2020, December 24). Before Ardern, Labour had been unstable, with four leaders in just six years, various policy flops, and little policy work done in opposition (Rashbrooke). Within the first half-hour of Ardern's leadership, Labour had received more favourable media coverage than it had in the past year under Little's leadership (Curtin & Greaves, 2020).

Ardern ran her entire election campaign on "hope" and "relentless positivity" and struck a nerve (Curtin & Greaves, 2020, p. 180). She wanted to evoke an emotional response and emphasised that politics had to reconnect to feelings of empathy and that "understanding the issues people in our communities face, their experiences, and never being satisfied that things…can't be changed or made better. That is why I chose politics. That is why I am here" (Ardern, 2017a, November 8). Her campaign images followed the same message of hope and were white instead of red, featuring a smiling Ardern dressed in white with the slogan "Let's do this" (Chapman, 2020, p. 102).

Ardern also had a different way of communicating (Chapman, 2020). Appearing authentically on social media and making politics more accessible to a broader audience was especially important to her. She went live on Facebook at least once a week to allow voters to ask questions and explain policy announcements, often in her private home. She reached audiences that typically did not engage with politics because she was easy to understand and relatable. She also posted many selfies, always smiling and signalling that she had a sense of humour and was genuine (Chapman). In a 90-second video to promote Labour, Ardern stated that this was "an opportunity to build a better, fairer New Zealand...to give everyone a voice...They will dismiss our optimism. They will say that kindness will stand in the way of progress...but we can do better" (New Zealand Labour Party, 2017). The message was picked up in memes and photos across social and traditional media and reached older and younger generations (Curtin & Greaves, 2020).

The subjects Ardern addressed in her campaign were equally important, focusing on human rights, economic wellbeing, social policies, climate change, and pro-abortion (Curtin & Greaves, 2020). According to election analyses, health, the economy, housing, education, and social welfare were the top five themes for the public, and the environment was the sixth most important (Lees-Marshment et al., 2018, p. 10). Polls showed that Labour's policies were thus more in line with public opinion than National's (Lees-Marshment et al). It further exposed how important a likable leader was to the public, as voters agreed with the Greens' policies most but found their leader less agreeable than Ardern (Vowles, 2020a).

Despite this positive outlook for Ardern, nobody won on election night (Chapman, 2020). The Left parties received 43.3 percent of the votes, the Right parties 45.1 percent, and the Centre 10.9 percent (Vowles, 2020a, p. 41). Although the New Zealand First Party only won 7 percent of the vote, the left and right blocks in parliament did not have enough votes to govern without them (Edwards, 2018, p. 215). Thus, they could decide on the future coalition and Prime Minister (Edwards). After weeks of negotiations, NZ First leader Peters announced his decision to coalition with the Labour and Green Party (Vowles et al., 2020). He based his decision on the fact that capitalism had become the enemy of many New Zealanders and that they wanted the change he found in the Labour Party and Ardern, who was equally critical of capitalism (Chapman).

In 2017, months before the election, Ardern did not want anything to do with the job because she was anxious, constantly worried, and hated letting people down (Clifton, 2017, June 15). Still, Ardern became Prime Minister and the world's youngest female head of government (Blackwell & Hobday, 2020). A few months into her first term, she also gave birth while in office and was only the second world leader to do so (Blackwell & Hobday). In the 2020 elections, she achieved another first with the Labour Party gaining an outright majority with 51 percent of the vote (Rashbrooke, 2021, p. 136).

Political convictions

Jacinda Ardern's leadership is driven by a deeply humanitarian view. She believes the world must find and remember its humanity again (Ardern, 2019b, September 25). To her, humans have more in common than differences, and we should focus on connecting to one another (Ardern). Along these beliefs, Ardern developed her well-known "politics of kindness" (Chapman, 2020): "Kindness is that sense of being aware of the environment around you, the people around you and the community around you" (Blackwell & Hobday, 2020, p. 29). She links kindness to the responsibilities of the State and the purpose of government to "care" for both people and the planet (Pacella et al., 2021). Concerning the latter Ardern holds that people are not just guardians of each other, but of the planet (Ardern) and to tackle climate change we must stand unified, keep pushing and bring all people along (Blackwell & Hobday, 2020).

Ardern makes the economic system and the State's (in-)actions responsible for the lack of wellbeing of both people and the planet. She openly declared capitalism is failing New Zealanders (Gurevitch, 2021, p. 495) and that "economic growth accompanied by worsening social outcomes is not success [but] failure" (McCarthy, 2019, September 25). She further holds that the neoliberal path New Zealand had embarked on was detrimental and the government must raise social conditions and wealth for all New Zealanders (Barnett & Bagshaw, 2020, p. 81). Thereby her mission is to conserve and develop long-term social welfare so that every New Zealander can have "access to world-class education and healthcare, live in a home that's healthy and in a community that is safe, and realise their potential" (Simpson et al., 2021, p. 9).

To overcome capitalist detriments and increase New Zealander's wellbeing, Ardern follows the approach of pragmatic idealism (Chapman, 2020): "I always strive for better. But I am pragmatic about how much time that sometimes takes" (Manhire, 2019 April 6). Respectively, she aims to implement incremental reforms, allow people to adjust, and gain a social license for further shifts (Rashbrooke, 2021). In line with this approach, she has expressed an open aversion to change she deems "too radical to stick" (Gurevitch, 2021, p. 497). Her approach of "radical incrementalism" implies that many small steps add up to something transformative (Rashbrooke, p. 136). This may be particularly suitable for New Zealand's political system. Due to three-year parliamentary terms, the frequency of government turnovers is fast (Lijphart, 2012), and the relatively short cycle gives citizens the chance to sanction political parties (Barker & Vowles, 2020). In addition, New Zealand is a small, intimate democracy, and New Zealanders have a special relationship with their politicians, their media coverage mirroring that of celebrities in other countries (Vani & Harte, 2021). The public expects politicians to be approachable, and because citizens have direct and easy access to politicians, they value high responsiveness to their concerns (Vowles et al., 2020). This leads to policy responsiveness that often turns into ad hoc pragmatism, real-time reactive decision-making, and a trajectory of incremental change (Barker & Vowles). In 2017, after nine years of National Party leadership, nearly two-thirds of New Zealanders believed that the country was heading in the right direction and regardless of their dissatisfaction with housing, poverty, or the environment, there was no demand for extensive reforms (Rashbrooke, 2021, p. 136). Hence, Ardern's approach was highly suitable for New Zealand's political culture.

Personality, skills, and leadership style

At the beginning of her political career, Jacinda Ardern believed she was not tough enough for politics (CNN, 2021, June 3). Indeed, she is typically described with mostly "soft" character traits such as caring, empathetic, sensitive, compassionate, intuitive, assuring, and kind (Blackwell & Hobday, 2020; Chapman, 2020; Vani & Harte, 2021). With time she, however, came to believe that thick-skinned politicians are not what the world needs but rather those who care. To her, society has placed too much emphasis on assertiveness and strength, but considering global challenges, the world needs kindness and empathy combined with strength (Blackwell & Hobday). In an interview with the BBC, she stated that she had "always said that it takes courage and strength to be empathetic, and I'm very proudly an empathetic, compassionately driven politician... I am trying to chart a different path..." (BBC, 2018, November 16). Respectively, Ardern wants to reshape what it means to be a politician and demonstrate that she can do things differently without changing her character traits and personality (Vani & Harte).

Ardern has coined a new type of leadership that the media and academics refer to as "empathetic" (Chapman, 2020, p. 250) or "compassionate" leadership (Simpson et al., 2021). What characterises this leadership style first and foremost is that Ardern acts along profound values and a moral compass rooted in deep humanitarianism (Malpass, 2021, December 9). It also goes hand in hand with the respect she holds for her political position. She sees it as a privilege to serve the nation (Chapman). She took on political leadership roles when others wanted her to lead and accepted these positions due to her inert responsibility and sense of duty for the people (Chapman).

Ardern wants New Zealand to be a compassionate and inclusive team, regardless of religion, race, and gender (Simpson et al., 2021). The government ought to represent the people's shared vision for a modern and prosperous New Zealand rooted in the concept of kindness. By communicating a vision of a better and kinder New Zealand, Ardern created a shared vision and identity for New Zealanders and a strong connection with the people. She provided them with a sense of identification, moral support, and belonging and built consensus across interests. She further increased their ability to collaborate, creating interdependent relationships that helped all parties develop resources of social welfare knowledge, socio-relational identification, and stability (Simpson et al.).

Ardern particularly demonstrated this in two crises New Zealand faced: the Christchurch attack and the COVID-19 pandemic. Her leadership style in both situations promoted "emotional intelligence and vulnerability alongside steel and resolve" (Chapman, 2020, p. 186). One of Ardern's greatest strengths was acknowledging people's fears and anxieties in her communication, opening space for them to feel heard and making them more receptive to her messages (Rashbrooke, 2021). This was especially the case due to her intuitive and deliberate language (Blake-Bear et al., 2020) and hopeful, optimistic, and inspiring rhetoric (Chapman, 2020).

After the Christchurch attack, for instance, she provided understanding and support to the victims and asked the nation to show compassion, love, and empathy rather than vengeance (Chapman, 2020). She further emphasised New Zealand's identity of diversity, kindness, and compassion, stating that everyone "are us" (Chapman, p. 202). She called the event a terrorist act by a white supremacist. This contrasted sharply with the communication of other nations where the media typically frame White mass shooters as killers and non-Whites as terrorists (Chapman). Ardern made further gestures, such as wearing a scarf around her hair to show respect or meeting the victims without the press (Blackwell & Hobday, 2020). She united New Zealanders in compassion and kindness and inspired them to offer security services outside mosques, make coffee and bake treats, or lay out flowers in the streets (Chapman). Within ten days of the attack, she changed the gun laws, which politicians had tried and failed at for decades (Rashbrooke, 2021). Shortly after, she brought the CEOs of major tech companies and 70 nations together to pledge to fight terrorism and violent extremism on social media (Chapman, p. 225). Her handling of the Christchurch attack moved Ardern and New Zealand into the international spotlight (Wahab et al., 2020). Her compassion and actions resonated with the Muslim community worldwide because it stood in contrast to many other leaders taking an anti-Muslim, xenophobic, or silent approach to immigration and Islam (Curtin & Greaves, 2020).

During the COVID-19 pandemic, Ardern equally excelled, primarily through her communication skills, empathy, direction-giving (Blake-Bear et al., 2020), role-modelling, and collaboration (Simpson et al., 2021). She asked New Zealanders to be "kind to one another" (Willis, 2021, p. 3), addressed them as a "team of 5 million", and framed the challenge so everyone understood their responsibility for each other considering the pandemic threat (Simpson et al., p. 10). Through this, she balanced tensions between individual and collective interests, presenting the lockdown as a joint endeavour for public health rather than an imposition on personal freedom (Simpson et al.). At the same time, she acted as a role model, e.g., when she and her ministers cut their pay by 20 percent during the first six months of the pandemic (Simpson et al., p. 10).

Ardern further demonstrated her belief in evidence-based decision-making (Maak, Pless & Wohlgezogen, 2021), basing all her decisions on scientists' analyses and recommendations (Rashbrooke, 2021). She kept reassuring the people of her government's approach via daily briefings, press conferences, and Facebook Live broadcasts (McGuire et al., 2020, p. 374). Her ability to communicate purpose and information clearly and frequently comforted the public rather than leaving a vacuum for misinformation (Dirani et al., 2020). Another leadership facet that stood out was her flexibility in adapting to unforeseen circumstances (Vani & Harte, 2021) and openness in admitting mistakes (Simpson et al., 2021). Ardern had first adopted a "spread the cases, flatten the curve" approach but quickly adapted to "eliminate" or "stop the virus in its tracks" (Simpson et al., p. 9). In this adaptive learning process, she transparently communicated what the government had learned and why it made the necessary changes (Simpson et al.).

This also connects to Ardern's general honesty and authenticity (Blackwell & Hobday, 2020). She holds herself accountable for her failings. According to her, the worst thing leaders can do is pretend that leading is easy and that they do not need help because that only alienates people (Blackwell & Hobday). In January 2023, Ardern demonstrated this again when she resigned as Prime Minister and Labour Party leader (Ardern, 2023, January 19). She openly stated that she recognised her responsibility of knowing she was no longer the right person to lead because she had run out of energy. She finished her announcement speech by stating, "I hope I leave New Zealanders with a belief that you can be kind, but strong, empathetic but decisive, optimistic but focused. And that you can be your own kind of leader – one who knows when it's time to go" (Ardern).

The case of New Zealand's political innovations

Jacinda Ardern and her Labour-led government were driving sustainable development via all three levers of the State explored in Chapter 3. The following sections provide a brief overview of exemplary measures.

Establishing a new narrative

Jacinda Ardern sought to redefine the State's role based on her narrative of radical humanitarianism. In her first speech from the Throne, she clearly stated the new focus of her government was inclusion, transformation, and aspiration (Ardern, 2017a, November 8). Inclusion means that every person living in New Zealand is entitled to respect, dignity, a meaningful life, care, and compassion. Transformation refers to the government lifting those who have been neglected, including the environment. Aspiration refers to making the nation one where all cultures and rights are valued, where ideas flourish, where children are encouraged to reach their full potential, and where they become leaders on social and environmental issues. To her, New Zealand had the opportunity "to become a kinder, more caring and confident nation. This will take courage. We will have to do things differently…This government invites you all to join us in creating a better future together". Ardern focused on what unites the people because, in this complex system, everything and everyone is interconnected and impacts each other (Ardern). This new narrative was also communicated frequently by the new government and coalition (Skilling, 2018). In most speeches, representatives employed a language that challenged capitalist realism, its focus on economic growth, and the homo oeconomicus theory (Skilling), and insisted on the State's role of providing for everyone within society (Weijers & Morrison, 2018).

Institutionalising sustainable development

The overarching mission-oriented framework: wellbeing

New Zealand's political approach was based on wellbeing (MPISOC, 2019) and Ardern's conviction that a prosperous economy serves its people, not the other way around (Skilling, 2018). This meant measuring success differently, i.e., going beyond surpluses and deficits to include social and environmental indicators (Skilling). In 2018 the Treasury published the "Living Standards Framework" as a basis for the Wellbeing approach. It identifies 12 wellbeing domains and more than 60 indicators, seeking to improve the long-term prospects of social, natural, human, and physical capital assets (Macaulay, 2021, p. 1268). The data for the domains and indicators are tracked in a dashboard available to the public. Wellbeing provides the basis for discussing individuals' holistic needs, the State's role, and vital public services that enable New Zealanders to live better lives (Rashbrooke, 2021). New Zealand became the first nation in the Western world to evaluate its economic health along wellbeing (Chapman, 2020).

In 2018, New Zealand entered the "Wellbeing Economy Governments" alliance with Scotland, Iceland, Finland, and Wales (WEALL, 2022). Together they engage in global norm entrepreneurship, aiming to inspire other governments and organisations to focus on wellbeing (WEALL). In 2019 Ardern and her government further installed an annual Wellbeing Budget, which builds on analyses of the Living Standards Framework indicators and allows for evidence-based decision-making (Macaulay, 2021). It also goes hand in hand with a social view on investments because the Wellbeing Budget makes investments that expand people's capabilities for creating and sustaining wellbeing (Dalziel, 2019). Thus, rather than seeing it as expenditures, the government invests in national wealth, i.e., economic, human, natural, and social capital (Dalziel).

Industry policies

Ardern's government followed the conviction that the State should take an active role in the economy to foster wellbeing (Rosenberg, 2021). The government's industrial policy centrepiece was their 2019 Industry Transformation Plan with which they sought to transition the critical industries of construction, food and beverage, agritech, digital technology, forestry, and wood processing to a lower-emissions, more sustainable and just economy (Rosenberg).

The sector-led plans took an inclusive and collaborative "Just Transition" approach (Rosenberg, 2021). They involved stakeholders from the government, education providers, non-Māori and Māori businesses, community organisations, unions, and workers in developing a shared vision for the future and plan to get there. The government further set up a Forum consisting of ministers and union representatives to focus on how changes brought about by technology, climate change, globalisation, and demographic change would affect the nature of work. Lastly, they formed specific working groups with Māori to learn from their ancient culture, address environmental issues and create sustainable jobs (Rosenberg).

Finally, the government set up a Green Investment Fund to promote low-emission transportation, mitigate agricultural emissions, end new offshore oil and gas explorations, and research renewable energy in a commitment to transition towards a net-zero-emission economy (Rosenberg, 2021).

Trade policies

New Zealand's economy strongly depends on foreign trade (Szöllösi-Circa, 2022). However, the public was no longer committed to unfettered free trade and protested the latest Trans-Pacific Partnership Agreement in 2015. Ardern was equally sceptical because she saw limits to accessing new markets and threats to the sustainability of the international trading system. They set up the trade policy review "Trade for All", in which a 22-member advisory board suggested reforms along New Zealand's broader economic, social, and environmental objectives (Szöllösi-Circa). In 2019, they launched the Agreement on Climate Change, Trade, and Sustainability with Costa Rica, Fiji, Iceland, Norway, and Switzerland (MFAT, 2019). Part of this first-of-its-kind agreement was the removal of tariffs on environmental goods to accelerate their access and uptake, the elimination of environmentally harmful and socially regressive fossil fuel subsidies, and the development of guidelines for eco-labelling programs and mechanisms to encourage their promotion and application (MFAT). These examples followed the Labour-led government's conviction that international trade remains integral to New Zealand's economy but should be a vehicle for an inclusive and sustainable society (Szöllösi-Circa).

Environmental legislation

The government also took a new approach to environmental legislation. Political debates on reforming climate policy had been ongoing since before 2008 (Bailey et al., 2021). Since then, growing climate concerns among the public strengthened the government's perception and room for action as the public debate around climate change shifted altogether (Rashbrooke, 2021).

One of the leading policy entrepreneurs driving the creation of a new legal framework regarding climate change was a youth-based NGO called Generation Zero (Bailey et al., 2021, p. 1165). In 2017 they launched a blueprint for a Zero Carbon Act. The intense public interest in the report subsequently led to a special debate in parliament in April 2017 (Bailey et al.). Once they were officially sworn in, Ardern's government took the chance to push for corresponding legislation. In 2019, the government implemented the Zero Carbon Act, which legally requires the nation to become carbon neutral by 2050, along with the targets of the Paris Agreement (Szöllösi-Circa, 2022, p. 109). This represented landmark legislation because of its intent and because it enjoyed cross-party support from both the Labour-led coalition and the oppositional National Party after a decade of climate policy debates (Bailey et al.). In 2021, New Zealand also became the first country in the world to introduce a law requiring the financial sector to disclose the impacts of climate change on their business and make it mandatory to explain how they will contribute to cutting emissions and transitioning to a low carbon future (Clark & Shaw, 2021, April 13).

Reshaping relations with Māori

Jacinda Ardern promised to make Māori values stand alongside European New Zealanders' (Ardern, 2017a, November 8). In 2019 the government announced that New Zealand's history, including the Māori arrival, colonisation and attempted genocide by the British, would be made compulsory in school curriculums across the nation (Chapman, 2020). Ardern further showed the government's appreciation for the Māori's ancient culture and values, e. g. by integrating Māori cultural concepts in her speeches and policy approaches or starting and ending speeches in Te Reo Māori (Chapman). In the latest evolutionary stage of the Wellbeing Budget in 2021, she also integrated the Māori view of wellbeing into the Wellbeing framework (Global Government Forum, 2021, May 20) and dedicated parts of the Wellbeing Budget to Māori wellbeing (Chapman). As a sign of gratefulness and respect for her commitment, the Māori loaned her a traditional feather cloak, which she wore to dinner in Buckingham Palace before the Crown. Pictures of her appearance spread around the world because Ardern represented the Māori in front of the monarch family that had colonised the country two centuries ago in an attempted genocide (Chapman).

Enabling leadership for sustainable development

As stated in Chapter 3, enabling others to become leaders for sustainable development is crucial. With her leadership approach, Ardern was innovating what it means to be a political leader. By being a role model inspiring global publicity, she encouraged other leaders to adopt a similar approach and showed citizens worldwide what empathetic and compassionate leadership is (Chapman, 2020).

Ardern also stimulated debates around sustainable development through the new wellbeing narrative and mission-oriented strategy that government agencies must follow (Chapman, 2020). She mobilised other actors for the objectives and encouraged learning processes through agenda setting and anticipating and involving all stakeholders' interests, e.g., with the "Just Transition" approach. She also inspired greater collaboration around these topics between parliamentary groups and political parties. As previously mentioned, Labour relied on New Zealand First and the Green Party to form a coalition and it was the first time that a party with the second-most votes gained the leading position in government (Vowles et al., 2020). That was partially due to Ardern's leadership as she spent weeks negotiating with New Zealand First leader Winston Peters (Chapman). Significant differences with New Zealand First remained on topics like gun laws, environmental policies, and immigration. Still, Ardern had set out to make the coalition successful (Chapman), knowing this would require compromises (Ardern, 2017a, November 8). Lastly, she successfully negotiated the political differences and maintained a stable three-party government that can look back at various achievements regarding sustainable development (Edwards, 2020, December 24; cf. MPISOC, 2019). When Labour won the majority in the 2020 elections, Ardern formed another coalition with the Greens (Reuters, 2020, November 1). Whilst coalitions are the norm in New Zealand (Reuters), it also supported Ardern's political conviction that the challenges of our time require collaboration and unity (Ardern, 2017b, November 8).

Finally, Ardern succeeded in integrating more diverse perspectives within the State. Following her election in 2017, diversity in Parliament increased significantly, which is also a prerequisite for an inclusive institutionalisation of sustainable development. Since Ardern's first term and re-election in 2020, almost half of the parliamentarians were women, twelve percent identified as LGBTQ+, sixteen were Māori, and two had a migration background from Africa and Asia (Malpass, 2021, December 9). In 2020, Ardern appointed Nanaia Mahuta as New Zealand's first female foreign minister and Indigenous woman to hold the position (Hollingsworth 2020, November 2). Most newly appointed members of Parliament were also younger than ever. According to political scientist Bronwyn Hayward, the traditional superiority of older white men had faded, reflecting New Zealand's diversity much better than before (Malpass) and making it one of the most diverse parliaments in the world (Hollingsworth).

Comprehending the interplay of structure and agency

Agency as an enabler and barrier to Jacinda Ardern's leadership

Judging from the exploration of Jacinda Ardern's personality and leadership and contrasting it with the framework for women's political leadership for sustainable development (see Appendix 1.0), Ardern matched most of the variables explored and her agency strongly contributed to her success. For one, Ardern has strong positional and strategic skills, demonstrated e.g., by reaching an executive position to drive change, developing a strategic vision, her high contextual intelligence, and ability to seize windows of opportunities. This became most evident in her political approach of radical incrementalism. Ardern also boasts personal traits and competencies relevant to inspiring and driving change, such as a high consciousness of self, a strong sense of citizenship, empathy, and the drive for change. She also has significant follower empowerment skills, setting a common purpose with her narrative of "politics of kindness," encouraging mutual support, and following a "power to" or "power with" approach. As explored previously, Ardern further boasts a variety of analytical, positional, strategic, organisational, and particularly communication skills, frequently communicating a shared vision or showing interpersonal diplomacy.

Despite Ardern's leadership strengths and successes, there were limitations to her agency and drawbacks to her political approach. Her gender and personality sometimes acted as a barrier. Like many women before her, Ardern found Parliament a toxic and hostile work environment for women (Vani & Harte, 2021). That is why she initially considered herself too soft for political positions and said she remained constantly anxious about making mistakes. Ardern also admits to suffering from imposter syndrome, typical for female leaders who do not want to disappoint others and thus strive to perform to the highest possible standards (Vani & Harte).

However, most of the critique directed at Ardern and her government was that her domestic achievements did not match her international reputation (Rashbrooke, 2021). She had promised "transformational" change but did not sufficiently translate this promise onto her policies, especially regarding wellbeing. Whilst the Wellbeing Budget got great international recognition, the government did not entirely embed it in public policy, and many decisions were still built on cost-benefit analyses (Rashbrooke). At the same time, systemic wellbeing problems prevailed. In setting high expectations but not spearheading more significant policy changes, Ardern failed to reach the standards she set for herself (Chapman, 2020). The critique specifically concerned high suicide rates and housing prices, slow progress on greenhouse gas emissions reductions, and access to mental health care (McClure, 2021, April 20). The former chief economist of the New Zealand Reserve Bank, Arthur Grimes, stated that "it was marketing as opposed to substance…but it came at a time when a number of other governments were so clearly not prioritising people's wellbeing…that it sort of looked like something novel and new and grand" (Gurevitch, 2021). Faltering wellbeing finally became an even greater problem with the COVID-19 pandemic and the Russia-Ukraine War (McKenzie, 2022, June 27). Like other leaders, Ardern lost further support with the economic challenges arising from both events (McKenzie).

But Ardern also backed down from some of her first election promises, including implementing a capital gains tax (Rashbrooke, 2021) and wealth taxes, after facing strong business and right-wing opposition (Edwards, 2020, December 24). Critics state that these failures may represent the limit to Labour's challenge of the neoliberal status quo, as large proportions of the country's wealth are locked in real estate, and a respective tax would have challenged capitalist elites (Gurevitch, 2021). Furthermore, critics stated that Ardern was good at managing external threats such as the virus or foreign capital flows but proved less radical and decisive on complex internal issues (Gurevitch). Ardern appeared to have missed out on actions relating to matters voters care about, such as rising food, fuel, and rental prices or the explosion of gang violence (McKenzie, 2022, June 27). Overall, New Zealanders were frustrated by the lack of change (McKenzie).

Structural enablers and barriers to Ardern's agency

During the 2017 election, the public initially preferred a National-led coalition based on incumbency and perception of competence (Vowles, 2020b). However, the people wanted Jacinda Ardern to lead (Vowles, 2020a). On average, Ardern scored higher on trust than her National Party competitor Bill English (Curtin & Greaves, 2020, p. 189). This was particularly relevant for New Zealanders because public trust in parties and politicians had not fully recovered from the legitimacy crisis in the late 1980s and early 1990s when both Labour and National pursued a neoliberal agenda (Vowles, 2020a). Ardern became known as a political ally to the communities throughout her campaigning and beyond (Vani & Harte, 2021). She represented the "people", coming together to make New Zealand better for everyone, providing hope and comfort, noticing followers' distress, and empathising with their experiences (Simpson et al., 2021). Ardern thus appears to have been a welcome change because she presented herself as accessible and relatable, shared her personal life openly on social media, and had an inclusive communication style (Simpson et al.).

Ardern further satisfied the need for New Zealanders to depart from their Anglo-Saxon heritage and define their own identity (Szöllősi-Circa, 2022). She did so by creating a new vision of New Zealand, framed in statements by her government wanting to "foster a kinder, more caring society" or working towards leaving "a legacy of a stronger, fairer, kinder New Zealand" (Curtin & Greaves, 2020, p. 205). Through her vision and policies, she played to the essential values from New Zealand's history: early settlers tried to escape the conflicts of Europe, felt entitled to self-governance, and wanted equality by law, striving for an equal, fair and honest society that inspires others (McDonald, 2020, May 19). In addition, desperate modesty is a virtue in New Zealand and Ardern fulfilled the public's demand for a modest and down-to-earth politician (Chapman, 2020). Respectively, the media described her as "an assured public speaker in that modest, natural way New Zealanders like" (Mills et al., 2018, p. 168).

Ardern also thrust New Zealand into the international spotlight with her leadership. Before her, New Zealand politics was considered relatively insignificant internationally, and New Zealanders were rarely proud of being mentioned in the media (Szöllősi-Circa, 2022). Any good press for Ardern was now regarded as good press for the country, which New Zealanders loved (Chapman, 2020). She instilled a new sense of pride in the public, which would later increase with the publicity she received for handling the Christchurch attack and the COVID-19 pandemic (Chapman). All of the above made for a great leader-society fit that enabled Ardern's success.

Traditionally, public support in New Zealand has also been strong for progressive policies (Szöllösi-Circa, 2022, pp. 90–114). The country lays claim to several political innovations: the creation of Indigenous parliamentary seats in 1857, granting women the right to vote in 1893, advocating the eight-hour working day in 1840, state-funded pensions in 1898, the world's most extensive welfare system in 1938, its no-fault accident compensation scheme in 1974 (McDonald, 2020, May 19), their nuclear-free policy in the 1980s, and the support for the establishment of the United Nations after World War II (Szöllösi-Circa). The small size and isolated geopolitical position provide New Zealand with the freedom to act as a norm entrepreneur. Under Ardern's leadership, New Zealand started engaging in norm entrepreneurship once again (Szöllösi-Circa).

As outlined in Chapter 6, gender can be a significant barrier for female leaders, but it also enabled Ardern. Recalling her rise to the office of Prime Minister, she says that her experience with sexism was pretty good relative to others (Blackwell & Hobday, 2020). She acknowledged this was the case because of the women before her, such as Helen Clark (Chapman, 2020). She entered New Zealand politics in the 1970s when only a few women were in politics and showed that "a woman who could be as effective and good as any man could be" (Chapman, p. 176). When Ardern entered New Zealand politics, women's representation was much higher, and the country had already witnessed two female Prime Ministers. Her gender fast-tracked her political career. Because there were not enough female members in the Labour Party, she became the leader of national and international young Labour organisations and stepped up in the Labour Party as quickly as she did (Chapman). In the 2017 elections, women's support for Labour was also up by 11 points and women were more likely to vote than men (Curtin & Greaves, 2020, p. 197).

Whilst Ardern's experience with sexism was better than that of Helen Clark and other female politicians before her, she still faced sexist rhetoric (Chapman, 2020). When she first ran for the MP position and was unknown, the media described her as "easy on the eye" and "at least as bright and at least as attractive" as her female opponent Nikki Kaye (Chapman, p. 54). But when she ran for the 2017 election, the media started discrediting her due to her looks, using statements such as "show pony," "all style no substance" or "pretty little thing" (Chapman, p. 179). In a live interview, Ardern was asked whether she had to make or had already made a choice between having babies or a career. Ardern always kept calm but stated that these types of allegations were a crux because she had the option of laughing them off and undermining the feminist cause, or speaking up and risking the public perceiving her as humourless and overly sensitive (Chapman). Her appointment as Labour leader, only seven weeks before the election, was also a typical "glass cliff" appointment. As described in Chapter 6, that is when women are appointed to executive positions in times of crisis or decline and have the highest chance of failure (Curtin & Greaves, 2020). Finally, when Ardern and her partner Gayford announced they were expecting a child, critics claimed she showed a lack of commitment, giving birth shortly after being sworn in as Prime Minister (Chapman). When she finally had her daughter, the opposition questioned how she would juggle being a mother within the demands of the office and going on maternity leave for six weeks (Chapman).

New Zealand's culture and innovation capacity may have also hindered a more transformative approach. The country ranks in the middle regarding uncertainty avoidance (Hofstede, 2022). The higher the uncertainty avoidance, the fewer innovations are promoted (Prim et al., 2017). It further ranks high on masculinity, which is unfavourable to innovation because it indicates a lower tolerance for errors and experimentation. The low long-term orientation score is also averse to innovation, revealing a short-term orientation that contrasts with sustainable development (Hofstede; Prim et al.). Thus, the nation's lack of innovation capacity may have hindered Ardern's wish to push for more significant political innovations. As previously mentioned, in 2017, New Zealanders did not demand extensive reforms, despite their dissatisfaction with housing, poverty, and ecological challenges (Rashbrooke, 2021).

A final structural barrier stemming from the public and parliamentary arenas was political opposition and unfavourable media framing, e.g., regarding the potential implementation of a capital gains tax (CGT). In the 2011 and 2014 elections, the CGT became the centrepiece of Labour's tax package (Chapman, 2020). The National Party, however, framed it as a death tax for ordinary New Zealanders, and Labour could not convince the public otherwise. In the 2017 election, Ardern learned from the mistake and took a cautionary path stating she would form a tax working group, and if the group recommended it, she would implement it before the 2020 election (Chapman, p. 113). However, once elected and despite a clear recommendation by the group, Ardern backed down from the CGT implementation following more business and right-wing opposition, as well as a decline in Labour's public polls due to the prospect of the tax implementation (Rashbrooke, 2021).

Another barrier to Ardern's agency was the administrative arena, as the bureaucracy in New Zealand can limit and slow social progress (Szöllösi-Circa, 2022, pp. 116–117). Whilst Ardern had implemented the Wellbeing Framework to increase cross-departmental collaboration and address challenges systematically, barriers to further implementation remained. NZ bureaucratic employees do not change with new governments. Because of their long-term approach and permanent employment, they rarely accept innovative thinking and can be an obstacle to establishing progressive social ideas, as their values are rooted in effectiveness, reliability, and professionalism. They are also not likely to diverge from the strict procedures that predict their work processes. The bureaucracy is also an obstacle for new government members, as they push for them to learn and respect the internal processes of the administration before supporting them in their strategies. Last, innovation initiation also comes from government decision-makers, and the bureaucracy only makes recommendations along these decisions. Thus, bureaucrats have no incentive to be more creative and drive transformative change, acting as a break on political innovations (Szöllösi-Circa).

In addition, before elections, opposing parties do not have equal resources and access to experts to elaborate feasibility studies on potential policy proposals (Szöllösi-Circa, 2022, pp. 120–121). In the elections, promises thus compete rather than feasible policy programs. Once a party is elected, three years of governing are typically insufficient for measures to be implemented and for the public to perceive advantages before the next election cycle (Szöllösi-Circa). This is especially important regarding the systemic crises New Zealand faced. These were born out of past political decisions, including the most significant welfare retrenchment in any country of the Global North but could not be reversed in a three-year election cycle.

Radical incrementalism had also been forced onto Labour because they had to rely on ordinary majorities with their coalition partners in their first government from 2017 to 2020 (Rashbrooke, 2021). It was New Zealand First especially, who put a handbrake on many plans (Rashbrooke). For example, when the government implemented the Zero Carbon Act, New Zealand First and the opposition watered it down from its initially ambitious targets (Chapman, 2020). They opposed the idea of carbon budgets set independently by the Climate Change Commission and obligations imposed on the agricultural sector (Bailey et al., 2021). Thus, Labour and the Greens had to accept significant compromises to secure opposition cooperation and industry support and eventually implement the bill (Bailey et al.).

Ardern's gender also became a barrier in the parliamentary barrier. For one, she was a victim of the "queen bee syndrome", where women resent the rise of other women and want to stop them (Vani & Harte, 2021, p. 171). Some of Ardern's female National Party opponents sought to put a break on Ardern's success by discriminating against her with statements such as "Zip it sweetie" and "Don't be so precious, petal" within the House of Representatives (Vani & Harte, p. 167). They also stated that her elevation to Labour Deputy was a "superficial, cosmetic facelift" for the party (Vani & Harte, p. 170) or referred to her as "my little pony" (Vani & Harte, p. 171).

Finally, the COVID-19 pandemic also represented a tremendous structural barrier since Ardern's government had to direct all attention and funding to COVID-19 relief measures.

To conclude, the qualitative analysis of Jacinda Ardern's case shows that a structure-agency interplay enabled her to become an agent for sustainable development. Still, it becomes evident from the research, that structures primarily acted as barriers to Ardern's success. On the contrary and in line with the findings in Chapter 6, her agency specifically enabled her to successfully drive political innovations.

References

Ardern, J. (2017a, November 8). Speech from the Throne. Delivered by her excellency the Rt Hon Dame Patsy Reddy, GNZM, QSO, Governor-General of New Zealand, on the occasion of the State Opening of Parliament, Wednesday 8 November 2017. *Beehive*. https://www.beehive.govt.nz/speech/speech-throne-2017

Ardern, J. (2017b, December 14). Delivering greater fairness with prosperity. *Beehive*. https://www.beehive.govt.nz/release/delivering-greater-fairness-prosperity

Ardern, J. (2019a, September 25). Wellbeing a cure for inequality. *Beehive*. https://www.beehive.govt.nz/speech/wellbeing-cure-inequality

Ardern, J. (2019b, September 25). New Zealand National Statement to United Nations General Assembly 2019. *Beehive*. https://beehive.govt.nz/speech/new-zealand-national-statement-united-nations-general-assembly-2019

Ardern, J. (2023, January 19). Prime Minister Jacinda Ardern announces resignation. *Beehive*. https://www.beehive.govt.nz/release/prime-minister-jacinda-ardern-announces-resignation

Bailey, I., Fitch-Roy, O., Inderberg, T. H. J., & Benson, D. (2021). Idealism, pragmatism, and the power of compromise in the negotiation of New Zealand's Zero Carbon Act. *Climate Policy*, *21*(9), 1159–1174. https://doi.org/10.1080/14693062.2020.1868393

Barker, F., & Vowles, J. (2020). Populism and electoral politics in New Zealand. In Vowles, J. & Curtin, J. (Eds.), *A populist exception? The 2017 New Zealand General Election* (pp. 9–34). Acton, Australia: Australian National University Press.

Barnett, P., & Bagshaw, P. (2020). Neoliberalism: What it is, how it affects health and what to do about it. *New Zealand Medical Journal*, *133*(1512), 76–84. PMID: 32242181.

BBC. (2018, November 16). *Jacinda Ardern: it takes strength to be an empathetic leader.* [Video]. YouTube. https://www.youtube.com/watch?v=ruDJp64prhc&t=70s

Blackwell, G., & Hobday, R. (2020). *Jacinda Ardern. I know this to be true.* San Francisco, CA: Chronicle Books.

Blake-Bear, S., Shapiro, M., & Ingols, C. (2020). Feminine? Masculine? Androgynous leadership as a necessity in COVID-19. *Gender in Management: An International Journal, 35* (7/8), 607–617. https://doi.org/10.1108/gm-07-2020-0222

Chapman, M. (2020). *Jacinda Ardern. A new kind of leader.* Cheltenham: The History Press.

Clark, D., & Shaw, J. (2021, April 13). NZ becomes first in world for climate reporting. *Beehive.* https://www.beehive.govt.nz/release/nz-becomes-first-world-climate-reporting

Clifton, E. (2017, June 15). Exclusive: Labour's Jacinda Ardern reveals why she doesn't want to be Prime Minister. *Now to love.* https://www.nowtolove.co.nz/news/current-affairs/jacinda-ardern-labour-deputy-leader-personal-story-in-next-32958

CNN. (2021, June 3). *Jacinda Ardern didn't feel like she was 'tough enough' for politics.* https://edition.cnn.com/2021/06/03/asia/axe-files-jacinda-ardern-interview-scli-intl/index.html

Curtin, J., & Greaves, L. (2020). Gender, populism and Jacinda Ardern. In Vowles, J. & Curtin, J. (Eds.), *A populist exception? The 2017 New Zealand General Election* (pp. 179–212). Acton, Australia: Australian National University Press. https://doi.org/10.22459/pe.2020.06

Dalziel, P. (2019). Wellbeing economics in public policy: A distinctive Australasian contribution? *The Economic and Labour Relations Review, 30*(4), 478–497. https://doi.org/10.1177/1035304619879808

Dirani, K. M., Abadi, M., Alizadeh, A., Barhate, B., Garza, R. C., Gunasekara, N., Ibrahim, G., & Majzun, Z. (2020). Leadership competencies and the essential role of human resource development in times of crisis: A response to Covid-19 pandemic. *Human Resource Development International, 23*(4), 380–394. https://doi.org/10.1080/13678868.2020.1780078

Edwards, B. (2018). New Zealand: political data and development for 2017. *European Journal of Political Research. Political Data Yearbook, 57*(1), 212–220. https://doi.org/10.1111/2047-8852.12229

Edwards, B. (2020, December 24). The secret of Jacinda Ardern's success lies in her conservatism. *The Guardian.* https://www.theguardian.com/world/2020/dec/25/the-secret-of-jacinda-arderns-success-lies-in-her-conservatism

Environment Guide. (2022). *New Zealand's Biodiversity.* https://www.environmentguide.org.nz/issues/biodiversity/

Globaia. (2022). *A safe operating space for Aotearoa New Zealand.* https://globaia.org/planetary-boundaries-new-zealand

Global Government Forum. (2021, May 22). *New Zealand sets out 2021 budget with new inclusive wellbeing framework.* https://www.globalgovernmentforum.com/new-zealand-sets-out-2021-budget-with-new-inclusive-wellbeing-framework/?shared=email&msg=fail

Gurevitch, L. (2021). The spectacle of competence: global pandemic and redesign of leadership in a post neo-liberal world. *Cultural Studies*, *35*(2–3), 489–504. https://doi.org/10.1080/09502386.2021.1898023

Hofstede, G. (2022). *Country comparison graphs.* https://geerthofstede.com/country-comparison-graphs/

Hollingsworth, J. (2020, November 2). New Zealand's Jacinda Ardern appoints country's first Indigenous female foreign minister. *CNN.* https://edition.cnn.com/2020/11/02/asia/new-zealand-foreign-minister-intl-hnk/index.html

La Placa, V., McNaught, A., & Knight, A. (2013). Discourse on wellbeing in research and practice. *International Journal of Wellbeing*, *3*(1), 116–125. https://doi.org/10.5502/ijw.v3i1.7

Lees-Marshment, J., Elder, E., Chant, L., Osborne, D., Savoie, J., & van der Linden, C. (2018). Vote Compass NZ 2017: Marketing insights into public views on policy and leaders. In Lees-Marshment, J. (Ed.), *Political marketing in the 2017 New Zealand election* (pp. 7–22). Cham, Switzerland: Palgrave Pivot.

Lijphart, A. (2012). *Patterns of democratic government forms and performance in thirty-six countries* (2nd ed.). Yale, CT: Yale University Press.

Maak, T., Pless, N. M., & Wohlgezogen, F. (2021). The fault lines of leadership: Lessons from the global Covid-19 crisis. *Journal of Change Management*, *21*(1), 66–86. https://doi.org/10.1080/14697017.2021.1861724

Macaulay, M. (2021). In search of the golden thread: Recent developments in public management across New Zealand and Australia. *Public Management Review*, *23*(9), 1265–1274. https://doi.org/10.1080/14719037.2020.1796289

Maharey, S. (2000, September 15). Social welfare in New Zealand. Address by the Minister of Social Services and Employment to the RNZAH Command and Staff College, No 41, Staff Course. RNZAF Whenuapai, Auckland. *Beehive.* https://www.beehive.govt.nz/speech/social-welfare-new-zealand

Malpass, L. (2021, December 9). Wie Jacinda Ardern die politische Kultur Neuseelands verändert [How Jacinda Ardern is changing New Zealand's political culture]. *NZZ.* https://www.nzz.ch/international/jacinda-ardern-premierministerin-veraendert-die-politische-kultur-ld.1582702

Manhire, T. (2019, April 6). Jacinda Ardern: 'Very little of what I have done has been deliberate. It's intuitive'. *The Guardian.* https://www.theguardian.com/world/2019/apr/06/jacinda-ardern-intuitive-courage-new-zealand

Marcetic, B. (2021, May 25). The New Zealand "Socialists" who govern like neoliberals. *Jacobin Magazine.* https://jacobinmag.com/2021/05/new-zealand-labour-party-socialists-jacinda-ardern

McCarthy, J. (2019, September 25). Jacinda Ardern says economic growth is pointless if people aren't thriving. *Global Citizen.* https://www.globalcitizen.org/en/content/jacinda-ardern-goalkeepers-unga-2019/

McClintock, B. (1998). Whatever happened to New Zealand? The great Capitalist restoration reconsidered. *Journal of Economic Issues*, *32* (2), 497–503.

McClure, T. (2021, April 10). New Zealand's 'wellbeing budget' made headlines, but what really changed? *The Guardian.* https://www.theguardian.com/world/2021/apr/10/new-zealands-wellbeing-budget-made-headlines-but-what-really-changed?utm_term=Autofeed&CMP=twt_b-gdnnews&utm_medium=Social&utm_source=Twitter#Echobox=1618035433

McDonald, E. (2020, May 19). Why is New Zealand so progressive? *BBC*. https://www.bbc.com/travel/article/20200518-why-is-new-zealand-so-progressive

McGuire, D., Cunningham, J. E. A., Reynolds, K., & Matthews-Smith, G. (2020). Beating the virus: An examination of the crisis communication approach taken by New Zealand Prime Minister Jacinda Ardern during the Covid-19 pandemic. *Human Resource Development International, 23*(4), 361–379. https://doi.org/10.1080/13678868.2020.1779543

McKenzie, P. (2022, June 27). Abroad, Jacinda Ardern is a star. At home, she's losing her shine. *The New York Times*. https://www.nytimes.com/2022/06/27/world/asia/new-zealand-jacinda-ardern-popularity.html?

MFAT. (2019). *Agreements on Climate Change, Trade and Sustainability (ACCTS) negotiations.* https://www.mfat.govt.nz/de/trade/free-trade-agreements/trade-and-climate/agreement-on-climate-change-trade-and-sustainability-accts-negotiations/

Mills, K., Berti, C., & Rupar, V. (2018). What kind of country we want for our children: An analysis of media coverage of the 2017 New Zealand General Election. *Kotuitui: New Zealand Journal of Social Sciences, 13*(2), 161–176. https://doi.org/10.1080/1177083x.2018.1476390

Ministry for the Environment. (2020). *Our marine environment 2019.* https://environment.govt.nz/assets/publications/Files/our-marine-environment-2019-summary.pdf

Ministry for the Environment. (2022a). *Our air quality.* https://environment.govt.nz/publications/our-air-2021/summary-of-key-findings/

Ministry for the Environment. (2022b). *Our atmosphere and climate 2020.* https://environment.govt.nz/publications/our-atmosphere-and-climate-2020/#our-atmosphere-and-climate-2020-summary

Ministry for Women. (2020, June 26). *New Zealand women.* https://women.govt.nz/about/new-zealand-women

Mintrom, M. (2019). New Zealand's Wellbeing budget invests in population health. *The Milbank Quarterly, 97*(4), 893–896. https://doi.org/10.1111/1468-0009.12409

MPISOC. (2019). *Towards wellbeing? Developments in social legislation and policy in New Zealand.* https://www.mpisoc.mpg.de/en/social-law/publications/detail/publication/towards-wellbeing-developments-in-social-legislation-and-policy-in-new-zealand/

New Zealand Labour Party. (2017). *Let's do this TV ad.* [Video]. YouTube. www.youtube.com/watch?v=E_kycR6u0Tg

New Zealand Parliament. (2020a, March 3). *The history of New Zealand's party system.* https://www.parliament.nz/en/get-involved/features/the-history-of-new-zealands-party-system/

New Zealand Parliament. (2020b, October 12). *Prime Ministers of New Zealand since 1856.* https://www.parliament.nz/en/visit-and-learn/mps-and-parliaments-1854-onwards/prime-ministers-of-new-zealand-since-1856/

New Zealand Parliament. (2021, June 29). *Quick history.* https://www.parliament.nz/en/visit-and-learn/history-and-buildings/quick-history/

OEC. (2022). *New Zealand.* https://oec.world/en/profile/country/nzl/

Pacella, J., Luckman, S., & O'Connor, J. (2021). Fire, pestilence and the extractive economy: Cultural policy after cultural policy. *Cultural Trends, 30*(1), 40–51. https://doi.org/10.1080/09548963.2020.1833308

Policy Commons. (2019, November 26). *Watch Helen Clark on the Sustainable Development Goals and their relevance to New Zealand.* https://www.policycommons.ac.nz/2019/11/26/watch-helen-clark-on-the-sustainable-development-goals-and-their-relevance-to-new-zealand/

Prim, A. L., Filho, L. S., Zamur, G. A. C., & di Serio, L. C. (2017). The relationship between national culture dimensions and degree of innovation. *International Journal of Innovation Management, 21*(1), 173001. https://doi.org/10.1142/s136391961730001x

Rashbrooke, M. (2021). Jacinda Ardern. Good in a crisis but cautious when not. *IPPR: Progressive Review, 28*(2), 134–139. https://doi.org/10.1111/newe.12258

Reuters. (2020, November 1). *New Zealand's Ardern forms government with Greens.* https://www.reuters.com/article/newzealand-election-government-idUSKBN27H10P

Rosenberg, B. (2021). Commentary: Unions and the evolution of trade and industry policy under the Ardern government. *Labour and Industry: A Journal of the Social and Economic Relations of Work, 31*(3), 343–351. https://doi.org/10.1080/10301763.2021.1979892

Ross, K. (2018). Jacinda Ardern – ready for global diplomacy? *New Zealand International Review, 43*(2), 2–5. https://nz.vlex.com/vid/jacinda-ardern-ready-for-725575185

Simpson, A. V., Rego, A., Berti, M., Clegg, S., & Pina e Cunha, M. (2021). Theorizing compassionate leadership from the case of Jacinda Ardern: Legitimacy, paradox and resource conservation. *Leadership, 18*(3), 337–358. https://doi.org/10.1177/17427150211055291

Skilling, P. (2018). Why can't we get what we want? Inequality and the early discursive practice of the sixth Labour government. *Kōtuitui: New Zealand Journal of Social Sciences, 13*(2), 213–225. https://doi.org/10.1080/1177083x.2018.1486328

Stats NZ. (2019, September 23). *New Zealand's population reflects growing diversity.* https://www.stats.govt.nz/news/new-zealands-population-reflects-growing-diversity

Stats NZ. (2021, February 16). *Household income and housing-cost statistics: Year ended June 2020 – corrected.* https://www.stats.govt.nz/information-releases/household-income-and-housing-cost-statistics-year-ended-june-2020

Szöllösi-Circa, L. (2022). *New Zealand's global responsibility. A small State's leading role in establishing progressive ideas.* Singapore, Singapore: Palgrave Macmillan.

UNDP. (2022). *Gender Inequality Index (GII).* https://www.hdr.undp.org/en/content/gender-inequality-index-gii

Vani, S., & Harte, C. A. (2021). *Jacinda Ardern. Leading with empathy.* London: Oneworld.

Vowles, J. (2020a). Populism and the 2017 election – the background. In Vowles, J. & Curtin, J. (Eds.), *A populist exception? The 2017 New Zealand general election* (pp. 35–70). Acton, Australia: Australian National University Press.

Vowles, J. (2020b). The unexpected coalition – challenging the norms of government formation. In Vowles, J. & Curtin, J. (Eds.), *A populist exception? The 2017 New Zealand general election* (pp. 247–270). Acton, Australia: Australian National University Press.

Vowles, J., Curtin, J., & Barker, F. (2020). The populist exception? The 2017 New Zealand General Election. In Vowles, J. & Curtin, J. (Eds.), *A populiste exception? The 2017 New Zealand general election* (pp. 1–8). Acton, Australia: Australian National University Press.

Wahab, S. A., Rasidi, N. M. F. M., & Wahab, S. (2020). Influences of women's leadership performance towards the corporate, political and social success: A review and research agenda. *Asian Journal of Research in Business and Management*, 2(4), 54–68. https://myjms.mohe.gov.my/index.php/ajrbm/article/view/11571

WEALL. (2022). *What's happening with the Wellbeing Economy Governments?* https://weall.org/whats-happening-with-the-wellbeing-economy-governments?utm_source=victoria%20times%20colonist&utm_campaign=victoria%20times%20colonist%3A%20outbound&utm_medium=referral

Weijers, D., & Morrison, P. S. (2018). Wellbeing and public policy. Can New Zealand be a leading light for the "wellbeing approach"? *Policy Quarterly*, 14(4), 3–12. https://doi.org/10.26686/pq.v14i4.5144

Willis, E. (2021). Editorial: Performance and radical kindness. *Performance Paradigm*, 16, 1–19. https://www.performanceparadigm.net/index.php/journal/article/view/PDF

World Data. (2022). *New Zealand.* https://www.worlddata.info/oceania/new-zealand/index.php

8

CAROLE DELGA

Championing regional political innovations

Understanding the context Carole Delga faced

The chapter starts by providing background information on the region of Occitanie to describe the context that Carole Delga faced. Since Occitanie depends on political choices on the national level, relevant information on France and national politics is added where they influence Occitanie's leeway for political innovation.

France is a unitary majoritarian democracy with a Presidential system (Lijphart, 2012). Historically, France had a long-standing tradition of centralist administration (Crespy et al., 2007). However, in light of globalisation and internationalisation, it could not evade the rise of the "Region State" (Crespy et al.). The political entity of the "region" was created in 1956 (Simoulin & Negrier, 2021, p. 1999) and since 2003, the region's status has been fixed in the French constitution (Kempf, 2017, p. 318). In 2016, the central government reduced the French mainland regions from 21 to 13 to simplify the nation's governance structures (Kempf, p. 318). In addition, the political system entails other forms of territorial groupings, including pays, departments, communes, and metropolises, keeping governance processes highly complex (Kempf). Occitanie emerged from the merger of the two regions Languedoc-Roussillon and Midi-Pyrénées. It is the second-largest region in area and population size, encompassing 13.2 percent of France's surface (Palgrave Macmillan, 2022, p. 453), and making it larger than 12 countries of the European Union (La Région Occitanie/ Pyrénées-Méditerranée, 2022a). The region boasts 13 départments, 161 intercommunalités, 2 metropolises, 4454 communes (La Région Occitanie/

DOI: 10.4324/9781003507666-12

Pyrénées-Méditerranée) and a population of around 5.9 million (Palgrave Macmillan, p. 453). Whilst the two former regions were similar in population size, budgetary capacity, institutions, and political culture, administrative staff first undermined the ability of the new institution to find a working order due to their resistance to the central government's imposition of the merger (Simoulin & Negrier).

Regional elections take place every six years by universal suffrage and work with lists on the level of departments and a mixed system of proportional and majority voting systems (Kempf, 2017). Elected regional presidents and regional councils manage the regions and Regional Presidents become the head of all administrative personnel (Kempf). One of the Regional President's most significant powers lies in preparing and implementing regional council resolutions (Jamet, 2007). The regional councils then work with the president and economic and social committees comprised of representatives from business and commerce, trade unions, and other organisations (Jamet). In recent years, the government expanded the list of regions' duties from economic development to fishing ports and transport planning, vocational training and apprenticeships, hospitals, as well as culture and education (Kempf). Since 2003, an experimental stipulation further allows regions to carry out a new competence for up to 5 years, if the central State approves. Examples include the management of EU grants or the shareholding of regional hospitals. Regional councils are thus the leaders of the region's development and planning, and communes and departments must follow their specifications (Kempf). Still, the power distribution between governance levels is complex, and many different levels of government get involved in the same areas simultaneously (Jamet). To cope with these shared responsibilities, a regional scheme typically coordinates the policies of the territorial entities within a region. Regional councils work out regional plans to be approved by central government entities. The central State is also present in each region via a regional prefect who heads the prefectorial services and is responsible for implementing central government policies in a system of "dual representation" (Jamet).

The constitution provides sub-national governments with some fiscal autonomy (Jamet, 2007). Half of sub-national governments' resources consist of tax revenues and 35 percent of grants from the central State (Jamet, p. 10). The primary local taxes include business, residency, and property taxes. Other local revenues include fees for authorising vehicles and driving licenses, fuel taxes, and EU grants. Regional governments further collect several indirect taxes, of which the two main ones are real estate transaction taxes and excise taxes on petroleum products. However, sub-national governments have little to no power over the latter, which the central State only partially transfers to them. Regions have become dependent on State grants, increasing the central States' influence over them (Jamet). In addition, regional competencies and budgets remain low and resources are monopolised in the central State (Le Galès, 2006). Respectively, mistrust thereof remains high in regional and local institutions (Le Galès). Furthermore, citizens remain largely unaware of the regions' activities, even though they are leading players in planning, economic development, and other responsibilities (Sauviat, 2017). The complicated territorial organisation favours communities of communes and departments over regions, making it challenging to institutionalise regional power (Sauviat).

Regarding political party politics, France's parties typically aligned clearly along the left and right poles, and from 1984 until 2004, the Right held the majority in parliament (Gougou & Labouret, 2010, p. 330). However, in the 2004 regional elections, this majority was shaken, as the moderate right weakened while the far right gained majorities, and the moderate left became the strongest group. A quest for dominance of the centre in the French party system has since been ongoing (Gougou & Labouret). In 2016, when Carole Delga was elected, the regional elections took place less than 18 months before the end of Socialist François Hollande's presidency, and due to his unpopularity, the National Front (NF) became one of the strongest parties (Shields, 2018, pp. 369–370). Since then, the NF keeps growing stronger, whilst the party landscape was shaken up by Emmanuel Macron and his new La République en Marche! Party that further reshaped the bipolar polity that traditionally dominated France (Evans & Ivaldi, 2018). In 2022, voter turnout was the lowest ever experienced (Warren et al., 2021, June 28). Political scientists read this development as an alarming sign of a crisis of democracy and political apathy (Momtaz, 2021, June 22). In turn, movements such as the "Yellow Vests" grew stronger, protesting policies and organising themselves in the absence of proper party structures and decreasing or abandoned traditional ideological positions (Liddiard, 2019).

Considering past neoliberal agendas, from the early 1970s onwards, France followed the same trends of economic liberalisation as its European neighbours (Brookes, 2021). However, it remained one of the most Interventionist regarding taxation and market regulation. There was even a substantial increase in Welfare State generosity during the 1980s. And even though social spending declined and stagnated since the early 1990s, France never experienced a neo-liberal turning point. Instead, at the beginning of the 2000s, France had become the European country with the most significant social spending budget (Brookes, p. 113). One of the reasons was public opposition, as the French are particularly attached to the notion of a strong Welfare State. Parties and politicians trying to implement public policies along the neoliberal path of deregulation, privatisation, and cuts in public spending faced high electoral costs due to a lack of popular legitimacy, especially since the ideology that French neoliberals promoted was much more radical than in countries like the United States and the United Kingdom. Therefore, parties and their leaders largely refrained from the neoliberal path (Brookes). France still boasts a State-intervened capitalist economic system with competitive to mildly regulated product markets, coordinated labour markets, a variance in employment protection, and a corporatist welfare model with mostly employment-based benefits (Amable, 2003). The State plays a pivotal role in the economy, even though President Emmanuel Macron liberalised the economy to some extent (O'Neill, 2021, October 26).

France boasts the second-largest economy in the European Union but has struggled with a lack of growth since the global financial crisis (O'Neill, 2021, October 26). Services comprised around 70.2 percent of France's GDP in 2019 and are the main contributor to growth (Palgrave Macmillan, 2022, pp. 458–459). Considering the regional and local levels, France faces significant inequalities, which increase with the level of territorial subdivision (Jamet, 2007). Occitanie was the region with the fourth largest GDP at €174 million in 2018 (Jeudy, 2021, November 30). Aeronautics, food, viticulture, tourism, and activities with high development potential, such as health, digitalisation, or eco-construction, drive the regional economy (La Région Occitanie/Pyrénées-Méditerranée, 2022d). Occitanie hosts 700 aeronautics companies that provide more than 90.000 jobs, including the Airbus and ATR headquarters (AD'OCC, 2022a). In the food sector, Occitanie has the largest surface area for appellation wines and agriculture globally, is the number one region for organics in France, the second-largest region for meat, and the third largest for fruit and vegetable production (AD'OCC, 2022b). Tourism makes up around 10 percent of the region's GDP (La Région Occitanie/Pyrénées-Méditerranée, 2022c). Occitanie is also the number one region in France regarding the share of GDP invested in research and development (La Région Occitanie/ Pyrénées-Méditerranée, 2022d). Its two metropolises, Toulouse and Montpellier, are among the most critical regions in Europe regarding industrial, cultural, and scientific fields and key drivers of regional development (La Région Occitanie/Pyrénées-Méditerranée, 2022d).

Unemployment remains a central challenge. In the first quarter of 2021, Occitanie had the highest unemployment rate in France at 9.4 percent (Statista Research Department, 2021, August 18). Half of Occitanie's households lived on an income of less than €19.200 per year, among the country's lowest median incomes (Insee, 2017, November 14). The region reduces income inequalities by about 43.5 percent with monetary compensation schemes, but still, 17.2 percent suffer from economic poverty (Insee).

There was also increased migration to the region, with a net migration of 773.000 people, i.e., 25 percent of net migration in France, between 1999 and 2011 (La Région Occitanie/Pyrénées-Méditerranée, 2022e, p. 16). But population development is unevenly distributed, rising in the metropolises and stagnating or declining in rural areas, which generally lag in development and quality of life. Dynamic and attractive territories coexist with precariousness, unemployment, and poverty that economic growth cannot level out (La Région Occitanie/Pyrénées-Méditerranée, 2022e).

Regarding its ecological state, France exceeded all but two planetary boundaries in 2015: ecological footprint, material footprint, land-use change, CO_2 emissions, phosphorus, and nitrogen (DEAL, 2022). The region of Occitanie is already strongly influenced by the consequences of climate change. However, people feel the effects differently due to the regions' varied ecology. Occitanie boasts two massifs, the Massif Central and the Pyrénées, and 220 kilometres of Mediterranean coastlines (La Région Occitanie/Pyrénées-Méditerranée, 2022a). The region's climate thus varies from mild Mediterranean winters and hot summers to mountainous rather opposite weather patterns. It is also one of the most elevated regions in France, with more than 2200 hours of sun per year and a lot of wind (La Région Occitanie/Pyrénées-Méditerranée, 2022a). Studies on the region show that by 2040, temperatures will rise significantly, precipitation will decrease, droughts will increase, and there is a high risk of marine submersion, threatening entire ecosystems (La Région Occitanie/Pyrénées-Méditerranée, 2022e). Agriculture will have to adapt to droughts and rising temperatures, and tourism will experience substantial changes. Population growth is further increasing pressure on the environment in the region, and the proportion of artificial soils has grown by 14.5 percent between 2005 and 2015 (La Région Occitanie/Pyrénées-Méditerranée, 2022b, p. 16). The artificialisation of soils divides up ecosystems and directly contributes to their degradation and biodiversity loss whilst simultaneously reducing agricultural production potential. Furthermore, the coast is subject to erosion and submersion, linked to rising sea levels of the Mediterranean Sea and sediment deficits. Finally, rainfall is less frequent and more violent, resulting in a reduction of water resources and significant flooding (La Région Occitanie/Pyrénées-Méditerranée, 2022b).

Due to the merger of the regions Midi-Pyrénées and Languedoc-Roussillon, it was difficult to find information on past sustainable development policies before Carole Delga's election and the merger of the Occitanie region. Still, Occitanie is influenced by the French State. It has developed various national sustainable development approaches (Gouvernement, 2022). President Emmanuel Macron prioritised combatting climate change for his administration and promised a budget of €50 billion for implementing the 2030

Agenda (Cobbe, 2021, February 4). The aim of creating a new, more inclusive ecological model of prosperity stands at the centre of his strategy. For this purpose, his government created the position of an Interministerial Delegate for Sustainable Development to organise and coordinate the implementation of the SDGs (Cobbe). The government has further set up a new governance mechanism along the SDGs, concerned with Interministerial coordination, public policy analysis, and monitoring (Monnoyer-Smith & Lorioux, 2017). In 2021, however, Oxfam, Greenpeace, and other environmental groups sued the government for climate inaction, and the Administrative Tribunal in Paris ruled that France had indeed fallen short of its promises (Cobbe, 2021, February 4).

In terms of women's rights and representation, women only gained the right to vote in 1945 (Smith, 1996). There has been slow progress since. In 2000, the government introduced legislation forcing the lists of regional, municipal, senatorial, and European elections to respect gender balance (Hird, 2022, June 22). However, they did not implement it for parliamentary elections, and parties merely face financial penalties when disregarding it. Women only occupy 37 percent of the 577 parliamentary seats, representing a drop of 2 percent since Macron was elected and made gender equality part of his campaign. In 2017, female MPs accounted for just 4 percent of speaking time in parliament. Up to 80 percent of ministerial cabinets, and two-thirds of advisers at the prime minister's office and Elysée are still male. There have been two female prime ministers and no female president thus far (Hird). On top of low representation in politics, only around 50 percent of women participate in the labour force, and just 81.7 percent have at least some secondary education (UNDP, 2022). Consequently, France only ranks 33rd on the global Gender Equality Index (UNDP).

Having set the scene with the most important information about the context Carole Delga faced as a political leader, we can now move on to understand her leadership.

Examining Carole Delga's leadership

Path to becoming Regional President

Delga was born on August 19th, 1971, in Toulouse (La Région Occitanie/Pyrénées-Méditerranée, 2022b). She grew up in Martres-Tolosane, where she still lives today, and which is part of today's Occitanie region (La Région Occitanie/Pyrénées-Méditerranée, 2022b). Delga was an only child, and her mother, formerly a secretary, worked as a housekeeper to support the two of them (Lafarge, 2021, September 24). Her grandmother raised Delga for the first six years and became a significant role model to her. Delga states that she nurtured her confidence in her abilities by show-ing her relentless love, idealising, and even idolising her. She further taught her that she could succeed at anything, gave her the courage to lead a fight until the end, and encouraged her to be considerate of others, caring for older and younger neighbours (Lafarge). Finally, her grandmother also advised that she could achieve her dreams only if she worked hard at school (Le Midi-Libre, 2015, December 13). Thus, Delga became an excel-lent student with the support of her teacher Mrs Ducos who promoted her self-confidence (Le Midi-Libre).

Delga obtained a license in economics, a legal science diploma, and a master's degree in local authority law in France (Lafarge, 2021, September 24). She financed her studies with summer jobs, working in the town hall and department for communal politics, finding a liking in these positions because she served others. After university, Delga passed the competitive exams for territorial public services. She then joined the territorial public service in 1994 as a territorial speaker at Limoges Town Hall, responsible for the historical and archaeological heritage of the city. In 1998 she became Director and General Manager of the Barousse Water Board. In 2005 she was appointed Deputy Director of Regional Planning for the former Midi-Pyrénées region and oversaw the regional planning, economic develop-ment, and sustainable development division (Lafarge). In 2007, two central political figures in Delga's hometown suggested that she should rejuvenate the municipality and become mayor (Idoux, 2021, October 27). Delga recalls that she knew this position would be a great springing board for her. Former Socialist mayor Brigitte Hippolyte also found Delga's dynamic exciting and endorsed her (Idoux). In 2008 Delga was elected mayor with 76 percent of the votes and remained in the position until 2014 (Lafarge). Back then, she was already described as a great and tenacious worker who was just as demanding of herself as everyone else (Idoux).

In 2010 Martin Malvy, a member of the Socialist Party and President of the Midi-Pyrénées region from 1998 to 2015, insisted that Delga become the director of his campaign (Merlet, 2021, February 19). Once he won the election, he appointed her Vice President in charge of rural issues and infor-mation and communication technologies (Merlet). In 2012, she was elected Deputy of Comminges-Savès in Haute-Garonne, part of the former Midi-Pyrénées region (Lafarge, 2021, September 24). From June 2014 to June 2015, she joined the French national government as Deputy Secretary of State for Commerce, Crafts, Consumption, and the Social and Solidarity Economy (Lafarge). On June 9, 2015, Delga announced that she would resign as Deputy Secretary of State to run for the Regional President posi-tion of the newly merged Occitanie region (Merlet). She based her decision on the realisation that she preferred to devote herself to her home region rather than national issues (Merlet). She had previously told Malvy, her mentor and President of the Midi-Pyrénées region, that she felt ready to become his successor, and he endorsed her plans (Idoux, 2021, October 21).

As previously laid out, the merger of the Midi-Pyrénées and Languedoc-Roussillon regions was an imposed threat to power, and many party officials ran in the 2015 election (Lafage-Coutens et al., 2019). Delga campaigned with propositions revolving around economic development, transport, the environment, agriculture, education, tourism, rurality, life, and culture (Le Midi Libre, 2015, December 13). Details included increasing the production of renewable energies, extending organic agricultural practices, passing new apprenticeships, supporting the start-up scenes in Toulouse and Montpellier, and expanding the number of nursing homes (Le Midi Libre). In the first round of elections, Delga and her Union of the Left only received 24 percent of the votes, while Louis Aldot's right-wing National Rally list received 32 percent (Shields, 2018, p. 374). Realising the threat from the Right and having poorly performed themselves, the list made up of the Union of Europe Ecology the Greens, the Left Front, the New Socialist Left, the Occitanie Party, and the Republican Left of Catalonia merged with Delga's list. Through the alliance, Delga won the second round with nearly 45 percent of the votes (Lafage-Coutens et al., p. 109) and became Regional President of Occitanie on January 4, 2016 (La Région Occitanie/Pyrénées-Méditerranée, 2022b).

With the election, Delga gained more power than a Minister due to the sheer size of the region and its dense population (Idoux, 2021, October 27). Her new task was immense because she had to merge two regions that were opposing the merger (Merlet, 2021, February 19). She had to build institutional legitimacy with her heterogeneous alliance and embody regional action and unity against the strong resistance (Lafage-Coutens et al., 2019). Furthermore, she had to revitalise democracy in the region since voter turnout had been less than 50 percent that year, correlating with the long-term decline in voter turnout and general discontent with politics in France (Shields, 2018, p. 375).

After her first term, Delga was re-elected as Regional President of Occitanie on July 2, 2021 (La Région Occitanie/Pyrénées-Méditerranée, 2022b) with nearly 58 percent of the vote (Le Parisien, 2021, July 9). She became France's best-elected Regional President (Mollaret, 2021, July 6). Due to this success and because she actively demanded the position (Idoux, 2021, October 27), she was further elected President of the Regions of France the same year (Lafarge, 2021, September 24).

Delga's career was a natural continuum (Lafarge, 2021, September 24). Looking at studies on regional political elites in France, Delga fits the profile, as previous regional and local experience is relevant in accession to regional leadership (Botella et al., 2010). In total, 9 out of 10 regional leaders in France previously held a municipal office (Botella et al., p. 49). There is also a significant presence of mayors among the heads of regional governments, which Delga was for six years. Experience in national government further helps accumulate political capital sufficient to ascend to regional leadership faster than through the local arena. Delga had also spent a year as Deputy Secretary of State and thus had all the prerequisites for the regional election and the positions she took on (Botella et al.).

Political convictions

Delga is a member of the Socialist Party and one of her central convictions is that there is a need for a strong Left (Devic et al., 2022, January 30) and its values of solidarity, social justice, and secularism (Métropolitain, 2022, March 23). She believes they are especially significant on a municipal, departmental, and regional level because that is where the values manifest in actual measures (Devic et al.). Delga's vision of politics further includes concrete acts, helpful to citizens, and adapted to the realities of each territory (Métropolitain).

To succeed in this new social project, she believes it is essential to provide the regions with more freedom and responsibility (Mari, 2022, March 3). Delga explicitly demanded the national government to respect regions' competencies and build a co-constructive partnership (Mari). She desired more autonomous regulatory power for the regions to make crucial decisions more quickly and adapt them to citizens' needs (Armand, 2022, March 8). This specifically concerns preserving territories' biodiversity, control over national parks, conservation strategies, climate change, charging station networks to promote electric vehicles, and agriculture (Armand). Delga holds that respective strategies are too centralised because they cannot be the same for France's North, East, South, and West. She feels that this is what the French expect: valuable and effective decisions that are as close to their reality as possible (Métropolitain, 2022, March 23). Furthermore, the regions need greater fiscal power and financial autonomy (Armand). The executive and legislative do not give regional councils power over regional taxation. Whilst the VAT accounts for half the regions' resources, the exact allocation depends on the National Finance Act. Delga finds this is also an issue of democracy because taxpayer money does not belong to the State, who is only its manager (Armand).

This conviction is one of the reasons, Delga opposes President Emmanuel Macron's political program. She believes that he divides the French because he does not know how to bring people together and how to speak to the people (Idoux, 2021, October 27). In her opinion, it is increasingly difficult for most French to live with dignity. They feel treated unjustly and betrayed, especially because Macron passed himself as a left-wing candidate but pursued right-wing policies that mainly benefitted the wealthy (Idoux). Finally, Macron is also against the greater independence of the regions, contrary to Delga's vision (Lafarge, 2021, September 24).

Delga further holds that a union of the Left and Green parties is needed (Métropolitain, 2022, March 23) to reconcile economic development and ecology, and maintain people's safety and the Republic's values in the future (Lafarge, 2021, July 9). Strategically, Delga first and foremost believes in a Green Deal as a new societal model (Merlet, 2021, February 19). With the Deal, she wants to guarantee a place for everyone, fight social and territorial downgrading, pay specific attention to understanding the needs of the French, and create a development model that consumes less energy (Métropolitain). She knows the transition toward a Green Deal will take courage and be painful, but believes society must pay this price for future generations (Métropolitain; Mari, 2022, March 3).

In line with the philosophy of the European Green Deal, Delga wants to promote economic development and anchor businesses in the territories, offer jobs both in the cities and countryside, create more balanced development between metropolises and rural areas, and be more respectful of social and environmental issues (Mari, 2022, March 3). On a similar note, Delga is highly critical of global giants such as Google and Amazon because their business models do not align with her plans to reconcile ecology and economy as they transport products worldwide and have harsh salary policies (Merlet, 2020b, November 18). In this sense, she holds that local purchases create local jobs and that citizens should commit to buying regional products from local shops to support Occitanie's merchants, artisans, and manufacturers. Delga's vision for Occitanie is thus built on economic patriotism to protect local development and the environment (Merlet).

Personality, skills, and leadership style

In her Twitter description, Delga (2022) describes herself as an engaged citizen of the territories, quality of life, employment, and transitions. In line with this description, she is said to cultivate the image of a simple and accessible woman (Dupont, 2021, June 23) and does not forget where she came from (Merlet, 2021, February 19). She embodies closeness and service to others, stemming from her deeply humanist motivation (Lafarge, 2021, September 24). Her upbringing in a modest rural environment shaped this aspect of her personality. She wants to be the same person in her political and private life and rather be able to take off her armour in her village and be herself, with sincere relationships. Her neighbours talking to her about everyday life, rather than politics, allows her to draft well-adapted policies that start from citizens' real problems (Lafarge). Delga feels attached to people and their fates because she knows how difficult life is for most of them and how resigned they have become (Idoux, 2021, October 27). A couple from her hometown said they had become reconciled with the political world because of her. Moments like this fuel her responsibility to fight for them. At the same time, she stays grounded by hiking, picking mushrooms in the woods, or cycling (Idoux).

Personality-wise, the media and colleagues describe Delga as modest, outgoing, controlled in her communication (Dupont, 2021, June 23), typically smiling (Lafarge, 2021, September 24), confident (Devic et al., 2022, January 30), and a woman of character (Merlet, 2021, February 19). She describes herself as anxious (Dupont et al.), an optimist by nature (Delga, 2020, October 16), grateful, determined, and passionate (Dubault, 2015, December 14). Her political opponents even admit to her strengths, stating she keeps her word, does not betray anyone, and when she commits to something, she does so wholeheartedly (Dupont, 2021, October 29). They further describe her as having a backbone, being consistent, and having but one face, whether you meet her in Paris or Toulouse (Dupont).

Considering her leadership style, Delga promises citizens to be consistent and exemplary in her words and actions (Dubault, 2015, December 14). In her first speech as Regional President, she stated that she would be a President for all without exception and with complete dedication (Dubault). She believes that it is essential to be sincere and authentic (Lafarge, 2021, September 24), which even her political opponents, such as Republican Laurent Wauqiuez, acknowledge (Dupont, 2021, October 29). The latter described her as a strong character and someone who has become rare in politics: she says what she does and does what she says and shows that politics can still be done well with proper values (Dupont).

Delga knows where she is going (Lafarge, 2021, September 24). She believes that where there is a will, there is a way and that politics is a matter of choice and decision (Métropolitain, 2022, March 23). Respectively, she prefers to act rather than hold grand speeches. She also never gives in to the ease of saying, "It's not me, it's someone else", nor to fatality or renunciation (Métropolitain). With that comes a strong work ethic and a desire to be well-prepared. Her team praised her capacity to work (Merlet, 2021, February 19), stating that she knows her dossiers so well that she can receive high-ranking politicians without preparation and still be informed about their work (Mollaret, 2021, July 6). She is also not shy to actively ask for what she wants. She is even said to impose herself around the table and the region (Idoux, 2021, October 27), e.g., when she actively told Malvy that she planned to become his successor. She also vigorously demanded to become President of the Regions because she was France's best-elected regional president. She is determined and claims that one must be calm and determined in politics and can either be weak or authoritarian. She chose to be the latter (Idoux).

Another strength of Delga is, as Martin Malvy recalls, her incredible spirit of synthesis (Merlet, 2021, February 19). According to him, she quickly exposes a subject's components with a global perspective whilst anticipating the potential consequences of each decision she considers (Merlet). However, Delga is not only analytical in a theoretical sense but believes in the need to be connected to the citizens' reality as a politician (Haddad, 2021, June 28). Correspondingly, her approach to politics is bringing together all relevant players, whether citizens, business leaders, employees, community activists, mayors, or Presidents of departments, to listen to their needs and expectations, co-jointly make decisions, and then act on them (Marco, 2022, February 10). Her conception of public action is to stay away from grand discourses and rather listen and make causes suitable for everyone so that they will put their energy into achieving the goals they collectively set out to reach. Her leadership style is thus one of shared leadership (Marco). A mayor of a 512-inhabitant town stated that he found it incredible that someone at Delga's political level came to his village to attend his strategic planning meetings (Idoux, 2021, October 27).

Delga also managed to overcome the initial opposition to the merger, demonstrating her narrative and communication skills. In her first speeches, she used the terms and concepts "collective," "unity," "working together," and "Republic of territories" in a territorial narrative that considered the regions' differences but simultaneously united them (Lafage-Coutens et al., 2019, p. 111). Through her skills, Delga succeeded in uniting the territories and did the same with the regions of France under a "Republic of Trust" as President (Mari, 2022, March 3). Together, they diplomatically and constructively asked the potential future President to share leadership with the regions (Lafage-Coutens et al.).

Finally, Delga also networks and connects well with the business world (Mollaret, 2021, July 6). Four hundred businesses supported Delga in her re-election in 2021. Three of the supporting companies' executives were among the 500 richest in France, namely Qair, Newrest and Nicollin Group, and the President of the National Federation of Banques Populaires. Delga's ability to unite stakeholders beyond her party makes her a synthesising leader. It has inevitably raised her national rating, with some even having proposed her for the Presidential race in 2022 (Mollaret). However, when asked about her national ambition, Delga emphasised that she has always been faithful to her region because her heart belongs to Occitanie (Merlet, 2021, February 19).

The case of Occitanie's political innovations

Carole Delga and the Regional Council were driving sustainable development via all three levers of the State explored in Chapter 3. The following sections provide a brief overview of exemplary measures.

Establishing a new narrative

When Carole Delga first ran for the position of Regional President, she mainly focused on social issues, a new type of political leadership, and promises of democracy, equality, and wealth for all (Dubault, 2015, December 14). She wanted to make Occitanie an exemplary region in France and Europe, constructing the vision of a region that protects, unites, and develops, and most importantly, relies on its inhabitants, the strength of its territories, high quality and local public services, and a happy and positive identity. She intended to stimulate dialogue, including consultation with citizens and economic, social, and associative actors. She also focused on considering all territories and building a robust, creative, and united region where no one is left behind, and wealth is shared equally regardless of gender and heritage. Delga stated it as her duty to unite and involve all in joint action to meet future challenges. She stressed that her desire as President was to work tirelessly on a new closeness with citizens and territories and a new contract of trust. Simultaneously she called on all elected officials from the metropolises, departments, and networks of towns to join her in this dynamic union and work for their region (Dubault).

Being in office, Delga's narrative changed, and she adopted a more socio-ecological perspective. She clarified her belief that the current economic model had shown its limits, especially during the COVID-19 pandemic (Soucheyre, 2021, June 17). During the crisis, her main priority was to stand with businesses and employees to maintain employment. But in the long run, she believes in a renewed economic model that creates a better life, not just dividends. Respectively, Delga favours a social and solidarity economy (Soucheyre). Along these beliefs, Delga started promoting her conviction that the environmental crisis requires the region to accelerate its ecological transition while ensuring that the new development model is fair and uniting (La Région Occitanie/Pyrénées-Méditerranée, 2022c). Delga sees an economic opportunity in the ecological transition to create green jobs (La Région Occitanie/Pyrénées-Méditerranée). This change in narrative went hand in hand with the ideological repositioning of the French Socialist Party. They broke with their past productivist vision and redefined their notion of growth and social progress to include respect for ecological balances and new indicators beyond GDP (Zappi, 2021).

Institutionalising sustainable development

The overarching mission-oriented framework: SRADDET

Since 2019, the French Ministry of Ecological Transition has made it mandatory for regional councils to develop a Regional Planning, Sustainable Development, and Territorial Equality Scheme (SRADDET) (Ministère de la Transition Ècologique, 2021, October 6). It is a long-term planning framework aiming for holistic development by 2040 (La Région Occitanie/Pyrénées-Méditerranée, 2022e). The plan strengthens the region's strategic role as an institution and provides a political vision and priorities for regional development along mid- and long-term objectives that go hand in hand with the State's priorities (Ministère de la Transition Ècologique). These include the balance and equality of territories, the establishment of infrastructures of regional interest, the development of transport, the protection and restoration of biodiversity, and waste management. Local development must then be compatible with the SRADDET's objectives, and this new legal requirement gives regional presidents and councils great power over departments and communes. Still, each SRADDET must also be approved by the regional prefect and thus be developed in consultation with the French State (Ministère de la Transition Ècologique).

Delga and the Regional Council set two main goals for Occitanie's SRADDET (La Région Occitanie/Pyrénées-Méditerranée, 2022e). One goes hand in hand with the focus area of the State, namely territorial rebalancing. The second follows Delga's political vision, new narrative, and strategic plan for a more virtuous development model. In developing the SRADDET, Delga, and the council involved all stakeholders, following the desire to co-create a plan that is not imposed but rather connected to the peoples' realities. For two years, they involved almost 2000 actors in the process, ranging from the French State to regional and local authorities, economic actors, and citizens (La Région Occitanie/Pyrénées-Méditerranée, p. 13). For citizens' consultation, they further experimented with new formats such as citizen cafés, online consultations, and Massive Open Online Courses, training nearly 1200 citizens in the planning process (La Région Occitanie/Pyrénées-Méditerranée). This demonstrates Delga's commitment to shared leadership because the co-creative approach was not mandatory.

Together they identified three major areas for the Occitanie region of tomorrow (La Région Occitanie/Pyrénées-Méditerranée, 2022e, pp. 16–21). The first area revolves around becoming attractive enough to sustain population growth and distribute it evenly across the region. This is necessary to drive business and balanced development. To become more attractive, Occitanie must also become a region of opportunity that guarantees equal access to resources and offers each the means for a successful future. In addition, they must preserve natural resources to provide quality of life to all inhabitants, whether current or future generations. The second area is for all territories to cooperate in their strategy development. The SRADDET, cooperative working methods, and a range of further measures aim to achieve that. And the third area is radiation and setting an example in terms of development. As previously described, climate change will substantially influence Occitanie, and respectively the SRADDET addresses the need for lifestyle and production changes. More specifically, it addresses the notion of sufficiency, e.g., by limiting energy consumption, as well as the need for adaptation and mitigation to be at the heart of regional development (La Région Occitanie/Pyrénées-Méditerranée). Sufficiency proposes a maximum level of consumption for environmental sustainability and policymakers remain the most prevalent actor in advancing sufficiency transitions and equally, one of its greatest barriers (Sandberg, 2021).

Delga and her team have made the SRADDET inclusive and strategically well-planned out with ambitious goals (La Région Occitanie/Pyrénées-Méditerranée, 2022e). Thereby, they also enabled greater leadership for sustainable development on the regional and local levels and went beyond traditional policymaking by including progressive sustainability concepts such as sufficiency (La Région Occitanie/Pyrénées-Méditeranée).

The Green Deal

In 2020, in response to the health and economic crises caused by the COVID-19 pandemic, Carole Delga and her council focused on a "Pacte Vert," or Green Deal, supported by the European Commission (Merlet, 2020a, July 15). Occitanie became the first region in the European Union to commit to a Green Deal (Merlet) and strives to be the first energy-positive region by 2050 (Moutarde, 2021, November 15).

In the Deal, they identified five key levers (La Région Occitanie/Pyrénées-Méditerranée, 2022a). These include a better evaluation of the regions' actions, e.g., via green budgets, citizen juries, labels for exemplary companies, and strengthening of citizen participation, e.g., via specific initiatives and conventions. They also seek to accelerate the digital transition, e.g., via support services and training, ensure a balance via the territories, e.g., via shared tools and more services in rural zones, and finally, open up to the world and reinforce Occitanie's European roots, e.g., by increasing the reception of foreign researchers and increasing international mobility of young people. The Deal specifies 300 measures for the short- to mid-run, revolving around creating a better quality of life, reconciling ecology and the economy, new jobs, and supporting the evolution of mobility concepts.

Some suggestions include the financial support of organic farmers, increasing aid for health staff, developing a value-based circular economy, research and development activities for the protection of biodiversity, the support of new energy sources such as hydrogen, renovating apartments, hotels, and resorts for increased energy efficiency, or offering training on new energy professions, renewables, ecology, and sustainable development (La Région Occitanie/Pyrénées-Méditerranée).

In 2021, the regional budget was €3,75 billion, and €2,2 billion were reserved for the Green Deal (Delga, 2021, December 17). Thereby €122 million were set out for health, €398 million for education orientation and youth, €900 million for transport and infrastructure, €544 million for the economy, employment, and professional training, and another €138 million for environmental protection (Delga). Delga also launched a Sovereign Energy Wealth Fund to develop renewable energies, create jobs in the sector, and fund industrial projects that respect the environment (Moutarde, 2021, November 15). For this purpose, she secured a further €2 billion from private national and international investors. By acquiring private funding for the ecological transition, Delga overcame the significant challenge of financial shortages due to the region's dependency on the French State (Moutarde).

Strengthening democracy

France is witnessing a severe crisis of democracy and whilst Occitanie remains one of the regions with the highest share of voters going to the ballot, during the last regional elections in 2021, only 44.7 percent went to the polls, compared to 63.6 percent in 2014 (Haute et al., 2021, p. 2). Delga is aware that France and Occitanie face a democratic crisis, so she has made it her mission to strengthen public trust in politics (Dubault, 2015, December 14). She believes that political leaders infantilise citizens when they ask to be recognised and have their voices heard (Berger, 2020, September 11). That is why she focuses explicitly on citizen participation processes for the democratic development of the region (Berger).

First, Delga let the citizens choose the name of the newly formed region in a participation process (Dumez, 2016, December 16). Secondly, she responded to the citizens' request to participate in Occitanie politics by forming the Occitanie Citizen Convention (Delga, 2020, October 16). It allows citizens to reflect and build fair and effective public policies together with the regional administration, particularly for the Green Deal. For that purpose, 100 citizens were drawn by lot so that they could bring in their expertise and ideas from their daily lives (Delga). Together they developed 294 proposals for the Green Deal in areas such as transport, high schools, biodiversity, or energy (Berger, 2020, September 11). The group then prioritised 52 proposals to guarantee a better quality of life for all (Delga). Three guarantors and a steering committee supervised the process (Berger). Next, all residents of Occitanie were able to vote on the proposals to be submitted to elected officials for approval and inclusion into the specific plans. The initiative thus represents a good complementary between representative and participatory democracy, as citizens enrich the ideas and approaches of elected officials (Berger).

Territorial rebalancing and integration

Delga set out to rebalance territorial development within her region. When entering a majority agreement with the EELV list to win her first election, they co-jointly agreed on institutional innovations regarding territorial balancing and, specifically, a Regional Assembly to promote democracy between the territories (Lafage-Coutens et al., 2019). This democratic body is unique to France (Lafage-Coutens et al.). Whilst the territories are represented in the Regional Council, the number of representatives depends on population size (Dumez, 2016, December 16). Thus, some territories only have one representative, whilst others have seventeen, creating an unequal distribution of power and interests (Dumez). The new Assembly brings together local elected officials according to the principle of one vote per territory, a much more representative approach favouring the less developed rural territories (Lafage-Coutens et al.).

The Assembly also fulfills a symbolic function and corresponds to Delga's narrative of a region that stands united behind its President (Lafage-Coutens et al., 2019). It helps local officials get to know other elected officials, their practices, and the policies the new region will prioritise. It is a space for creating mutual knowledge and learning to bridge the vast distances across the region. Delga and her team further created departments along the different needs within the region. Amongst them are the Department of the Sea for specificities of territories along the sea, and the Department of Solidarity and Equality, which highlights missions concerning all territories and promotes solidarity on a regional level. Finally, they created other measures around shared missions, such as a food pact to unite the region by establishing a regional identity around eating and the Sud de France brand (Lafage-Coutens et al.).

Enabling leadership for sustainable development

The various initiatives mentioned above also per significantly enable greater leadership for sustainable development within the State and beyond. Another of Delga's significant initiatives is a white paper she drew up with France's other regional authorities in her position as President of the Regions of France (Mari, 2022, March 3). It is titled "Republic of Trust," and they distributed it to all Presidential candidates in 2022. The report aimed for the candidates to seek greater trust in local elected officials and consider them good executors rather than their worst political enemies (Mari). It comprised 64 pages with 64 proposals with which Delga aimed to strengthen local power and autonomy, restore meaning to democratic life, and react to the multiple crises regions face, including the climate crisis, social crisis, health crisis, and international economic crisis (Galiero, 2022, March 8). As stated in the paper, this requires new ways of working together, and respectively Delga invited the Presidential candidates to embark on a path of greater decentralisation. By addressing the future President in a constructive tone and offering to forge new partnerships between local authorities and the State on constitutional, legislative, governance, and financial levers, the regions hoped to increase their room for action in service of the citizens (Galiero). Amongst others, the paper included propositions for more effective and individual governance, better access to financial means, retaining cultural heritage, reviving democracy, protecting biodiversity, mitigating climate change, transitioning to a circular economy, creating better health services, and building stronger ties with the European Union (Régions de France, 2021). Delga thus strives to enable leadership for all locally elected officials to ensure their territories' sustainable development.

Comprehending the interplay of structure and agency

Agency as an enabler and barrier to Carole Delga's leadership

Regarding the framework for women's political leadership for sustainable development (see Appendix 1.0), not all variables could be evaluated due to a lack of information on Delga. Still, her personality and leadership style fit most of the evaluated leadership models. For one, Delga appears to have a high consciousness of her values and strengths, acts consistently along them, and has a strong sense of citizenship, motivating her to drive change and strive for excellence along a shared vision with a strong future orientation. She is also highly empathetic to stakeholders' needs and extroverted and agreeable in bringing stakeholders together to collaborate. In this, she demonstrates strong follower empowerment skills, by setting a common purpose, encouraging them to work together, and giving support. Overall, she chooses an approach of "power to" and "power with," although there are indications that on necessary occasions, she also makes use of the top-down "power over" approach. Overall, her personality and leadership style are praised and seem to match the challenges she faced in Occitanie and significantly enabled her.

Due to the lack of information available, it is difficult to judge whether Delga's agency also represented a barrier. The only information to be found were critiques from political opponents. The former head of the regional EELV list, Antoine Maurice, voiced concerns about Delga's leadership (Idoux, 2021, October 27). Maurice resigned his list in the 2015 elections so that Delga could win against the National Front candidate with his support. He stated that she forced him to withdraw and concluded that she would stop at nothing for her political success. Another male opponent from the NF described Delga as dogmatic, closed, sectarian, and discriminatory against other political ideas (Idoux). Still, as explored previously, Delga was the only female candidate and the first female head of the region. Both politicians may have thus tried to use her gender and seemingly nonfemale qualities of determination and resolve to discredit her but this could not be validated.

Structural enablers and barriers to Delga's agency

A key structural enabler for Delga's agency was key figures and role models who supported her. For example, Delga's grandmother taught her to have a strong feminist stance (Lafarge, 2021, September 24). For her, being turned down because of being a woman was simply not an option. The only limit and confinement to her was a lack of education, and so she pushed for Delga to become an excellent student (Lafarge). Thus, having a feminist grandmother enabled Delga to look beyond her gender to focus on her political career. Delga quickly rose to various political ranks, and today she is one of France's most well-known female figures (Mamet, 2018, March 8). Her gender was mainly an asset to her and when asked about sexism in her political career, Delga felt that being a woman was an advantage. Women were rare in politics in her early career, so she embodied renewal simply by being a woman. In her hometown Martres-Tolosane, the former deputies asked her to run for office because they wanted a young woman to become mayor and bring renewal to local politics (Mamet). Gender was thus very much enabling for Delga.

Still, Delga felt sexism when she ran for Regional Presidency in Occitanie, with all other candidates being male (Mamet, 2018, March 8). She found real male solidarity and allyship against her and faced low-level comments from her competitors and high-ranking officials who tried to discredit her based on her gender and age. The comments included the likes of her shoulders not being wide enough, her being too young, and having a pretty face but no brains (Mamet). This was the first time Delga realised that being a woman could signal a lack of legitimacy to the people (Le Midi Libre, 2015, December 13). She is further aware that women must work twice as hard in politics and be twice as competent and present to be heard (Mamet). Thus, gender also acted as a break in her efforts.

It is not clear, whether the public acted as an enabler or barrier for Delga's success. On the one hand, she was the best-re-elected regional president in France in 2021 (Occitanie Tribune, 2022, February 14). In the corresponding award speech, Delga stressed how the price reflected the inhabitant's trust in her and her team (Occitanie Tribune). She may have been the best re-elected regional president because of her leadership and a high leader-society fit. Still, on the other hand, voter turnout was at a historical low that year (Cérez & Dorandeu, 2021, June 20), with only around 38 percent of eligible voters participating in the election. Thus, we cannot substantiate whether citizens voted for her for the reasons she described or whether low turnouts were due to Delga's past political program, other structural factors such as discontentment with the Socialist Party's national politics, or distrust in politics and democracy in general.

France's culture and innovation capacity were not highly favourable to progressive political agendas. France ranks high on uncertainty avoidance and power distance, indicating a culture of obedience and little promotion of innovation (Hofstede, 2022; Prim et al., 2017). Masculinity and indulgence rank around the middle (Hofstede, 2022), suggesting some but not much room for innovation (Hofstede, 2011). The nation further scores high on individualism (Hofstede, 2022), meaning there is a strong mentality of everyone having to provide for themselves rather than a collective approach to life (Hofstede, 2011). Whilst high individualism is good for innovation output (Prim et al.), it may not be for sustainable development since concepts of justice, equity, and collaboration contrast individualism. Finally, France's high long-term orientation may be advantageous for sustainable development, as they may favour long-term strategic planning in line with sustainable development (Hofstede, 2011). Still, overall, the cultural dimensions in France are not highly favourable to innovations for sustainable development. These cultural factors cannot be specified for the region of Occitanie but may be applicable to one degree or another.

Regarding the administrative arena, despite an ongoing decentralisation process, regional autonomy from national politics, power over political issues, and financial independence remained limited for Delga. Thus, to some extent, her and the Regional Council's control over sustainable development plans and funding remained restricted and dictated by the national government. At the same time, the decentralisation process led to the newly formed region of Occitanie, which represented a barrier at first since the administrative staff of the two regions met the imposed merger with resistance and sabotaged a smooth transition. Still, a significant advantage Delga had and still currently has as President of Occitanie is that she formed a majority agreement with other parties, such as the Greens. The Left held the majority of seats on the Regional Council during both of Delga's terms (Belaubre, 2021, June 30; L'Express, 2015). This majority enabled Delga to successfully implement her ambitious transformation plans for Occitanie.

A final barrier particular to Occitanie is its geographics. The region is larger than many EU countries and highly diversified, ranging from a Mediterranean coastline to mountainous Massif regions. Creating sustainable development plans suitable to all individual requirements is a challenge, for which Delga and the Regional Assembly had to set up specific working groups.

To conclude, the qualitative analysis of Carole Delga's case shows that a structure-agency interplay enabled her to become an agent for sustainable development. Still, it was especially agency that acted as an enabler rather than structures, which aligns with the theoretical and empirical findings in Chapter 6 on agency being key to women leaders' success.

References

AD'OCC. (2022a). *Aeronautics/Space.* https://www.invest-in-occitanie.com/en/business-sectors/aeronautics-space/

AD'OCC. (2022b). *Food/Wine.* https://www.invest-in-occitanie.com/en/business-sectors/food-wine/

Amable, B. (2003). *The diversity of modern capitalism.* Oxford: Oxford University Press.

Armand, C. (2022, March 8). "L'argent des contribuables n'appartient pas à l'État ni aux collectivités" [Tax money does not belong to the state or collective]. *La Tribune.* https://www.latribune.fr/economie/france/l-argent-des-contribuables-n-appartient-pas-a-l-etat-ni-aux-collectivites-carole-delga-regions-de-france-905638.html

Belaubre, N. (2021, June 30). Occitanie, la composition nouveau conseil regional classée par départments [Occitanie, the composition of the new regional council by department]. *Le Journal Tolousain.* https://www.lejournaltoulousain.fr/occitanie/la-composition-du-nouveau-conseil-regional-par-departements-124605/

Berger, E. (2020, September 11). Carole Delga: "L'objectif, c'est que les citoyens participant aux decisions de la Région" [Carole Delga: "The objective is that citizens participate in regional decisions"]. *La Depeche.* https://www.ladepeche.fr/2020/09/11/lobjectif-cest-que-les-citoyens-participent-aux-decisions-de-la-region-9063503.php

Botella, J., Teruel, J., Barberà, O., & Barrio, A. (2010). A new political elite in Western Europe? The political careers of regional prime ministers in newly decentralized countries. *French Politics*, 8(1), 42–61. https://doi.org/10.1057/ fp.2009.40

Brookes, K. (2021). *Why neo-liberalism failed in France. Political sociology of the spread of neo-liberal ideas in France (1974-2012)*. New York, NY: Palgrave Macmillan.

Cérez, G., & Dorandeu, G. (2021, June 20). *Régionales en Occitanie: une abstention record au premier tour [Regionals in Occitanie: A historic abstention in the first round]*. Mediacités. https://www.mediacites.fr/decryptage/toulouse/2021/ 06/20/regionales-en-occitanie-un-abstention-record-au-premier-tour/

Cobbe, E. (2021, February 4). Paris court finds France guilty of failing to meet its own Paris climate accord commitments. *CBS News*. https://www.cbsnews.com/ news/paris-climate-agreement-france-court-government-guilty-failing-commitments/

Crespy, C., Herauf, J. A., & Perry, B. (2007). Multi-level governance, regions and science in France: competition and equality. *Regional Studies*, 41, 1069–1084. https://doi.org/10.1080/00343400701530840

DEAL. (2022). *National Doughnuts Data Explorer*. https://doughnuteconomics. org/tools-and-stories/22

Delga, C. (2020, October 16). *Une belle énergie cityoenne pour l'Occitanie [Beautiful civil society energy for Occitanie]*. http://caroledelga-occitanie.fr/2020/10/ 16/une-belle-energie-citoyenne-pour-loccitanie/

Delga, C. (2021, December 17). *Un budget solide et ambitieux [A solid and ambitious budget]*. http://caroledelga-occitanie.fr/2021/12/17/un-budget-solide-et-ambitieux/

Delga, C. (2022). Carole Delga. *Twitter*. https://twitter.com/caroledelga?lang=de

Devic, E., Berger, E., & Servant, J. (2022, January 30). Carole Delga: 'Il y a un besoin de gauche, ses valeurs ne sonst pas pérmées' [Carole Delga: "We need a left, its values are not expired"]. *La Depeche*. https://www.ladepeche.fr/2022/01/28/ carole-delga-il-y-a-un-besoin-de-gauche-ses-valeurs-ne-sont-pas-perimees-10074776.php

Dubault, F. (2015, December 14). Régionales 2015: Carole Delga, une femme socialiste à la tête de la region [Regionals 2015: Carole Delga, a Socialist woman as head of the region]. *France Info*. https://france3-regions.francetvinfo.fr/ occitanie/herault/montpellier-metropole/montpellier/regionales-2015-carole-delga-femme-socialiste-tete-region-882649.html

Dumez, H.-O. (2016, December 16). Occitanie: un an après l'élection de Carola Delga, la fusion jugée par des élus de la Région [Occitanie: One year after the election of Carole Delga, the merger is judged by the elected officials of the region]. *Actu Toulouse*. https://actu.fr/occitanie/toulouse_31555/occitanie-un-an-apres-lelection-de-carole-delga-la-fusion-jugee-par-des-elus-de-la-region_3788317.html

Dupont, B. (2021, June 23). Régionales Occitanie: le portrait "intime" des trois candidats du second tour [Regionals Occitanie: the "intimate" portrait of the three candidates of the second tour]. *France Bleu*. https://www.francebleu.fr/ infos/politique/regionales-en-occitanie-le-portrait-intime-des-trois-candidats-du-second-tour-1624456351

Evans, J., & Ivaldi, G. (2018). *The 2017 French presidential elections: A political reformation?* Cham, Switzerland: Springer Nature. https://doi.org/10.1007/978-3-319-68327-0

Galiero, E. (2022, March 8). *Décentralisation: les regions posent 64 propositions sur la table des candidats à la présidentielle [Decentralisation: The regions put 64 propositions on the table of the presidential candidates].* Le Figaro. https://www.lefigaro.fr/politique/decentralisation-les-regions-posent-64-propositions-sur-la-table-des-candidats-a-la-presidentielle-20220308

Gougou, F., & Labouret, S. (2010). The 2010 French regional elections: Transitional elections in a realignment era. *French Politics, 8*(3), 321–341. https://doi.org/10.1057/fp.2010.17

Gouvernement. (2022). *Sustainable Development.* https://www.gouvernement.fr/en/france-sustainable-development

Haddad, M. (2021, June 28). *Régionales en Occitanie: Carole Delga se dit proche de la gauche d'Hidalgo et de Cazeneuve [Regionals in Occitanie: Carole Delga says she is close to the Left of Hidalgo and Cazeneuve].* RTL. https://www.rtl.fr/actu/politique/regionales-en-occitanie-carole-delga-se-dit-proche-de-la-gauche-d-hidalgo-et-de-cazeneuve-7900049980

Haute, T., Kelbel, C., Briatte, F., & Sandri, G. (2021). Down with Covid: patterns of electoral turnout in the 2020 French local lections. *Journal of Election, Public Opinion and Parties, 31*, 69–81. https://doi.org/10.1080/17457289.2021.1924752

Hird, A. (2022, June 22). *Drop in the number of female MPs shows ongoing battle for gender parity in French politics.* rfi. https://www.rfi.fr/en/france/20220622-drop-in-female-mps-shows-ongoing-battle-for-gender-parity-in-french-politics-feminism-chamboncel

Hofstede, G. (2011). Dimensionalizing cultures: the Hofstede model in context. *Online Readings in Psychology and Culture, 2*(1), 1–26. https://doi.org/10.9707/2307-0919.1014

Hofstede, G. (2022). *Country comparison graphs.* https://geerthofstede.com/country-comparison-graphs/

Idoux, G. (2021, October 27). Enquete. Comment Carole Delga, présidente de Région, est devenue l'un des plus solides espoirs du PS [Investigation. How Carole Delga, President of the Region, became one of the PS's strongest hopes]. *Le Journal du Dimanche.* https://www.lejdd.fr/Politique/enquete-comment-carole-delga-presidente-de-region-est-devenue-lun-des-plus-solides-espoirs-du-ps-4073228

Insee. (2017, November 14). *Malgré les revenus de transfert, l'Occitanie Figure parmi les regions métropolitaines les plus pauvres [Despite income transfers, Occitanie is among the poorest metropolitan areas].* https://www.insee.fr/fr/statistiques/3181926

Jamet, S. (2007). Meeting the challenges of decentralisation in France. *OECD Economics Department Working Papers, 571.* https://doi.org/10.1787/127050885680

Jeudy, L. (2021, November 30). *Gross domestic product of France between 2017 and 2018, by region.* Statista. https://www.statista.com/statistics/1085639/gdp-france-region/

Kempf, U. (2017). *Das politische System Frankreichs [The political system of France]* (5th ed.). Wiesbaden, Germany: Springer.

L'Express. (2015). *Résultats des élections regionals 2015 Occitanie [Results of the 2015 election in Occitanie]*. https://www.lexpress.fr/actualite/politique/elections/regionales-2015/resultats-elections/region-occitanie.html

La Région Occitanie/Pyrénées-Méditerranée. (2022a). *Le Pact Vert pour l'Occitanie [The Green Deal for Occitanie]*. https://www.laregion.fr/pactevert

La Région Occitanie/Pyrénées-Méditerranée. (2022b). *La présidente: Carole Delga [The president Carole Delga]*. https://www.laregion.fr/La-presidente-Carole-Delga

La Région Occitanie/Pyrénées-Méditerranée. (2022c). *Le Pact Vert pour l'Occitanie [The Green Deal for Occitanie]*. https://www.laregion.fr//pactevert

La Région Occitanie/Pyrénées-Méditerranée. (2022d). *Les atouts économiques [The economic advantages]*. https://www.laregion.fr/Les-atouts-economiques-35340

La Région Occitanie/Pyrénées-Méditerranée. (2022e). *SRADDET – Occitanie 2040*. https://www.laregion.fr/-occitanie-2040-

Lafage-Coutens, A., Prenat-Ville, C., & Simoulin, V. (2019). La construction politique et organisationelle de la region Occitanie [The political and organizational construction of the Occitanie region]. *Cairn Info*, *50*, 105–120. https://www.cairn.info/revue-pole-sud-2019-1-page-105.htm

Lafarge, R. (2021, September 24). *Carole Delga, l'adroite [Carole Delga, the clever one]*. France Culture. https://www.franceculture.fr/emissions/comme-personne/carole-delga-l-adroite-de-la-gauche

Le Galès, P. (2006). The ongoing march of decentralisation within the Post-Jacobin State. In Culpepper, P., Hall, P., & Palier, B. (Eds.), *Changing France. The politics that markets make.* (pp.198–219). New York, NY: Palgrave Macmillan.

Le Midi Libre. (2015, December 13). *Régionales: ce qu'il faut savoir sur Carole Delga [Regionals: What you need to know about Carole Delga]*. Midi Libre. https://www.midilibre.fr/2015/12/13/regionales-tout-ce-qu-il-faut-savoir-sur-carole-delga,1257110.php

Liddiard, P. (2019). *The trouble with political parties and the rise of the Yellow Vests*. Washington, DC: The Wilson Center.

Lijphart, A. (2012). *Patterns of democratic government forms and performance in thirty-six countries* (2nd ed.). Yale, CT: Yale University Press.

Mamet, L. (2018, March 8). *Carole Delga: "En politique, les femmes sont habituées à travailler deux fois plus" [Carole Degla: "In politics, women are used to fighting twice as hard]*. L'Independant. https://www.lindependant.fr/2018/03/08/carole-delga-en-politique-les-femmes-sont-habituees-a-travailler-deux-fois-plus,3905603.php

Marco, J.-M. (2022, February 10). *Carole Delga, présidente de la Région Occitanie, reçoit le prix de l'élue locale 2021 [Carole Delga, President of the Occitanie region, receives the price for locally elected 2021]*. France Bleu. https://www.francebleu.fr/infos/politique/carole-delga-presidente-ps-d-occitanie-recoit-le-prix-de-l-elue-locale-2021-1644476832

Mari, N. (2022, March 3). *Sommet européen des régions et des villes: Carole Delga demande plus de liberté pour les régions [European summit of regions and municipalities: Carole Delga demands more liberty for the regions]*. Corse Net Infos. https://www.corsenetinfos.corsica/Sommet-europeen-des-regions-et-des-villes-Carole-Delga-demande-plus-de-liberte-pour-les-regions_a63286.html

Merlet, P. (2020a, July 15). *Le Green New Deal de la Région Occitanie en quatre questions [The Green New Deal of the Occitanie region in four questions]*. La Tribune. https://toulouse.latribune.fr/politique/territoires/2020-07-15/le-green-new-deal-de-la-region-occitanie-en-quatre-questions-852867.html

Merlet, P. (2020b, November 18). *Green New Deal: "Amazon est le conte-modèle de ce que nous voulons" [Green New Deal: "Amazon is the counter model of what we want"]*. La Tribune. https://toulouse.latribune.fr/politique/2021-02-19/regionales-qui-est-carole-delga-celle-qui-veut-prendre-part-au-debat-en-2022-878134.html

Merlet, P. (2021, February 19). *Régionales: Qui est Carole Delga, celle qui veut prendre part au débat en 2022? [Regionals: Who is Carole Delga, the one who wants to take part in the 2022 debates?]*. La Tribune. https://toulouse.latribune.fr/politique/2021-02-19/regionales-qui-est-carole-delga-celle-qui-veut-prendre-part-au-debat-en-2022-878134.html

Métropolitain. (2022, March 23). *Interview: Carole Delga, élue locale 2021: "Notre région est solide et solidaire" [Interview: Carole Delga, elected local 2021: "Our region is solid and united"]*. https://actu.fr/occitanie/montpellier_34172/interview-carole-delga-elue-locale-2021-notre-region-est-solide-et-solidaire_48896714.html

Ministère de la Transition Ècologique. (2021, October 6). *SRADDET: un schema stratégique, prescriptif et intégrateur pour les regions [SRADDET: a strategic, prescriptive and integrating plan for the regions]*. https://www.ecologie.gouv.fr/sraddet-schema-strategique-prescriptif-et-integrateur-regions

Mollaret, G. (2021, July 6). *Qui est vraiment Carole Delga, boostée nationalement par son triomphe? [Who is Carole Delga really, boosted nationally for her triumph?]*. Challenges. https://www.challenges.fr/femmes/qui-est-vraiment-carole-delga-reelue-triomphalement-en-occitanie_772182

Momtaz, R. (2021, June 22). *'French democracy is sick.' Low election turnout sparks grave concern*. Politico. https://www.politico.eu/article/french-democracy-crisis-election-low-turnout/

Monnoyer-Smith, L., & Lorioux, S. (2017). La mise en oeuvre des objectifs de développment durable (ODD) en France: Indicateurs de suivi et financement [The implementation of the Sustainable Development Goals (SDGs) in France: Monitoring and financing indicators]. *Responsabilité & Environnement, 88*, 32–36. https://doi.org/10.3917/re1.088.0032

Moutarde, C. (2021, November 15). *La Région Occitanie lance trois nouveaux dispositifs pour accélérer la transition écologique [The Occitanie region launches three new schemes to accelerate the ecological transition]*. France Bleu. https://www.francebleu.fr/infos/environnement/la-region-occitanie-lance-trois-nouveaux-dispositifs-pour-accelerer-la-transition-ecologique-1636722805

O'Neill, A. (2021, October 26). *France: real gross domestic product (GDP) growth rate from 2016 to 2026*. Statista. https://www.statista.com/statistics/263604/gross-domestic-product-gdp-growth-rate-in-france/

Occitanie Tribune. (2022, February 14). *Occitanie – Carole Delga se voit remettre le prix de l'élue locale de l'année 2021 [Occitanie – Carole Delga is awarded the prize for local elected representative of the year 2021].* https://www.occitanie-tribune.com/articles/35848/occitanie-carole-delga-se-voit-remettre-le-prix-de-l-elue-locale-de-l-annee

Palgrave Macmillan. (2022). *The stateman's yearbook 2022.* Berlin, Germany: Springer Nature.

Le Parisien. (2021, July 9). *Carole Delga (PS) élue présidente des Régions de France pour trois ans. Le Parisien [Carole Delga (PS) elected President of the Regions of France four three years].* https://www.leparisien.fr/politique/carole-delga-ps-elue-presidente-des-regions-de-france-pour-trois-ans-09-07-2021-JDQCVXQWWBDT5P52FTKX37RLFI.php

Prim, A. L., Filho, L. S., Zamur, G. A. C., & di Serio, L. C. (2017). The relationship between national culture dimensions and degree of innovation. *International Journal of Innovation Management, 21*(1), 173001. https://doi.org/10.1142/s136391961730001x

Régions de France. (2021). *Vers une république de la confiance. Le livre blance des regions [Towards a republic of trust. The regions' white book].* https://regions-france.org/wp-content/uploads/2022/03/Livre-blanc-des-r%C3%A9gions-finalis%C3%A9-1.pdf

Sandberg, M. (2021). Sufficiency transitions: A review of consumption changes for environmental sustainability. *Journal of Cleaner Production, 293*, 1–16. https://doi.org/10.1016/j.jclepro.2021.126097

Sauviat, A. (2017). Decentralisation in France: A principle in permanent evolution. In Ruano, J. M., & Profiroiu, M. (Eds.), *The Palgrave Handbook of decentralisation in Europe* (pp. 157–200). New York, NY: Palgrave Macmillan.

Shields, J. (2018). Winner loses all: The 2015 French regional elections. *Regional & Federal Studies, 28*(3), 367–381. https://doi.org/10.1080/13597566.2018.1440389

Simoulin, V., & Negrier, E. (2021). Merging regions in contemporary France: A policy perspective. *European Planning Studies, 29*(11), 1999–2016. https://doi.org/10.1080/09654313.2020.1791054

Smith, P. (1996). *Feminism and the Third Republic. Women's political and civil rights in France, 1918-1945.* Oxford: Oxford University Press.

Soucheyre, A. (2021, June 17). *Carole Delga: Je propose de créer un "revenue écologique jeune" [Carole Delga: I suggest the creation of a "ecological youth revenue"].* L'Humanité. https://www.humanite.fr/politique/occitanie/carole-delga-je-propose-de-creer-un-revenu-ecologique-jeune-711269

UNDP. (2022). *Gender Inequality Index (GII).* https://www.hdr.undp.org/en/content/gender-inequality-index-gii

Warren, H., Alexander, C., & Nussbaum, A. (2021, June 28). *Republican rivals emerge for Macron, Le Pen.* Bloomberg. https://www.bloomberg.com/graphics/2021-france-regional-elections/

Zappi, S. (2021, April 8). *Le Parti socialiste renouvelle sa vision de l'écologie [The Socialist Party renews its' ecological vision].* Le Monde. https://www.lemonde.fr/politique/article/2021/04/08/le-ps-renouvelle-sa-vision-de-l-ecologie_6076079_823448.html

9

VALÉRIE PLANTE

Driving local political innovations

Understanding the context Valérie Plante faced

The chapter starts by providing background information on Montréal to outline the context Valérie Plante faced. The city of Montréal is Canada's second-largest city and located in the province of Québec (World Population Review, 2022). Its islands' population was roughly 2 million in 2021 (Gouvernement du Québec, 2022a), and almost 5 million live in the greater Montréal metropolitan area (Canada Population, 2022), making up around 24 percent of Québec's total population (Ville de Montréal, 2018, p. 6). However, the population is shrinking due to an aging population, and the city has one of the slowest growth rates among major cities in Canada (Canada Population).

The political system in Canada builds on the Westminster model with a decentralised federal system and ten provinces (Lijphart, 2012). The Canadian federal State encompasses sub-central provincial governments with their own bureaucracies, parliaments, and, in most cases, courts and coercive apparatuses (Stevenson, 2019). Canadian federalism is considered a pact between the federal government and provinces, significantly limiting municipal authorities' autonomy and capacity to be central political actors (Turgeon, 2009). The Constitution defines the relationship between the federal government and provinces, whereas amendable statutory laws define those between provinces and municipalities. The former is a relationship of equals, whereas the latter is one between superiors and subordinates. Respectively, Canadian municipalities remain without any real extra-local political power, and political scientists define them as "outcasts of Canadian federalism" (Turgeon, p. 358). It is characteristic of Canadian

DOI: 10.4324/9781003507666-13

provinces to be comprised of many municipalities, leading to low budgets and a shortage of skilled staff in each of them (Sancton, 2009). In addition, the municipalities' scope of intervention and capacity to generate revenue remains limited (Turgeon, p. 358). In combination, the paternalism and number of municipalities further lead to inefficient decision-making, unclear accountabilities, poor coordination, unclear cost-sharing, patchy planning, inefficiencies, and poor overall accountability (Hachard, 2020).

Municipal governments' finances are constrained, and there is a mismatch between their responsibilities and ability to pay for them, leading to diminished service quality and deteriorating fiscal health (Hachard, 2020). Municipalities mainly depend on property taxes, making up around half of their revenues (Turgeon, 2009, p. 363). Other sources of income include user fees and provincial transfer payments. These revenues, however, never caught up with inflation rates, and federal and provincial transfer payments dropped significantly in the 2000s (Turgeon). Still, municipalities must pass balanced budgets, and provinces limit the amount and purpose of debts (Hachard). These restrictions and limitations put municipalities in a difficult position, even though responsibility-wise, they are at the front lines of significant national challenges such as climate change, homelessness, transit development, and policy areas once reserved for provinces and federal government, including immigrant services, childcare, and health care infrastructure and services (Hachard). Still, because 80 percent of Canadians live in urban areas, and the seven largest municipalities generate more than 45 percent of Canada's GDP, the federal and provincial governments cannot ignore local representatives' wills (Turgeon, p. 363).

The public directly elects its mayors, and there is a double vote: one for the office of mayor and the second for the office of municipal councilor for the district where voters reside (Belley et al., 2009). In the city of Montréal, the mayor heads the city council, agglomeration council, and executive committee (Ville de Montréal, 2022, June 2). Under the executive committee, a president manages the "direction génerale," which is involved in the boroughs and heads specified services, such as finances or human resources, bureaus, such as for racism and discrimination, and further "direction génerales" for issues such as citizen services or quality of life (Ville de Montréal).

Regarding party politics, in Canada, political parties are typically weak, and systemic party operations seldom govern Canadian municipalities (Lightbody, 2006). Instead, they are leader- and executive-dominant, have few local associations, centralised candidate selection, and little to no grassroots participation (Tolley & Paquet, 2021). They are rather centred on brokerage and follow the primary task of organising and financing election campaigns, with almost no presence in the periods in between (Tolley & Paquet). In Québec, potential parties must request recognition from the

Chief Electoral Officer (Belley et al., 2009). By 2020, the Québec registry listed more than 130 authorised municipal political parties (Tolley & Paquet, p. 42). The speed at which parties change is also noteworthy. In the 2021 elections, 13 parties were competing, and only five of them had already existed in the previous 2017 election (Montreal Gazette, 2021, March 15). Projet Montréal is currently the oldest political party in Montréal, founded in 2004 (Montreal Gazette). The three mayors that governed before Valérie Plante declined public trust in mayors since they became known for corruption, electoral misspending, fraud, and disconnection from citizens (Bruemmer, 2017, January 27; CBC News, 2012, November 5; Montreal Gazette). Respectively, voter turnout rates stood only at 42.5 percent in the 2017 municipal elections (Ville de Montréal, 2020b, December 8, p. 71).

It is also important to understand Québec's and Montréal's political course over the past 50 years. During the early 1960s, the Quiet Revolution period, Québec's political and cultural institutions adopted State-centred nationalist views and drove liberal economic reforms (Blad, 2011). The nationalist approach promoted the idea of an autonomous and independent Québécois identity rather than a French-Canadian one. Between World War II and the 1970s, the State took control over social and educational services from Church institutions. Officials now followed Keynesian State-centred economic modernisation strategies (Blad, p. 106). In the 1980s and 1990s, like many other countries of the Global North, Canadian federal and provincial governments underwent a decade of restructuring as they struggled with deficits and debts. Typical for neoliberal programs at the time, policies aimed at minimising the States' role by cutting back State programs, downsizing public sector employment, deregulating the economy, expanding international markets, and shifting responsibilities and debts from the federal to provincial and municipal governments (Clark, 2002). The province of Québec still took on a unique position. The government first extolled the benefits of the neoliberal economy and, since the 1980s, practised social and public sector wage restraint (Blad). In the 1990s, the Liberal and Québecois Parties advocated trade liberalisation to attract foreign capital, promoted economic growth, and sought to modernise the public sector. They amalgamated school boards, closed hospitals, and regionalised the provincial health care system. Still, they refrained from ideological reforms and a more significant restructuring of the larger public sector (Blad). Their measures were generally rather pragmatic than ideological, rooting for Neostatism as opposed to neoliberalism in their strive to modernise the province (Clark).

Canada's GDP was $1.58 billion in 2021 (Statista Research Department, 2022) and the nation has one of the fastest growth rates of the G7 nations, set between 0.8% and 1.2% for the past ten years (World

Population Review, 2022). Despite significant growth, labour shortages continuously hamper economic growth as the country remains underpopulated. It has thus long welcomed significant numbers of immigrants (Blad, 2011). In 2017, the city of Montréal welcomed more than 52.000 new permanent immigrants, which is 18 percent of all permanent residents admitted to Canada (Atak, 2021, p. 105). The top origins were Haiti, Algeria, Italy, France, and Morocco. According to the 2016 census, 645.000 of the roughly 4.9 million inhabitants of the greater Montréal area are immigrants, representing a 74 percent increase from 1981 (Atak). Around 70 percent of Montréalers speak French at home, 14 percent English, and roughly 17 percent another language (Canada Population, 2022). English and French are declining as first languages due to increasing diversity (Canada Population). Canada also has a rich Indigenous heritage. Yet, the province of Québec has the lowest percentage of Indigenous inhabitants out of all Canadian provinces (Page, 2017, October 25).

Immigration has enabled significant growth and economic prosperity in Montréal (Blad, 2011). In 2017, employment was at a record high, with 61.1 percent of the population aged 15 years and older working and unemployment at a record low of 8.2 percent (Ville de Montréal, 2018, p. 10). One of the reasons was that between 2012 and 2017, more than 60 international companies chose Montréal as their location for leading-edge business sectors such as artificial intelligence, research and development in life sciences, financial technologies, and data centres (Ville de Montréal, p. 11). Montréal is known for its higher education establishments, research centres, and creative drive (Ville de Montréal). In 2020, 86.9 percent of all jobs in Montréal were in services, whilst 9.9 percent were in production, 2.9 percent in construction, and 0.3 percent in the primary sector (Gouvernement du Québec, 2022b). In 2018, the Greater Montréal area's economy achieved a real GDP growth rate of 3.6 percent, which was the highest among major Canadian cities (Montréal International, 2019, February 6) and generated around 35 percent of Québec's GDP (Ville de Montréal, p. 6). Still, due to the COVID-19 pandemic, in 2021, the city faced immense financial challenges (Shingler, 2021, November 8).

Canada generally faces strong income inequalities, which are almost exclusive to cities and have risen over time (CPA Canada, 2021). In Montréal, the disposable income per capita averaged at $31.290 in 2021, which is higher than Québec's average of $30.721 (Gouvernement du Québec, 2022c). Considering the average disposable income of €37.494 in Canada, it however remains among the lowest in the country (Serebrin, 2018, July 26). Due to low income, in 2020, the most significant priority for Montréal's citizens was the cost of housing (Labbé, 2020, October 26). In 2017, 11.6 percent of Montréalers did not have enough income to purchase essential goods and services, and 13.6 percent were food insecure. In 2018, 3.000 people were homeless, representing an increase of 8 percent since 2015. Other priorities included the conditions of roads and streets at 31 percent, public transit at 30 percent, social housing and the fight against poverty at 25 percent, and fluidity of transport, road congestion, and management of road work at 24 percent (Ville de Montréal, p. 66).

Aside from significant social challenges, Canada also faces ecological crises as it exceeded all planetary boundaries in 2015: ecological footprint, material footprint, land-use change, CO2 emissions, phosphorus, and nitrogen (DEAL, 2022). Conditions regarding CO2 emissions, phosphorus, and nitrogen are especially dire (DEAL). This also reflects on the ecological conditions of Montréal. The city sits on an island encompassing 500 km² (Ville de Montréal, 2018, p. 63). Ninety percent of this area is urbanised, with 30 percent being used for residential purposes and only 8 percent for parks and green spaces (Ville de Montréal, 2018, p. 63). From 1986 until 2001, Montréal lost over 50 percent of its forests to new development (Hague, 2021, July 12). Due to urban sprawl, it has the lowest parkland per capita among all major cities in Canada (Hague). Montréal is also affected by climate change with floods and heat waves, and due to its geographic position, is at risk of flooding and shoreline erosion (Berkowicz & Hecht, 2022, May 12), droughts, destructive storms, and a rise in average temperatures (Ville de Montréal, 2020a, p. 34). From 1981 until 2010, the average annual temperature was 6.9°C but is projected to rise to 10.1°C by 2041. At the same time, freeze-thaw episodes decreased from 71 to 58 days, and precipitation increased from 72mm maximum to 78mm (Ville de Montréal, p. 34). Compared to 1990 levels, the city reduced its GHG emissions by 23 percent in 2014 but increased its transportation-related emissions by 14 percent in the same period (Ville de Montréal, 2018, p. 64). Forty percent of total GHG emissions in the Montréal area stem from transportation, 28 percent from industrial production, 16 percent from commercial sites and institutions, 12 percent from residential buildings, 4 percent from waste, and 0.06 percent from agriculture, forestry, and other land use (Ville de Montréal, 2020a, p. 37).

To counter these developments, the provincial government of Québec passed its first Sustainable Development Act around ten years ago, intending to improve the quality of life for future generations (Gouvernement du Québec, 2022d). It revolves around rethinking humans' relationship with each other and nature and critically examining the current mode of development, which damages the environment and relegates most of humanity to poverty (Gouvernement du Québec, 2022e). In the provincial governments' understanding, sustainable development must remedy the shortcomings of a social model solely based on economic growth (Gouvernement du

Québec, 2022e). The government has a 2030 Plan for a Green Economy, including an Energy Transition, Innovation and Efficiency and Sustainable Mobility plan, as well as strategies for critical sectors such as batteries and minerals, all of which they will measure along specific indicators (Gouvernement du Québec, 2022f). In the city of Montréal, former mayor Gérald Tremblay conceptualised the first sustainable development plan in 2005, following the 2002 Montréal Summit (Corriveau, 2005, April 21). The Regional Council for the Environment even defined specific indicators to measure the state of the environment (Corriveau). Former mayor Denis Coderre also developed a sustainable development plan. As President of the North American section of United Cities and Local Governments, he specifically promoted the 11th UN Sustainable Development Goal, "Making cities and human settlements inclusive, safe, resilient and sustainable" (Coderre, 2016, January 29). In 2019, however, when Valérie Plante was already in office, more than 500.000 people marched the streets, urging the city council to prioritise the fight against climate change, reinforce the city's strategic plans, and focus on its ecological transition (Ville de Montréal, 2020b, December 8).

Considering women's rights and representation, women in Canada were granted the right to vote at different times, depending on the province (Tremblay & Everitt, 2020). In Québec, it was 1791, even though rights were restricted to women who fulfilled specific land ownership conditions. The government repealed the regulation in 1849 (Baillargeon, 2019, p.vii). After that, women fought until 1940 to regain their rights but Indigenous, Inuit, and Asian women were excluded for as long as 1969 (Baillargeon, p. 138). The first woman was only elected to the Québec assembly in 1961, and it took another twenty years before there were more than six female members (Baillargeon, p. 136). It was also only in 2012 that a woman became the first and thus far only female first minister of the province of Québec (Canada Guide, 2022). Overall, the political system in Canada remains mono-gendered. Heterosexual and cisgender men occupy most legislative, executive, and judicial roles, and still dominate political ideologies, institutional culture, and public policies (Tremblay & Everitt). Before the 2017 election, Montréal had also not had a female mayor. Shortly before the election, the #MeToo movement gained broad traction in North America (Surridge, 2018, February 15). Many prominent men in Montréal faced allegations because they had used their power to bully subordinates into sexual actions. These scandals helped spur the feminist movement (Surridge) and demands for gender balance in politics (Tolley & Paquet, 2018). At the same time, reports on the municipal election showed strong gender stereotypes in the media (The Conversation, 2020, October 20). They slanted opinions toward female candidates' ability to balance work and family and questioned their skills and credibility more than those of male colleagues (The Conversation). Thus, the state of women's representation was relatively low but on the rise at the time of Valérie Plante's election.

Assessing Valérie Plante's leadership

Path to becoming mayor

Valérie Plante was born in Rouyn-Norana, Québec, on June 14, 1974, and grew up in Abitibi-Témiscamingue (Kucharsky, 2017, November 28). Her mother considered herself a feminist and was a stay-at-home mother before studying administration when Plante and her older sister became teenagers (Gyulai, 2017, October 14). Plante says her mother taught her to go for the things she believed in (Médium large, 2018, March 8). Her father, on the other hand, was a traveling salesman, selling knick-knacks and greeting cards out of his converted bus to provide the family with modest means (Gyulai). Plante spent much time traveling with her father and learned the ease of connecting with (Gyulai) and her love for people in general from him (Médium large).

Plante received her high school diploma in 1991 and was engaged in a group concerned with recycling (Kucharsky, 2017, November 28). In her yearbook, she stated that she dreamed of becoming President of Greenpeace (Kucharsky). During high school, Plante also started working early onward at the age of 12. Her first jobs included babysitting, washing dishes, pumping gas, selling ice cream, and working as a tour guide in France (Gyulai, 2017, October 14).

In 1994 Plante moved to Montréal to pursue a bachelor's degree in Anthropology at Université de Montréal (Kucharsky, 2017, November 28). She developed critical thinking on social inequalities, became an activist, and was first interested in politics (Gyulai, 2017, October 14). Later, she obtained a certificate in multi-ethnic intervention and a master's degree in Museology. At university, Plante also met her husband, an economist with the teacher's union Centrale des syndicats du Québec, and together, they have two sons (Gyulai).

Valérie Plante states that she had never dreamed of becoming a mayor or politician (Berkowicz & Hecht, 2022, May 12) and did not join a political party for long because she did not like their top-down nature (Gyulai, 2017, October 14). One day, she, however, figured that she would have to move to its epicentre and bring her values of justice and feminism, her drive to create equal opportunities for all, and her will to break down systemic barriers (Gyulai). Thus, Plante is not a typical career politician.

After completing her master's degree in 2001, Plante started working as a project and communications coordinator for several organisations, including eight years with the non-profit Girls Action Foundation (Kucharsky, 2017, November 28). On the side, she helped immigrant women and victims of domestic violence navigate the Canadian justice system, taught self-defense classes, organised programs for immigrant and Indigenous women, and engaged as an activist. Moreover, she was on several boards, including the left-of-centre think tank Broadbent Institute and Groupe Femmes Politique et Démocratie, promoting women's political participation (Kurcharsky).

In 2013, Plante came in touch with the left-leaning municipal political party Projet Montréal and applied as a candidate for the 2013 municipal election shortly after (Kucharsky, 2017, November 28). She was successfully elected city councilor in the Sainte-Marie district in downtown Montréal's borough Ville-Marie (Kurcharksy). As a city councilor, Plante was further named Deputy Leader of the opposition, critic for all issues related to downtown, tourism, and women, Vice-President of the city council, and Substitute Mayor for Ville-Marie (Epaper News, 2022). In 2016, three years after Plante joined the party, Projet Montréal sought to replace its interim leader and Plante stepped up because no other woman did (Kucharsky). She ran against an established fellow councilor and defeated him by 79 votes, becoming party leader of Projet Montréal on December 4th, 2016. As a logical consequence of her success, in 2017, Plante ran for the mayoral office (Kucharsky).

In the election, eight candidates competed (Tolley & Paquet, 2021). In the end, it was a race between incumbent Denis Coderre with Èquipe Denis Coderre pour Montréal and Valérie Plante with Projet Montréal. Coderre's campaign was typical for an incumbent, demonstrating his administration's successes while showing what he would still do. Also typical for Canadian municipal politics, Coderre's party was leader- and executive-dominant, with little grassroots participation, few local associations, and almost no presence in between elections (Tolley & Paquet, 2021). Projet Montréal, on the other hand, was the opposite, cultivating local engagement, internal democracy, gender parity, and participation beyond election campaigns (Tolley & Paquet, 2018). Plante positioned herself as the best candidate to steer Montréalers through a necessary ecological transition and to counter climate change (Shingler, 2021, November 8). She thereby presented Projet Montréal and herself as a progressive alternative to Coderre, stating that "our party is not about the status quo. I leave that to the other team. For us, it's about having courage, about raising the quality of life of citizens, of workers, of families, of the middle class" (Scott, 2021, June 29).

Regarding gender, Plante's strategy was one of "degendering" (Tolley & Paquet, 2021). She did not emphasise her womanhood and did not promote herself as a feminist. Instead, she downplayed her gender and deployed it strategically. She limited gender-specific proposals in the party's platform and focused on gender-neutral concerns such as public transportation, housing prices, equitable taxation, and construction management. She also chose not to promote her engagements in feminist organising and political efforts to increase women's political representation, to not evoke the perception that she was running solely for female voters. She further highlighted her policy choices rather than her personality to overcome stereotypical voter concerns about a female mayor. Still, it was advantageous to her that feminism and equality concerns were already embedded principles in Projet Montréal's structure and organisation. Plante and Projet Montréal did however play with gender stereotypes. The first campaign poster showed Plante wearing a grey suit jacket with her arms crossed and the slogan "man for the job". This sense of humour was to play towards Plante's bold and irreverent personality and to get ahead of the gender issue. In another example, Plante suggested a new metro line they called the "pink line", but otherwise framed as gender-neutral. Via these strategic and playful deployments, Projet Montréal and Plante engaged with stereotypes in politics and depersonalised her candidacy, putting the focus on policy issues and appealing to those who hesitated to vote for a female Mayor (Tolley & Paquet).

Plante and Projet Montréal thus offered voters a viable alternative to Coderre and his leader-centric party by positioning themselves as policy-forward and non-traditional (Tolley & Paquet, 2021). At the same time, Plante's personality and leadership style helped. She became popular by connecting with and inspiring her electorate and not shying away from saying, "we can do better" (Noakes, 2017, November 8). Overall, her messages were always cheerful and forward-thinking, and she intensely engaged with social media and the public (Noakes). Montréalers saw how Plante shook hands with citizens until the very last minute and appreciated her drive and earnestness (Drimonis, 2017, November 6). In addition, Projet Montréal's local associations provided the campaign with great organisational capacity and strength as grassroots members joined the campaign on behalf of Plante. Finally, because they depersonalised the party and did not focus on Plante in a leader-centric manner, voters could conceive the vote for Plante as one for the entire party. This may have also helped to neutralise the potentially adverse effects of her gender (Drimonis).

On November 5, 2017, Plante won the election with 51.4 percent of the vote, compared to 45.7 percent for Denis Coderre (Labbé, 2020, October 26). This was the first time in 57 years that citizens did not re-elect a mayor for a second term (Noakes, 2017, November 8). Plante also became the first female mayor in Montréal's 375-year history, and Projet Montréal won the majority of seats on the city council (Labbé). In the 2021 election, Plante won the race against Denis Coderre again, with 52.07 percent of the vote (Lau, 2021, November 8). Projet Montréal also increased its city council seats (Nerestant, 2021, November 8). The same year, Plante was awarded Canada's Top Sustainability Leader price in the category of Mayors (Pitchford, 2021, September 16) and elected to the C40 Cities Steering Committee (C40 Cities, 2022, February 25). She remained the only woman leading a major North American city and has become one of Canada's most influential people (Noakes).

Political convictions

Valérie Plante was already concerned with the environment as a young student when she dreamt of becoming President of Greenpeace. As mayor, she believes in an ecological transition and holds that cities must become its' frontrunners (Berkowicz & Hecht, 2022, May 12). To her, it is the cities' and the mayor's responsibility to protect ecosystems and biodiversity and restore humanity's relationship with it (Berkowicz & Hecht) by proactively bringing nature back into rapidly urbanising worlds (Plante, 2020, May 18). Respectively, she believes in nature-based solutions, green infrastructure, and green open spaces to improve the quality of life for all (Plante). She particularly wants Montréal to stand out as a metropolis of ecological resilience and transition in Canada and North America (Berkowicz & Hecht). In line with this conviction, Plante became part of the C40 Cities Leadership Group, a network based on the idea that cities are at the frontline of the ecological transition (C40 Cities, 2022, February 25).

Before her political career, Plante also showed her concern for people, volunteering with the elderly as a teenager and discovering critical thinking about social injustice during university. Plante had become particularly active for girls' and women's equality, both as an activist and professionally. In her graphic novel "Ok, universe. Chronicles of a woman in politics," she addressed the need for social cohesion, compassion, and society as a collective endeavour (McGillis, 2020, November 27). She wants Montréal to maintain its diversity and allow anyone, whether artists, the elderly, students, or families, to afford a roof over their head (McGillis). She describes herself as a social democrat (Cherry, 2016, December 4).

Plante thus fights for a social and ecological transition (Berkowicz & Hecht, 2022, May 12). Thereby she believes it is necessary to have a detailed vision and clear plan for the city's future and path of how to get there, thinking about today without neglecting what is important for tomorrow (Projet Montréal, 2021). However, Plante also knows that Montréal is like a big ship and that many people will have to row in the same direction for quite some time to change its direction (Médium large, 2018, March 8). She is also aware that she cannot change the entire system but at least bring a new approach to municipal politics (Montreal Gazette, 2017, April 20). Thereby she acknowledges governance challenges, e.g., by creating good relations with the Québec provincial government, on which she depends for financial assistance (Riga, 2018a, February 25). Still, to her, these relations also include the federal government (Riga) and the mobilisation of the entire community, city employees, businesses, and civil society organisations (Ville de Montréal, 2020a). That is why a strong and direct democracy is a critical concern for her (Women-4Climate, 2022).

Finally, Plante believes in a social investment approach and that investing in the public is an engine of wealth creation (Médium large, 2018, March 8). She wants to promote a paradigm change, so others start seeing major projects as contributions to the community (Médium large). And via these investments, she hopes that her vision of improving the quality of life for all Montréalers will become reality in the short, medium, and long term (Ville de Montréal, 2020a).

Personality, skills, and leadership style

What is possibly mentioned most about Valérie Plante's personality and leadership is her spirit, smile, joyfulness, energy, and dynamic (Gyulai, 2017, October 14). Ed Broadbent, the founder of left-of-centre thinktank Broadbent Institute, whose board Plante joined, describes her as "exuberant, imaginative and thoroughly pleasant to work with" (Gyulai). Others describe her as having an effortless way of being herself, smiling non-stop, laughing loudly, not afraid to be silly, and hard to dislike (Drimonis, 2017, November 6). Others add that she is engaging, upbeat (McGillis, 2020, November 27), generous, cheerful, lively, and hyperactive, but with relaxation about her (Berkowicz & Hecht, 2022, May 12). Her easy laugh and smile have become her trademark (Berkowicz & Hecht), and Plante is proud of her positive attitude and that she proved that one could lead Montréal with a smile (Shingler, 2021, November 8). At the same time, she says it is often a self-deprecating laugh because she does not have a big ego (Gyulai).

Plante first became famous by connecting and inspiring the citizens of Montréal (Noakes, 2017, November 8) as a natural campaigner with a laid-back, cheerful approach (Kucharsky, 2017, November 28). The press confirmed that she has a different, open, and upbeat charisma about her that represented a new kind of voice for the city of Montréal (Surridge, 2018, February 15). Her contagious passion and energy helped rally people around her progressive vision (Women4Climate, 2022), and her victory demonstrated a new way of presenting and conceiving authority (Surridge). With Plante, leadership no longer meant overwhelming opponents or smacking those who think differently (Surridge). Unlike traditional male politicians, Plante remained true to herself and proved that women could succeed in the political arena without becoming more like men (Drimonis, 2017, November 6).

At the same time, Plante is not only about laughs and smiles but also has strong willpower and stamina. According to her, she can keep pace in politics, mainly because of her athletic engagement as a swimmer and marathon runner (Scott, 2021, June 29). She also got her decisiveness from her mother, who said to persistently pursue what she believed was right (Médium large, 2018, March 8). When asked how she stays true to her values and handles harsh critiques, Plante replied that she fundamentally believes in what she does (Berkowicz & Hecht, 2022, May 12). And once she steps into the political arena, she puts on her boxing gloves, ready to fight. She believes you need a thick skin in politics, and her steely resolve enables her to thrive in the competitive political arena (Berkowicz & Hecht), as does her bold and irreverent character (Tolley & Paquet, 2018). Plante further suggests that when you have solid convictions and make explicit promises, sometimes you have to bang your fist on the table to move things forward (Berkowicz & Hecht). For example, she turned a significant shopping street into a bike highway, and business owners were angry, thinking it would kill their businesses. Instead, it became the city's busiest road, and business owners were grateful. During her first mandate, Plante also felt citizens were angry with her because she pushed them too much. Still, she firmly believes that she must take actions that shake things up, especially regarding the environment. And people re-elected her, proving to her that she was doing it right (Berkowicz & Hecht).

Plante claims that she does not want to disappoint the people (Drimonis, 2017, November 6; cf. Lau, 2021, November 8; cf. Nerestant, 2021, November 8; cf. Riga, 2018b, November 3), and she sees the position of mayor as a privilege and honour (CBC News, 2021, November 8). It gives her the energy to do her best and solve as many problems as possible (Riga, 2018a, February 25). Her profound care for people drives her and makes her an excellent listener (Gyulai, 2017, October 14). Projet Montréal elected her as leader precisely for that reason – to bring her "human touch" to politics (Gyulai). When she won the second election, Plante focused on how honoured she was by Montréalers re-electing her, promising that she would represent them all, not disappoint them, and always listen to what they had to say (Lau). She had proven this approach to be accurate, e.g., during the pandemic, when she started taking her bike to work so she could take the chance to stop and talk to workers, police officers, or the homeless and feel connected to their needs (Carpenter, 2020, May 21). Plante believes that her ability to care and genuine desire to improve the city and make a difference in the lives of Montréalers is her advantage (Montreal Gazette, 2017, April 20). In that way, people can easily relate to her. As a mother of two young boys, running marathons, taking the metro, and cycling through the city, she seems in touch with the average citizen (Drimonis). She also shares much about her private life on social media, which has served her well (Schué, 2022, February 8). This connects to Plante's authenticity. Those who know her say that she is always the same person, whether you see her at home, at dinner, or on TV (Gyulai).

In line with her authenticity, Plante also admits to mistakes. For example, when she promised not to increase taxes during her first campaign and stated that she should have chosen her words more carefully, unaware of the financial hole left by the prior administration (Riga, 2018a, February 25). Her learning curve as mayor has been "amazing" and "crazy," and she felt more ready to be Mayor the second time around (Nerestant, 2021, November 8). This statement goes hand in hand with her desire to show others, especially young girls, that they should go for things they believe in, even without having all the solutions yet (CBC News, 2020b, November 28).

Plante thereby follows a shared leadership approach and made this clear early on in her victory speech in 2017 (Kucharsky, 2017, November 28). She criticised her opponent and former Mayor Denis Coderre for his autocratic style, stating "Montréal deserves better" and that it has had "enough of a one-man show" (Kurcharsky). In her second victory speech in 2021, Plante again held that she and her grassroots political party Projet Montréal will "continue to be a team of all Montrealers." She especially emphasised that she is not a one-woman show but part of a team responsible for Montréalers' wellbeing (CBC News, 2021, November 8). Her collaborative leadership style and capacity for reaching out rather than issuing directives from the top are acknowledged widely (Gyulai, 2017, October 14). Her whole career has been about building bridges (Drimonis, 2017, November 6). Once elected in 2017, she started precisely doing that by launching an appeal for the city's francophone, anglophone, and allophone communities to work together (Drimonis) and making sure they knew she would include them in all political processes by consulting them (Berkowicz & Hecht, 2022, May 12). Plante also took a collaborative approach when tackling crises such as the COVID-19 pandemic or climate change, frequently speaking to other mayors in Canada to learn from their practices (Carpenter, 2020, May 21).

Plante further appears to pursue an adaptive approach to many of her political decisions (Carpenter, 2020, May 21). This became especially clear during the pandemic. To her, the challenge was that it simultaneously required a long-term strategy and constant reorientation, so she made most of her choices based on the day's events (Carpenter). Plante further demonstrated her adaptive ability regarding borough-specific challenges, aware that each borough requires an individual strategy regarding matters such as fighting climate change, based on their daily reality (Nerestant, 2021, November 8).

The case of Montréal's political innovations

Establishing a new narrative

Valérie Plante and her administration have a clear vision for the future of Montréal, around which they created a respective narrative. It is one where Montréal is a carbon-neutral, resilient city that is renowned across the globe for its quality of life (Ville de Montréal, 2020a). A city where the population respects the planet's ecological limits, e.g., via local agriculture and a circular economy, where districts have been transformed along sustainability principles, and where people forge ties of mutual aid (Ville de Montréal, 2020a). All citizens have equal access to housing, employment, services, and support from the community, and no one is left behind (Ville de Montréal, 2020b, December 8). It is also a city where parks and gardens thrive, and citizens are making public spaces their own, moving around freely on foot, by bike, or via electric vehicles. Finally, it is also a dynamic, open, and creative city that celebrates history, culture, and diversity, and has a strong reputation that attracts citizens, tourists, and investments (Ville de Montréal, 2020b, December 8).

At the same time, Plante and her administration refer to the challenges the future holds, including finite resources and global warming, emphasising that the transition requires the will to change ways of living, working, producing, and consuming (Ville de Montréal, 2020c, December 20). They address sobriety in a search for less whilst improving quality of life and wellbeing via respective approaches such as frugality, zero waste, and deconsumption. Regarding the economy, this means developing a new economic model based on respect for people and the environment, which considers the planet's limitations and finds new ways for production and employment (Ville de Montréal, 2020c, December 20). In line with this, the administration aims for a green and inclusive economy to fight socio-economic inequalities and environmental issues (Ville de Montréal, 2020b, December 8). For Plante, the COVID-19 crisis specifically showed the need for a new social and economic model that respects the environment and increases community resilience and solidarity (Ville de Montréal, 2020c, December 20).

Moreover, part of the narrative shows citizens that they are essential to the city's future and should be involved in defining it collectively (Ville de

Montréal, 2020c, December 20). Respective messages are based on irrefutable scientific evidence, emphasising unity and the capacity to act, along with phrases such as "We can lead the battle by working together" and "solutions exist to make our cities more resilient and ensure that no one gets left behind. We still have time to take collective action" (Ville de Montréal 2020c).

The overarching mission-oriented framework: Montréal 2030

To implement the narrative, Plante developed the Montréal 2030 plan that sets the stage for a continuous cycle of strategic planning and respective process of analysis, prioritisation, and alignment of policies, programs, and projects (Ville de Montréal, 2020b, December 8). The plan focuses on 4 orientations, 3 scales, and 20 priorities (Ville de Montréal, p. 17). The critical orientations include "accelerating ecological transition," "reinforcing solidarity, equity and inclusion," "amplifying democracy and participation," and "stimulating innovation and creativity." They ought to be applied on three scales of intervention: the level of the metropolis, neighbourhoods, and individuals. All municipal plans, policies, programs, and services must align with these four orientations. Governance rules are revisited to ensure that the administration considers the orientations in fiscal, budgetary, administrative, and regulatory decisions (Ville de Montréal).

Each of the four orientations specifies particular priorities. The ecological transition includes reducing GHG emissions by 55 percent below 1990 levels by 2030, becoming carbon neutral by 2050, or developing a greener and more inclusive economy (Ville de Montréal, 2020b, December 8, p. 22). Solidarity, equity, and inclusion priorities revolve around eliminating hunger, improving access to affordable and nutritious food, or combatting racism and discrimination within the city administration (Ville de Montréal, p. 28). Priorities to amplify democracy and participation include increasing citizen participation and involvement in municipal public life, leveraging transparency, and data sharing (Ville de Montréal, p. 32). Priorities for stimulating innovation and creativity include supporting Montréal's cultural vitality and creative heart or bolstering Montréal's status as a living laboratory and city of knowledge (Ville de Montréal, p. 36).

To ensure that plans and projects, will be implemented successfully, the administration defined steps for renewed governance and processes (Ville de Montréal, 2020b, December 8). These include linking budget processes to the plans' priorities, developing matrix structures, pooling resources within the administration and civil society, and transforming and maximising the use and benefits of internal advances in the digital technology sector. They further aim to monitor the progress through a performance measurement framework that presents priorities, targets, key performance indicators, and baseline data, all as a process for accountability to the population, city staff, and elected officials (Ville de Montréal).

For implementation, the framework is broken down into a variety of more specific plans, such as the Urban Planning and Mobility Plan, an Economic Recovery Plan, a Diversity and Social Inclusion Plan, and a Climate Plan, some of which will be highlighted in the following sections.

Climate Plan 2030

In 2018, Valérie Plante signed the One Planet Charter on behalf of Montréal, pledging, amongst others, to develop an action plan to support the implementation of the Paris Agreement, make Montréal carbon-neutral by 2050, and set an interim target for 2030 (Ville de Montréal, 2020a, p. 30). Along with the Montréal 2030 Plan and the pledge, the city developed a Climate Plan 2030, which includes 46 measures to set Montréal on a path to becoming a resilient, inclusive, and carbon-neutral city (Ville de Montréal, 2020c, December 15). Resilience, in this sense, means building the capacity to resist sudden shocks such as pandemics or severe flooding and chronic issues such as rising temperatures and heavy rainfalls. Inclusivity means ensuring no one is left behind and everyone benefits from the Climate Plan's measures (Ville de Montréal, 2020a).

The Plan includes the four fundamental orientations from the overall Montréal 2030 Plan and the climate-related priorities "GHG reduction," "nature in the city," "sustainable mobility," "zero waste," "green and inclusive economy," and "living environments and proximity" (Ville de Montréal, 2020a, p. 15). Respectively, the city also defined five key sectors in which to act first, namely "Mobilization of the Montréal community," "Mobility, urban planning, and urban development," "Buildings," "Exemplarity of the city," and "Governance" (Ville de Montréal, 2020c, December 15, p. 5).

In these sectors, specific actions are highlighted. The city wants to mobilise the community through access to information, deploy strategies to promote the adoption of eco-responsible practices, or launch plans to reduce food waste and facilitate textile donation and recycling (Ville de Montréal, 2020c, December 15, p. 19). Other key actions include promoting public transport via the Pink metro line, car-sharing, carpooling, converting parking lots into open green spaces, and planting trees (Ville de Montréal, p. 20). In addition, they want to favour renewable energies, support property owners in healthy and environmentally friendly renovations, and improve the energy performance of large buildings through rating and disclosure systems (Ville de Montréal, p. 21). Finally, they plan to apply a climate test to all city decisions, make all city buildings carbon neutral, and publish annual reports on the progress of the city's actions (Ville de Montréal, p. 23).

These actions are then further specified with key indicators and targets to make them specific and reporting transparent. They include reducing GHG emissions by 55 percent, reducing solo car trips by 25 percent, increasing the number of registered electric vehicles to 47 percent, planting 500.000 trees, or turning 10 percent of the territory into a protected zone (Ville de Montréal, 2020c, December 15, p. 25).

Diversity and Inclusion Plan

Following citizens' pressure on the city, Plante and her administration recognised systemic racism as an issue in Montréal and committed to fighting it (Kucharsky, 2017, November 28). Respectively, the city developed a Diversity and Inclusion Plan. Again, it is structured around a vision, an objective, three priorities, and 26 main projects (Ville de Montréal, 2021, p. 4).

The vision presented is once more that of an inclusive, united, and fair city that reflects the diversity of the population with its personnel and fights racism and systemic discrimination (Ville de Montréal, 2021). The administration knows its success depends on socio-professional integration and being a responsible employer. The main objective is to proactively build a public service representative of the population in all jobs and at all levels and, in doing so, optimise its services. Three priorities revolve around recognising and valuing diversity, developing an inclusive culture, and strengthening communication and consultation. Projects include developing new candidate identification methods and hiring processes, setting performance objectives for senior management related to diversity and inclusion, or collaborating on projects that promote the employment and inclusion of people with disabilities (Ville de Montréal).

Reconciliation Strategy

Whilst the Indigenous population in the Greater Montréal area remains relatively low, Plante and her administration committed to First Nations and Inuit with a Reconciliation Strategy (Ville de Montréal, 2020d, November 4). In 2018 they substantiated this commitment by appointing a Commissioner for Indigenous Relations in charge of the strategy's implementation and further corresponding efforts (Ville de Montréal).

The strategy itself revolves around seven strategic objectives (Ville de Montréal, 2020d, November 4). The first concerns recognising Indigenous governments as partners in regional dialogues and Indigenous civil society organisations as actors to collaborate with when developing solutions for urban issues of Indigenous concern. The second aims to improve the Indigenous populations' visibility in the city by showcasing their heritage in urban landscapes, design, and toponymy. The third objective revolves around supporting Indigenous community organisations' maintenance, development, and growth, whilst the fourth aims to improve Indigenous peoples' feeling of safety. A fourth objective seeks to support Indigenous cultural development in the urban environment by recognising the historical ethnocidal violence that caused the suppression of their language and cultural transmission mechanisms so that they may witness a renaissance. The fifth objective aims to support Indigenous economic development by recognising and fighting systemic racism and discrimination as significant obstacles to employability. Finally, the sixth objective seeks to acknowledge and build on the richness and relevance of Indigenous knowledge regarding preserving natural environments and ecosystems (Ville de Montréal).

Enabling leadership for sustainable development

Plante's administration is trying to enable leadership on many scales, both within the administration and beyond. For one, they document sustainability challenges and respective strategies thoroughly and comprehensively in documents such as the Climate Plan 2030 or the Montréal 2030 strategy. These reports enable all stakeholders to educate themselves, follow the cities' plans regarding sustainable development, and act accordingly. Plante and her team know that transparency and educating, mobilising, engaging, and equipping stakeholders are necessary to achieve behavioural changes, e.g., regarding climate change (Ville de Montréal, 2020a). We can also see this awareness along the stakeholder participation processes they implemented for all strategic plans. For one, to create the Climate Plan, the city consulted stakeholders so that they could express their opinions on important issues such as dependence on fossil fuels and waste management. They also formed a climate advisory committee whose suggestions contributed to the plan. Via these measures, the city aimed to ensure that the plan "belongs to the citizens, community organisations, merchants, businesses and city staff" (Ville de Montréal, 2020a, p. 9). They also monitored all progress and setbacks and reported on them in an annual report. In 2019 alone, ten public consultations, 63 public events, 70 public meetings, and 98 working sessions took place (Ville de Montréal, 2020b, December 8). Subsequently, the city presented 157 written or oral opinions to committees and tabled 123 reports (Ville de Montréal, 2020b, December 8).

The administration is also implementing measures for better governance. They know they must renew governance roles, responsibilities, and processes to implement their strategy for a more sustainable Montréal (Ville de Montréal, 2020b, December 8). For example, they seek to link budget processes to strategic plans, increase collaboration within the municipal administration and civil society, encourage the sharing of data, information, analyses, and reports, and integrate stakeholders in decision-making and planning processes. In addition, they are trying to improve change management and capacity building so that the administrative staff may implement the suggested transformations for Montréal 2030. They build municipal administrative actors' capacities via workshops and tools, encourage ownership, and train and nurture an organisational culture open to experimentation, errors, and learning (Ville de Montréal).

Finally, Plante's administration knew they must mobilise more than the city for the necessary transformations. Therefore, they wish to stimulate a collective movement and collaboration inside and outside Montréal by developing mechanisms for emerging, supporting, and deploying collaborative projects (Ville de Montréal, 2020b, December 8). This includes ongoing dialogues with other municipalities and the provincial and federal governments (Ville de Montréal).

Comprehending the interplay of structure and agency

Agency as an enabler and barrier to Valérie Plante's leadership

Regarding the synthesised leadership model for women's leadership for sustainable development (see Appendix 1.0) Valérie Plante's personality, skills, and leadership style fit the theoretically derived qualities and significantly enabled her success. For example, she holds strong beliefs and values and shows a strong commitment and sense of citizenship. This heightened her determination to drive change to enable a better quality of life, protect the environment, and adapt to the challenges the city faces. She does this with a strong vision in which she actively involves all stakeholders. Personality-wise she is empathetic, open, and likable and follows a "power to" or "power with" approach, although she is also known to occasionally apply "power over", where she finds it necessary to drive change. She has strong contextual intelligence and is a systemic thinker with a broad range of strategic and communication skills. Last, she empowers stakeholders and her organisation by sharing and fostering knowledge, preparing and mobilising for change, and driving collective values as a source of creative energy.

Still, Plante's leadership also acted as a barrier on several occasions, where her actions faced strong criticism. During her first campaign, she had stated she would not raise taxes above inflation. Still, she needed to make investments despite the financial hole the previous administration had left (Riga,

2018b, November 3). Consequently, she increased property taxes by an average of 3.3 percent, worsening the housing crisis as landlords passed the tax hike on to their tenants (D'Alimonte, 2018, January 11). At first, Plante denied that she had gone back on her word, but eventually, she had to acknowledge that she had broken her promise (Riga, 2018b, November 3). Another election promise Plante broke concerned the new Pink metro line for $6 billion. The proposal had to go through the provincial and federal governments which chose not to finance the line. Plante had to admit that she was "too excited" during the campaign and that work on it could probably only start during a second mandate (Riga, 2018a, February 25).

The media further criticised her for being out of touch with Montréalers, e.g., by closing commercial streets for bike lanes during the pandemic (CBC News, 2020a, September 4). She was even pointed out as imposing new projects on the population and as underestimating the pandemic's toll on them (Schué, 2022, February 8). An expert on municipal politics believes Plante had tried to implement her program too quickly during a period when citizens were first and foremost looking for stability and that she had pursued questions of mobility, whilst citizens were mostly concerned with the cost of housing (Labbé, 2020, October 26).

Finally, other politicians questioned her integrity and leadership qualities on multiple occasions. For example, she removed a female chief of staff from her caucus for refusing to take responsibility for a hostile work environment, and a court finally ruled in favour of the staff member (Hanes, 2020, December 23). Plante was also said to have booted a party member over siding with the wrong people and following different convictions, signalling there is little room for dissent within Projet Montréal (Hanes).

Structural enablers and barriers to Plante's agency

Before Plante's election, two previous male mayors had to resign due to corruption allegations. According to the media, citizens were "made cynical by years of wasteful spending, mismanagement and high-profile fraud scandals" (Noakes, 2017, November 8). Thus, before the 2017 election, there was a solid anti-Coderre sentiment due to his mistakes and top-down leadership (Drimonis, 2017, November 6). At the same time, there was a renewed sense of pride in Montréal, and Plante stood for hope and openness, attracting voters to her due to a strong leader-society-fit (Drimonis).

Party structures also enabled Plante's success. Incumbent Mayor Denis Coderre's political party represented a traditional Canadian municipal political party (Tolley & Paquet, 2021). Projet Montréal broke with this model and introduced a less-leader-centric model instead. It had a stable internal organisation via a decentralised model that gave greater power to grassroots members via local associations through which party members could elect district and borough candidates. Most Projet Montréal members are also active in community groups and political action communities and thus are actively embedded in civic and political life all year round. Most importantly, however, the party had developed a clear policy agenda beyond gaining power, guided by a vision statement and critical principles of sustainable development, that had been developed collectively in a bi-annual Congress with all party members. Projet Montréal's approach was thus a clear departure from Montréal's traditional municipal political parties and exactly what citizens were looking for. In addition, research on the non-partisan specificity of Canadian municipal politics suggests that women benefit from being political party members because they are judged less along their characteristics and stereotypes. At the same time, parties provide financial and organisational capacity, which facilitates campaigning. Both aspects were especially enabling for Plante's election (Tolley & Paquet).

Finally, regarding gender, a survey showed that gender was not a salient predictor of the public's mayoral choice and that Plante's success was not the result of the gender affinity effect (Tolley & Paquet, 2021). Still, the context was favourable to Plante because there were strong feminist movements and a desire for more women in politics (Tolley & Paquet). During Plante's first election, out of the 294 candidates, 127 were women, and a record number of female borough mayors and city councilors were elected (Drimonis, 2017, November 6). Thus, Plante may have been "the right woman at the right time" (Drimonis).

Whilst structural factors also enabled Valérie Plante, they mostly hindered her. Asked about going into politics, Valérie Plante states that she immediately felt she was a woman in a male-dominated environment (Berkowicz & Hecht, 2022, May 12). Thus, she and Projet Montréal chose not to focus on her gender during the campaign but instead employed the method of "degendering". Still, like many other women in politics, Plante was criticised based on her gender (The Conversation, 2020, October 20). Three major daily newspapers had endorsed Plante's opponent Denis Coderre and used her gender to discredit her (Drimonis, 2017, November 6), even labeling her "Madame Sourire" or "Mrs Smiles" (Labelle & Sullivan, 2020, October 20). Thereby, the media linked her seemingly flawed personality and overly enthusiastic smile to a perceived lack of competence (The Conversation). She was also called out as a neophyte, even though she had just as much political experience as many former mayors before they stepped into office (Drimonis).

Plante's gender was also used against her later, e.g., when she released an autobiographic graphic novel showing women's double standards in politics (CBC News, 2020b, November 28). In the novel, she highlighted a particularly sexist incident (McGillis, 2020, November 27). A supporter introduced Plante at an event, asking "Wouldn't you like to have a pretty city councilor for a change?" Plante frequently experienced situations like that and called them "the relentless sexism, the small things" that wore her out in the long run (McGillis).

Another barrier was the administrative arena. Canada follows the principle of provincial supremacy, and municipalities are subject to relatively close administrative control (Lightbody, 2006). In addition, they depend on provincial and federal governments for financial support. As an example, Plante planned for the new Pink metro line, but failed to secure funding from the provincial and federal governments and thus could not deliver on the promise (Shingler, 2021, November 8). To increase the quality of life, Montréal also needed to increase pay for low-wage workers, foster more stable workplaces, and improve housing affordability and access to social and health services (Jonas & Shingler, 2021, November 3). Still, these matters could only be partially addressed by the city, as it falls into the responsibility of the provincial or federal governments (Jonas & Shingler). During the COVID-19 pandemic, Québec also decided on various measures, such as closing and reopening economic sectors, some of which directed the public's anger at Plante, who was not responsible (Carpenter, 2020, May 21). In 2022, the national government further released a new federal budget. While Plante was happy with the focus on affordable housing and investments to accelerate the electrification of transport, she criticised a lack of funding to fight climate change and commitment to preventing the proliferation of firearms (Carpenter). These examples show that Plante's political plans were severly restricted by Canada's political system.

Another barrier relates to previous administrations. As mentioned, Denis Coderre's administration left a projected deficit of $358 million, which was seven percent of the budget (Riga, 2018a, February 25). The deficit forced Plante to raise taxes and draw the citizens' anger at her for breaking her election promise. The COVID-19 pandemic did not aid the city's financial situation, and the Québec government had to bail out Montréal for $263 million (Shingler, 2021, November 8). Plante further points to a lack of investments in the city's infrastructure, such as the water system or the metro stations, which had not seen investments in 25 years (Berkowicz & Hecht, 2022, May 12). These structural deficits resulted from past political decisions that Plante was not responsible for and could not overcome (Carpenter, 2020, May 21).

The COVID-19 pandemic further acted as a barrier because it highlighted and amplified existing urban problems, from socio-economic inequalities to a lack of shared public spaces and issues related to economic and cultural vitality (Ville de Montréal, 2020b, December 8). Plante says the pandemic represented her most significant dissatisfaction during her first mandate (Berkowicz & Hecht, 2022, May 12). For her, projects were no longer moving fast enough, especially regarding mobility, i.e., the need to reduce cars, develop public transport, and expand cycling lanes (Berkowicz & Hecht). A report further revealed that the pandemic harmed the public's opinion of Plante and her team's work (Labbé, 2020, October 26). Still, Plante felt like the public anger was over the pandemic itself and not her actions (CBC News, 2020b, November 28). She believes the media wrongly depicted the public's feelings towards her initiatives in the papers (CBC News, 2020a, September 4). For example, when stating citizens were angry about new city initiatives such as cycling lanes or pedestrian-only streets, she observed the opposite when talking to them (CBC News, September 4).

Finally, Canada's culture and innovation capacity were not highly suitable for the transformative politics Plante and her administration aimed for, especially regarding the ecological transition. Long-term orientation and power distance are low in Canada (Hofstede, 2022) and thus not favourable to innovation in general and political innovations for sustainable development in particular (Prim et al., 2017). The nation also scores high on individualism and indulgence (Hofstede, 2022), which favour innovation output but contrast innovations regarding sustainable development and concepts like equity and justice (Prim et al.). Overall, the cultural dimensions in Canada do not necessarily speak for transformative politics for sustainable development. However, the dimensions are not specified for Montréal and thus we cannot know the exact implications for the city.

To conclude, the qualitative analysis of Valérie Plante's leadership and respective patterns shows that a structure-agency interplay enabled her to become an agent for sustainable development and successfully drive political innovations. Still, judging from the summary, it was especially agency that acted as an enabler rather than structures.

References

Atak, I. (2021). "A responsible and committed city": Montréal's sanctuary policy. In Faret, L. & Sanders, H. (ed.), *Migrant protection and the city in the Americas* (pp. 105–130). Cham, Switzerland: Palgrave McMillan.

Baillargeon, D. (2019). *To be equals in our own country. Women and the vote in Quebec*. Vancouver, Canada: UBC Press.

Belley, S., Bherer, L., Chiasson, G., Collin, P., Hamel, P., Hamel, P. J., Rivard, M., & Archambault, J. (2009). Quebec. In Sancton, A. & Young, R. (Eds.), *Foundations of governance: Municipal government in Canada's provinces* (pp. 70–137). Toronto, Canada: Toronto University Press.

Berkowicz, S., & Hecht, L. (2022, May 12). Interview: recontre avec Valérie Plante, mairesse de Montréal [Interview: Meeting with Valérie Plante, mayor of Montréal]. *The Good Life*. https://thegoodlife.thegoodhub.com/2022/05/12/interview-rencontre-avec-valerie-plante-mairesse-de-montreal/

Blad, C. (2011). *Neoliberalism and national culture. State-building and legitimacy in Canada and Québec*. Leiden, Netherlands: Brill.

Bruemmer, R. (2017, January 27). Former Montreal mayor Michael Applebaum found guilty of corruption and fraud charges. *Montreal Gazette*. https://montrealgazette.com/news/local-news/former-montreal-mayor-michael-applebaum-found-guilty-of-corruption-and-fraud-charges/

C40 Cities. (2022, February 25). *Mayor of Montréal elected to C40 Cities Steering Committee*. https://www.c40.org/news/montreal-join-c40-steering-committee/

Canada Guide. (2022). *Premiers of Canadian provinces and territories*. https://thecanadaguide.com/data/provincial-premiers/

Canada Population. (2022). *Montreal Population 2021/2022*. https://canadapopulation.org/montreal-population/

Carpenter, L. (2020, May 21). Montreal Mayor Valérie Plante on how COVID-19 has transformed her job. *Cult Montréal*. https://cultmtl.com/2020/05/montreal-mayor-valerie-plante-on-how-covid-19-has-transformed-her-job-coronavirus-epicentre/

CBC News. (2012, November 5). *Montreal mayor steps down amid corruption allegations*. https://www.cbc.ca/news/canada/montreal/montreal-mayor-steps-down-amid-corruption-allegations-1.1166132

CBC News. (2020a, September 4). *Valérie Plante senses 'big gap' between media coverage and how residents actually feel about bike paths*. https://www.cbc.ca/news/canada/montreal/montreal-valerie-plante-daybreak-bike-paths-1.5712254

CBC News. (2020b, November 28). *Montreal Mayor Valerie Plante publishes graphic novel detailing her political journey*. https://www.cbc.ca/news/canada/montreal/mayor-plante-graphic-novel-1.5820620

CBC News. (2021, November 8). *"We will continue to be team of all Montrealers": Valérie Plante speaks after re-election as mayor*. [Video]. https://globalnews.ca/video/8357353/we-will-continue-to-be-team-of-all-montrealers-valerie-plante-speaks-after-re-election-as-mayor/%20%20(%E2%80%98We%20will%20continue%20to%20be%20team%20of%20all%20Montrealers%E2%80%99_%20Val%C3%A9rie%20Plant,%20S.%203:%20143)

Cherry, P. (2016, December 4). *Valérie Plante wins Projet Montréal leadership race*. *Montreal Gazette*. https://montrealgazette.com/news/local-news/valerie-plante-wins-projet-montreal-leadership-race/

Clark, D. (2002). Neoliberalism and public service reform: Canada in comparative perspective. *Canadian Journal of Political Science / Revue Canadienne de science politique*, 35(4), 771–793. https://doi.org/10.1017/S0008423902778438

Coderre, D. (2016, January 29). We need to make our cities inclusive, sustainable and safe. *UCLG*. https://www.uclg.org/en/media/news/we-need-make-our-cities-inclusive-sustainable-and-safe

Corriveau, J. (2005, April 21). Développement durable: Montréal établit ses objectifs [Sustainable development: Montréal establishes its objectives]. *Le Devoir*.

https://www.ledevoir.com/politique/regions/79902/developpement-durable-montreal-etablit-ses-objectifs

CPA Canada. (2021). Income inequality in Canada: The urban gap. *Huffington Post.* https://www.huffpost.com/archive/ca/entry/canada-income-inequality-montreal-study_n_1415838

D'Alimonte, M. (2018, January 11). Everything Valérie Plante has done wrong (thus far) as mayor of Montreal. *Mmontréal blog.* https://www.mtlblog.com/everything-valerie-plante-has-done-wrong-thus-far-as-mayor-of-montreal

DEAL. (2022). *National Doughnuts Data Explorer.* https://doughnuteconomics.org/tools-and-stories/22

Drimonis, T. (2017, November 6). The secret of Valérie Plante's Montreal success. Canada's National Observer. https://www.nationalobserver.com/2017/11/06/opinion/secret-valerie-plantes-montreal-success%20%20

Epaper News. (2022). *Valérie Plante.* https://en.epapernews.org/en/Valérie_Plante-4688880226

Gouvernement du Québec. (2022a). *Région Montréal [Montréal region].* https://www.economie.gouv.qc.ca/pages-regionales/montreal/

Gouvernement du Québec. (2022b). *Secteur des entreprises [Enterprise sectors].* https://www.economie.gouv.qc.ca/pages-regionales/montreal/portrait-regional/secteur-des-entreprises/

Gouvernement du Québec. (2022c). *Conditions de vie [Living conditions].* https://www.economie.gouv.qc.ca/pages-regionales/montreal/portrait-regional/conditions-de-vie/

Gouvernement du Québec. (2022d). *Le development durable au CAG [The sustainable development in CAG].* https://www.quebec.ca/gouvernement/ministeres-et-organismes/centre-dacquisitions-gouvernementales/developpement-durable-cag/

Gouvernement du Québec. (2022e). *À propos du développement durable [Speaking of sustainable development].* https://www.environnement.gouv.qc.ca/developpement/definition.htm

Gouvernement du Québec. (2022f). *About the Plan.* https://www.quebec.ca/en/government/policies-orientations/plan-green-economy/about-the-plan

Gyulai, L. (2017, October 14). The people person. *Montreal Gazette.* https://www.pressreader.com/canada/montreal-gazette/20171014/281487866576307

Hachard, T. (2020). *It takes three: Making space for cities in Canadian federalism.* Institute on Municipal Finance and Governance. https://tspace.library.utoronto.ca/bitstream/1807/103012/3/IMFG_%20No.31%20Perspectives_Hachard_Nov2020.pdf

Hague, M. (2021, July 12). Protecting biodiversity in Montreal with Canada's largest city park. Canada's National Observer. https://www.nationalobserver.com/2021/07/12/protecting-biodiversity-montreal-canadas-largest-city-park

Hanes, A. (2020, December 23). Allison Hanes: Valérie Plante's terrible, horrible, no good, very bad year. *Montreal Gazette.* https://montrealgazette.com/opinion/columnists/allison-hanes-valerie-plantes-terrible-horrible-no-good-very-bad-year

Hofstede, G. (2022). *Country comparison graphs.* https://geerthofstede.com/country-comparison-graphs/

Jonas, S., & Shingler, B. (2021, November 3). The pandemic exposed Montreal's inequalities and residents say it's time to tackle root causes. *CBC News*. https://www.cbc.ca/news/canada/montreal/covid-19-montreal-disparity-solutions-1.6232359

Kucharsky, D. (2017, November 28). Valérie Plante. *The Canadian Encyclopedia*. https://www.thecanadianencyclopedia.ca/en/article/valerie-plante

Labbé, J. (2020, October 26). Montrèal: l'électorat de Valérie Plante se fragilise [Montréal: Of Valérie Plante's electorate weakens]. *ICI Grand Montréal*. https://ici.radio-canada.ca/nouvelle/1743385/sondage-intentions-vote-satisfaction-montrealais-elections-mairie-2021

Labelle, A., & Sullivan, K. V. R. (2020, October 20). "Madame Sourire": que dit la couverture médiatique de Valérie Plante? ["Madam Smile": What does media coverage say about Valérie Plante?]. *The Conversation*. https://theconversation.com/madame-sourire-que-dit-la-couverture-mediatique-de-valerie-plante-146287 (« Madame Sourire » _ que dit la couverture médiatique de Valéri, S. 1: 91).

Lau, R. (2021, November 8). Valérie Plante outlines priorities one day after reelection as Montreal Mayor. *CTV News*. https://montreal.ctvnews.ca/valerie-plante-outlines-priorities-one-day-after-reelection-as-montreal-mayor-1.5656603

Lightbody, J. (2006). *City politics, Canada*. Peterborough, Canada: Broadview Press.

Lijphart, A. (2012). *Patterns of democratic government forms and performance in thirty-six countries* (2nd ed.). Yale, CT: Yale University Press.

McGillis, I. (2020, November 27). Drawn to public office: Valérie Plante revisits first campaign in graphic novel. *Montreal Gazette*. https://montrealgazette.com/entertainment/local-arts/drawn-to-public-office-valerie-plante-revisits-first-campaign-in-graphic-novel

Médium large. (2018, March 8). Entrevue avec la mariesse de Montréal, Valérie Plante [Interview with mayor Valérie Plante]. *ICI Radio*. https://ici.radio-canada.ca/ohdio/premiere/emissions/medium-large/segments/entrevue/62418/valerie-plante-nouvelle-vie

Montreal Gazette. (2017, April 20). *Mega vision: Projet Montréal leader Valérie Plante*. https://montrealgazette.com/news/local-news/mega-vision-projet-montreal-leader-valerie-plante/

Montreal Gazette. (2021, March 15). *Parties multiplying ahead of Montreal municipal election*. https://montrealgazette.com/news/local-news/parties-multiplying-ahead-of-montreal-municipal-election

Montréal International. (2019, February 6). *Greater Montréal leads the pack for economic growth in Canada*. https://www.montrealinternational.com/en/news/greater-montreal-leads-the-pack-for-economic-growth-in-canada/

Nerestant, A. (2021, November 8). Valérie Plante says housing a top priority to kick off 2nd term. *CBC News*. https://www.cbc.ca/news/canada/montreal/valerie-plante-election-victory-1.6241158

Noakes, T. C. (2017, November 8). Montreal election: Valérie Plante's giant leap forward. *Rabble*. https://rabble.ca/politics/canadian-politics/montreal-election-valerie-plantes-giant-leap-forward/

Page, J. (2017, October 25). More Quebecers identifying as Indigenous, 2016 census Figures show. *CBC News.* https://www.cbc.ca/news/canada/montreal/census-report-2016-quebec-indigenous-population-1.4370938

Pitchford, G. (2021, September 16). *Canada's Top Sustainability Leaders announced for 2022. Clean, 50.* https://clean50.com/canadas-top-sustainability-leaders-announced-for-2022/ (Canada's Top Sustainability Leaders Announced for 2022 | Clean5, S. 1: 82).

Plante, V. (2020, May 18). Greetings. *ICLEI.* https://citieswithnature.org/wp-content/uploads/2020/05/Letter-from-Mayor-Plante_English_20200518.pdf

Prim, A. L., Filho, L. S., Zamur, G. A. C., & di Serio, L. C. (2017). The relationship between national culture dimensions and degree of innovation. *International Journal of Innovation Management, 21*(1), 173001. https://doi.org/10.1142/s136391961730001x

Projet Montréal. (2021). *Projet Montréal 2021 platform. A city for today and for tomorrow.* https://projetmontreal.org/assets/common/Platform_PM_2021.pdf

Riga, A. (2018a, February 25). Mayor Valérie Plante's first 100 days: In her own words. *Montreal Gazette.* https://montrealgazette.com/news/local-news/mayor-valerie-plantes-first-100-days-in-her-own-words/

Riga, A. (2018b, November 3). One-on-one with Mayor Valérie Plante one year later. *Montreal Gazette.* https://montrealgazette.com/news/local-news/one-on-one-with-mayor-valerie-plante-one-year-later/

Sancton, A. (2009). Introduction. In Sancton, A., & Young, R. (Eds.), *Foundations of governance: Municipal government in Canada's provinces* (pp. 3–19). Toronto, Canada: Toronto University Press.

Schué, R. (2022, February 8). "Mairesse et poseuse de céramique": des rénos qui soulévent des questions. ["Mayor and ceramic tile setter": Renovations that render questions]. *ICI Grand Montréal.* https://ici.radio-canada.ca/nouvelle/1860513/mairesse-montreal-travaux-construction-locataires

Scott, M. (2021, June 29). Valérie Plante launches re-election campaign with transit fare cuts. *Montreal Gazette.* https://montrealgazette.com/news/local-news/valerie-plante-launches-re-election-campaign-with-transit-fare-cuts

Serebrin, J. (2018, July 26). Incomes are rising in Montréal: Where do you fit in? *MontrealGazette.* https://www.cbc.ca/news/canada/montreal/quebec-disposable-income-1.3409683

Shingler, B. (2021, November 8). After a big victory, Valérie Plante returns as Montreal mayor with even bigger challenges ahead. *CBC News.* https://www.cbc.ca/news/canada/montreal/valerie-plante-montreal-wins-1.6240848

Stevenson, G. (2019). Federalism and the political economy of the Canadian State. In Panitch, L. (Ed.), *The Canadian State. Political economy and political power* (pp. 71–100). Toronto, Canada: University of Toronto Press.

Surridge, M. (2018, February 15). Valérie Plante, #MeToo, and a new kind of authority. *Splice Today.* https://www.splicetoday.com/politics-and-media/valerie-plante-metoo-and-a-new-kind-of-authority

The Conversation. (2020, October 20). *"Madame Sourire": que dit la couverture médiatique de Valérie Plante ["Madame Smiles": What does media coverage of Valérie Plante say].* https://theconversation.com/madame-sourire-que-dit-la-couverture-mediatique-de-valerie-plante-146287

Tolley, E., & Paquet, M. (2018). Madam Mayor: Gender, Montréal and the election of Valérie Plante. *CMES Conference*, Montréal, Canada. https://www.cmes-eemc.ca/conference

Tolley, E., & Paquet, M. (2021). Gender, municipal politics and Montreal's first woman mayor. *Canadian Journal of Urban Research*, *30*(1), 40–52. https://cjur.uwinnipeg.ca/index.php/cjur/article/view/323/150

Tremblay, M., & Everitt, J. (2020). Introduction: Approaching Canadian politics through a gender lense. In Tremblay, J., & Everitt, J (Eds.), *The Palgrave Handbook of gender, sexuality and Canadian politics* (pp. 1–12). Cham, Switzerland: Palgrave Macmillan.

Turgeon, L. (2009). Cities within the Canadian intergovernmental system. In Turgeon, L. (Ed.), *Contemporary Canadian Federalism* (pp. 359–378). Toronto, Canada: University of Toronto Press.

Ville de Montréal. (2018). *Montreal. Geared up for tomorrow.* https://montreal.ca/en/articles/2018-2022-economic-development-strategy-13816

Ville de Montréal. (2020a). *Climate Plan 2020-2030.* https://montreal.ca/en/articles/montreal-climate-plan-objective-carbon-neutral-2050-7613

Ville de Montréal. (2020b, December 8). *Montréal 2030. Citywide strategic plan.* https://montreal.ca/en/articles/montreal-2030-first-strategic-plan-8318

Ville de Montréal. (2020c, December 15). *Montréal Climate Plan: Objective carbon-neutral by 2050.* https://montreal.ca/en/articles/montreal-climate-plan-objective-carbon-neutral-2050-7613

Ville de Montréal. (2020d, November 4). *2020-2025 strategy for reconciliation with indigenous peoples.* https://montreal.ca/en/articles/2020-2025-strategy-reconciliation-indigenous-peoples-7760

Ville de Montréal. (2021). *Plan directeur pour la diversité, l'équité et l'inclusion en employ [Master plan for diversity, equity and inclusion in the workplace].* https://montreal.ca/en/articles/master-plan-employment-diversity-equity-and-inclusion-14942

Ville de Montréal. (2022, June 2). *Ville de Montréal – organisation municipal 2022.* https://ville.montreal.qc.ca/pls/portal/docs/page/prt_vdm_fr/media/documents/organigramme.pdf

Women4Climate. (2022). *Valérie Plante.* https://w4c.org/profile/pioneer-valerie-plante

World Population Review. (2022). *Canada population 2022.* https://worldpopulationreview.com/countries/canada-population

PART IV

Practical research implications

10

PRACTICAL LESSONS FOR WOMEN POLITICAL LEADERS

Structures are a central barrier for women's political leadership for sustainable development

Jacinda Ardern, Carole Delga, and Valérie Plante had a similar responsibility regarding how many citizens they governed and they were embedded in democratic political systems. Still, the leaders' power and responsibilities differed substantially due to the configurations of their political systems and the governance levels they were on. As explored in Chapter 4, the literature shows that national actors typically determine the success of transitions (Fischer & Newig, 2016). In contrast, regional actors are potentially limited in their opportunities but remain little researched, and local actors have the weakest agency (Fischer & Newig). Indeed, Jacinda Ardern potentially held the most significant power for transformative changes, as authority and power resided entirely with her and her national government. Carole Delga potentially wielded considerable power because France has a decentralised political system and the federal government installed a broad range of responsibilities for regional presidents. Still, Delga was more limited than Ardern because she depended on the central government's approval of strategic plans and finances. According to the literature, Valérie Plante had the most limited opportunities to implement transformative changes, as municipalities are on the lowest governance level of Canada's decentralised political system. They have little autonomy and, in contrast to Delga's and Ardern's governments and administrations, rely on both local and national governments regarding strategic planning and finances.

DOI: 10.4324/9781003507666-15

Regarding political parties, coalition arrangements generally promote innovation (Bischoff & Christiansen, 2021). However, the specific literature findings were inconclusive. On the one hand, innovation capacity may be highest when there is a recent alternation in governing political parties (Bischoff & Christiansen) and a significant ideological difference between past and current governments (Schmidt, 2002). In addition, a coalition consisting of new but few parties with similar and not opposing positions is favourable to progressive policy changes (Bischoff & Christiansen). On the other hand, coalitions with a higher number of parties may represent more diverse interests, leading to lower legislative output but potentially more innovative solutions. Short election cycles hamper the willingness to depart from the status quo (Bischoff & Christiansen), and significant policy changes are more likely, the longer governments stay in office (Schmidt). In contrast, if a replacement does not threaten party players, they may have fewer incentives to innovate and depart from the status quo (Bischoff & Christiansen).

For all three women, the configuration of the party system enabled their accession to office. In her first term, Ardern formed a coalition with New Zealand First and the Greens to become Prime Minister. Delga also formed a majority agreement with the EELV list to become Regional President, and Plante was voted Mayor because of her party's significantly differing positioning to former governing parties. In Jacinda Ardern's first term, the alternation of the governing parties, the ideological difference to the past government, and the number of parties in the coalition potentially promoted progressive policies. However, on the one hand, in Ardern's first coalition, the Labour and Green Parties held similar positions. On the other, they were partially opposite to New Zealand First, who watered down many of their proposals and thus posed a significant barrier to a more progressive agenda. Furthermore, the short election cycle may have hampered the coalition's innovation capacity and room for implementation. In Carole Delga's case, the coalition consisted of the Parti Socialiste and Green Party, with similar political positions, potentially beneficial to a progressive agenda in addition to the fact that they held a majority in the regional council. However, the PS had already governed the two former regions pre-merger, and thus there was only a partial alternation. In addition, Delga and her administration held their position for six years, which may both promote and hamper innovation. For Valérie Plante, the factors differed altogether. Projet Montréal held the majority without a coalition, which is only partially suitable for transformative policy agendas. Still, her electoral term was four years, potentially long enough to implement innovations but short enough to fear replacement. Considering these strongly varying observations and the fact that we cannot quantify the degree of political innovation pursued, no general conclusions can be drawn.

The individual party level also plays a significant role in the literature, but the findings are equally inconclusive. One body of literature suggests that parties with top-down decision-making may have a more substantial innovation capacity, but only if leadership is motivated to drive a progressive agenda (Bischoff & Christiansen, 2021). Another stated that wicked problems require collective leadership and horizontal, open, and democratic decision-making to promote innovation (Helms, 2016). Finally, parties with distinct ideologies are more likely to adopt innovative policies, while parties with broad, vague, and more centred ones may do the opposite (Bischoff & Christiansen). Ardern's Labour and Delga's Parti Socialiste both follow a centrist ideology, unfavourable to political innovation. Still, the more top-down leadership procedures of both parties and the leader's political will to promote a progressive agenda may have been favourable. For Plante, this again differed altogether, as Projet Montréal had a progressive ideology and open, democratic organisational structures that promoted political innovation. Judging from the literature, all three women had similar chances of promoting transformative agendas.

The state of the political leader's parties played a significant role in all three cases and was an enabling factor that helped the leaders ascend to office. New Zealand's Labour Party faced constant internal fighting and hostile public reception. Thus, several of its leaders resigned after a relatively short time, which allowed Ardern to rise quickly within the party. For Delga, the state of the Socialist Party was also favourable to some degree because Socialist politicians had been Regional Presidents of the two former regions, Midi-Pyrénées and Languedoc-Roussillon, for more than a decade. Thus, citizens had already demonstrated trust in her party before she ran for office. For Plante, the state of Projet Montréal was decisive in that the party positioned itself very differently from traditional leader-centric municipal parties, and citizens were seeking a new leader. Having a solid political program and party members engaged in grassroots activities throughout the years, the party inspired new trust and confidence in them. In addition, political parties are mobilising institutions for female political leaders in the Canadian municipal context. The state of the leader's parties thus played a central role in enabling the women to become agents for sustainable statehood.

Regarding the administrative sphere, hierarchies, silo structures, and closed top-down bureaucratic processes often hamper progressive agendas (Bommert, 2010). This applied to all three cases and was particularly true regarding past political decisions, which created path dependencies difficult for the women to overcome. Each case's introductory section provided a glimpse at past political decisions and the context the leaders faced, e.g., the influence of past neoliberal politics on social conditions. The leaders all met systemically rooted issues, such as environmental degradation and wealth inequality, which may require a time frame longer than one elective cycle to overcome. Ardern faced a bureaucracy designed to limit or slow progress. It was somewhat unfavourable to long-term progressive approaches, rooted in values of effectiveness and reliability rather than innovation and creativity. In addition, the short three-year electoral cycles hinder governments because bureaucrats and parliament take time to start working together. The 3-year cycle is also typically not long enough to implement long-term measures and for the public to perceive their results within the election cycle. For Carole Delga, the administrative sphere also represented a barrier, as the regions of France do not have enough autonomy and power over political decisions and finances but depend on the federal government for both. For Delga, the imposed merger of the former regions also led to opposition by staff, which initially hindered the development and implementation of a regional political program. Governance barriers equally restricted Valérie Plante. She and her administration relied on federal and provincial governments for financing and strategies, significantly limiting her scope to address systemic issues. In Plante's case, past administrative decisions were also particularly mentioned as a barrier. For example, her predecessor left a financial deficit that limited the implementation of her political agenda and made it necessary for her to raise taxes, leading to a public outcry. In addition, previous administrations had not invested in the city's infrastructure for around 25 years, leaving investment gaps Plante and her administration had to fill in the face of high debts. Thus the cases confirmed the findings from the literature that the administrative sphere can act as a significant barrier to political innovations.

However, the administrative sphere also acted as an enabler for all three women but only regarding past political decisions for sustainable development. Jacinda Ardern built on the Wellbeing Framework that the Labour Party government under Helen Clark had developed. Delga was enabled by the central government making it mandatory for regions to create the SRADDR, thus allowing her to develop a mission-oriented sustainable development plan obligatory for communes, departments, and territories. Regarding Plante, the Québec provincial government had a progressive vision of sustainable development and developed an extensive strategic planning framework that Plante mirrored with her approach. All three leaders thus built on a solid foundation. In addition, all three places had significant deficits regarding sustainable development, thus leaving even more leeway for respective political innovations.

The cases of New Zealand and Montréal further confirmed the decisive role of the public in creating pull factors for innovation by exerting significant pressure on political leaders to develop new, innovative policy agendas (Fukuyama, 2004; Kingdon, 2011). In two cases, the public demanded more significant environmental action, enabling Ardern's government to install, amongst others, the Zero Carbon Act and Plante's administration to drive the city's ecological transition. This could not be observed in the literature on Occitanie. Nonetheless, in all three cases, dire social conditions, such as housing crises and rising inequality, gave the leaders leeway for corresponding political innovations. However, overall, the cases suggest an unsuitable public arena for transformative agendas. This was especially true with the outbreak of the COVID-19 pandemic which acted as a break on the leader's transformative agendas. They had to direct most attention and finances toward relief measures. Thus, other projects were moving slower or stopped altogether. In addition, the pandemic led to the public's general dissatisfaction, which may have skewed the perception of the leader's actions.

The literature revealed a paradox for achieving sustainable statehood, which requires two preconditions: socio-institutional transformation via political innovations, i.e., progressive and potentially transformative agendas, and hegemony, specifically, as Francis Fukuyama (2004) reveals, in terms of sufficient social demands, which are crucial to expanding State scope and strength. Yet transition literature suggests that society is risk-averse and inexperienced at steering in fundamentally new directions (Patt et al., 2010). Instead of progressive or even transformative agendas, they typically accept incremental reforms in response to social, environmental, and economic pressures (Nalau & Handmer, 2015). In all three cases, culture did not fully promote innovation capacity (Prim et al., 2017). This may have led to the media framing progressive measures negatively, playing to the lack of innovation capacity, influencing public perception, and taking an active role in the political process (Cohen et al., 2008). Amongst others, this was the case with Jacinda Ardern's suggestion of a capital gains tax and Plante's closing of busy high-street roads to expand cycling lanes. In New Zealand, the people did not demand extensive reforms, despite their dissatisfaction with housing, poverty, and ecological challenges (Rashbrooke, 2021). However, they criticised Jacinda Ardern for promising a transformative government and not acting on her promises enough. The paradox between the public potentially knowing what needs to change and actually demanding these changes appears challenging to overcome and further supports the notion that citizens expect political leaders to justify their decisions and actively listen and respond to their ideas and demands (Rosanvallon, 2011).

These insights go hand in hand with the literature suggestion that governments tend to innovate in one-time big shots rather than ongoing and incrementally to minimise risks in fear of potential public failures and an image of gambling with public money (Bommert, 2010). The cases of Carole Delga and Valérie Plante confirmed this finding with transformative mission-oriented agendas along their Green Deal and Montréal 2030 programs. However, Jacinda Ardern's case contradicts the finding, as she pursued an approach of "radical incrementalism".

Finally, it is significant to contrast the state of women's rights and representation in all three cases because it strongly influenced how the women were perceived and their leeway for innovation. New Zealand was the most progressive as in 1893 the nation's women were the first in the world to gain the right to vote. Since then, New Zealanders have prided themselves on being leaders in the field of gender equality. In contrast, in Québec, women only gained voting rights in 1940, and in France, only in 1945. This also reflects on women's political representation. New Zealand has had three female prime ministers, and women comprise almost half of the current parliament's members. There has been no woman president in France, only two women prime ministers, and six women Regional Presidents in 2022. Canada has had only one woman prime minister, but she was appointed to office only after the former Prime Minister resigned and the public did not re-elect her. In 2023 only two out of ten provinces' first ministers were women, both of whom were the first to be elected in their provinces. Women also only held 18 percent of mayoral positions in the country. To conclude, Ardern thus faced a context that long recognised women's rights, where women's representation was relatively strong, and the public was already used to women prime ministers. Plante faced the opposite context because women's representation on all political levels, especially in municipalities, remained low. Finally, Delga met a political context where women were already present but not yet the norm. Solely judging by women's representation, Ardern thus had the best chances of being elected and accepted as prime minister. At the same time, gender presented more of a barrier to Delga and especially Plante. These differences led to all three leaders adopting different gender positioning strategies.

All three women came true to expected female stereotypes to some extent, including being kind, gentle (Klenke, 2017), sensitive (Eagly & Karau, 2002), and compassionate (Brooks, 2011). They were, however, also discriminated against by the media based on these traits and a perceived lack of fortitude related to male leadership (Montecinos, 2017). For

Ardern, it related to her good looks and being a mother. For Delga, it was based on her looks and young age. For Plante, it was based on her personality, looks, and lack of experience. Delga felt further hindered by the media because they paid less attention to women's opinions, and she had to work twice as hard to be heard. If the women, however, adopted stereotypical male qualities such as resolve and failed to be congruent with female stereotypes, they found themselves at a disadvantage, just as the literature suggested (Klenke, 2017). Thus, all three cases confirm that it is challenging for women leaders to perform required masculine, rational leadership while simultaneously subjecting to female ideals (Fletcher, 2004). The "female advantage" only partially applies to the male-dominated political sphere (Pullen & Vacchani, 2020). Respectively, all three women adapted their gender positioning and impression management to their contexts.

Despite gender acting as a barrier for the women, it was an enabler for Ardern's and Delga's succession to office and at least favourable for Plante. Ardern rose in Labour Party youth organisations and the party itself because they sought young women to join their leadership ranks. In addition, Ardern's experiences with sexism were relatively good because Helen Clark had previously shown the nation that women could be as good at politics as men. Therefore, Ardern could play more to her feminine side. When Ardern ran in the 2017 elections, a gender gap also appeared, with the women's voting share increasing significantly and women becoming more likely to vote than men. Gender equally aided Delga, as when she first ran for the mayor's office, the town actively sought a young woman candidate. In addition, citizens wanted something new in politics, and since French politics did not yet represent women well, Delga embodied renewal simply by being a woman. For Plante, however, gender was not necessarily favourable due to low women's representation on the municipal level. Correspondingly, she chose a degendering strategy for her campaign. In contrast to Ardern, there was no gender gap in the elections, and polls showed that gender was not the voters' essential selection criterion. Still, Plante ran for election in a context favourable to women because, at the time, the feminist movement was strong, and there was an increasing desire to see more women in politics. Since this movement was strong all over Canada, research suggested it favoured her campaign.

A further factor that helped the three women with gender-based discrimination was that they all had inspiring role models who taught them to be feminists and go for what they sought. For Ardern, it was her feminist and Labour Party-centred family background, her parents, and her favourite teacher. For Delga, it was mainly her grandmother and a schoolteacher. For Plante, it was both her parents and her university context. Accordingly, it is also fruitful to explore leaders' childhood and upbringing to fully understand how they could become successful agents for sustainable development, especially as women are faced with gender-based discrimination.

To conclude, the case analysis demonstrated that structures were often hindering the leader's efforts to drive political innovations even though the decisiveness for the leader's actions varied significantly. Still, several structures were both decisive and enabling for all three leaders, including their childhood and upbringing, social and ecological conditions, gender equality and women's representation, the state of the leader's parties and leadership, and past political decisions for sustainable development.

Agency is the key enabler for women political leaders' success

Jacinda Ardern, Carole Delga, and Valérie Plante all came true to the Aristotelian notion of Greek democracy, as they were political entrepreneurs who acted as orators, shaping public opinion, persuaders, convincing society of the need for change, and public-opinion leaders, creating political agendas for sustainable development (Körösényi, 2005). All three followed the latest notion of political leadership research, namely "collective" leadership, which shifts the focus to collective processes and practices to advance shared missions that the leaders could not achieve as individuals (Ospina & Foldy, 2016). Ardern, Delga, and Plante engaged various stakeholders in political decision-making processes, including political parties, businesses, administrative staff, and the public, enabling them to pursue more significant program innovations (Sørensen, 2020) via empowered participatory governance processes (Fung & Wright, 2003). They frequently conveyed that they are part of a greater team, working together towards a shared vision, and played to their informal authority, pointing out the privilege of acting in service of the public, and thereby generating trust, admiration, and respect for their executive position (Heifetz, 2010).

The literature suggested that political leaders and heads of ministries most often promote political innovations relating to systemic challenges (Borins, 2001). The research could not explicitly reveal where the cases' political innovations originated. Only in the case of the Living Standards Framework did the literature emphasise that the New Zealand Treasury initiated it. Still, following the three leaders' strong political convictions and visions, the findings suggest that political leaders have substantial influence over political agendas and thus drive respective innovations. Another essential suggestion regarding public sector innovation was that processes must be more open and collaborative, especially to external networks and communities, to increase the quantity and quality of innovations (Bommert, 2010). This is particularly relevant when dealing with complex, large-scale, and pressing social issues such as climate change or mental health (Harris & Albury, 2009). All three cases confirmed this finding. The leaders drove their innovations via respective processes, e.g., through mission-oriented strategy frameworks that contributed to overcoming silos within the administration, enabled greater cooperation on systemic issues, and integrated various stakeholders in participation processes.

Relating the theoretical findings on transformative leadership styles to the case studies, it becomes evident that Ardern's, Delga's, and Plante's leadership styles matched the traits and competencies of the reviewed models. They demonstrated Authentic Leadership, including positive psychological capacities, a positive ethical perspective, self-awareness, self-regulatory behaviours, and veritable and sustained performance in dynamic and emergent contexts (Avolio et al., 2004; Avolio & Gardner, 2005). They employed Transformational Leadership by building trust, acting with integrity, encouraging people and innovative thinking, and rewarding achievements (Bass & Riggio, 2006). Regarding the five-factor personality model, all three leaders displayed Openness, Extraversion, Agreeableness, and Conscientiousness traits. The cases thus support past findings that Extraversion and Agreeableness are predictors of Transformational Leadership (Judge & Bono, 2000). The cases further confirmed the nexus between female leaders, Transformational Leadership (Stempel et al., 2015), and Authentic Leadership (Ruderman et al., 2002). Finally, regarding the Social Change Model of Leadership, the women displayed the individual values consciousness of self, congruence, and commitment, as well as the collective values for collaboration, a common purpose, controversy with civility, citizenship, and change (Roberts, 2017). To conclude, the case findings imply that women leaders may be specially cut out for transformative leadership styles.

Regarding specific competencies, the leaders matched all three explored leadership models: Meta-governance, Institutional Entrepreneurship, and the Collective Leadership Compass. The women acted as meta-governors, engaging in network design, framing, management, and participation activities (Ottens & Edelenbos, 2018; Sørensen & Torfing, 2009). Still, the cases suggest that executive political leaders are not likely to engage in the more project management-oriented meta-governance tasks, such as setting deadlines or designing specific procedures. Instead, their focus may lie more on tasks such as agenda setting, reducing tensions amongst conflicting actors, and creating a sense of ownership, trust, and commitment. In the case of Institutional Leadership (Battilana et al., 2009; Walker et al., 2004), Ardern, Delga, and Plante followed the three critical steps of change implementation by developing a vision, mobilising actors, and motivating them to achieve and sustain the vision both within their coalitions and beyond the State (Battilana et al., 2009). Furthermore, they all demonstrated remarkable communication skills, using discourse to convince and mobilise others of the need for change. The three leaders also engaged in resource mobilisation, e.g., by strengthening their social position and, in Delga's case, financial resources, as she obtained national and international private business funding for the Green Deal (Batillana et al.). They further built trust and legitimacy via their leadership, developed or at least facilitated the implementation of political innovations, and Ardern and Delga specifically facilitated conflict resolutions and negotiations within their coalition (Westley et al., 2013). Finally, regarding the Collective Leadership Compass, Ardern, Delga, and Plante promoted collective leadership, which is essential for improving the status quo (Künkel, 2019). They all played to the six dimensions of future possibilities, engagement, innovation, humanity, collective intelligence, and wholeness. As I demonstrated, these dimensions primarily manifest in soft skills such as empathy, optimism, and a drive to advance the common good. All three leaders demonstrated these to a great extent.

Whilst the previous leadership models are gender-neutral, some capabilities are specifically relevant for women leaders. The most fundamental was political savvy, referring to leaders who live by a code of ethics, do not follow self-serving goals and agendas, have low ego needs, and know the importance of forming coalitions and alliances (Klenke, 2017). All three women clarified their motivation for the common good, laid out their code of ethics, emphasised that their executive positions and service to the public were a privilege, and sought to form alliances. They further demonstrated that they believed in and cared about the issues at hand, played above the board to legitimise their tasks to build momentum for change, and showed interpersonal diplomacy on many occasions (Klenke). Valérie Plante represented an exception in some cases, where her words and actions did not match, and Ardern and Delga further stood out in terms of their coalition-building skills, and Delga in terms of building alliances beyond her region and administration.

Another skill the leaders managed was impression management (Klenke, 2017), including exemplification (Gardner & Clevenger, 1998), ingratiation (Ambler, 2005), and contextual intelligence (Ambler). However, only Ardern engaged in supplication (Klenke), i.e., presenting herself as vulnerable to secure empathy. None of the women used intimidation strategies, i.e., aggressively showing anger to get voters' attention, achieve higher performance ratings, and convey the ability to get the job done (Klenke).

Finally, referring to power exercise, the literature stressed that exercising "power with" rather than "power over" is more typical for women leaders (Coleman, 2011) because they do not want power for power's sake but to improve the lives of others (Klenke, 2017). The case studies only partially supported these findings. Jacinda Ardern, who positioned herself as the most feminine of the three and followed an incremental change approach, was the only one to primarily exercise "power with". In personal interviews, both Delga and Plante stressed that sometimes they needed to exercise "power over," especially when pushing for changes they deemed essential, but stakeholders may have perceived differently. This finding may be particularly relevant for more progressive and transformative policy programs since humans tend to be risk-averse, avoiding changes they do not feel comfortable with (Patt et al., 2010). Transformations for sustainable development require a fundamental redistribution of values, which some stakeholders may be uncomfortable with (Patt et al.). The two cases thus suggest that women political leaders pursuing more progressive policy agendas may occasionally have to use "power over" to drive transformation.

There were also limits to the women's agency. For both Ardern and Plante, the election promises they made but could not keep led to dissatisfaction with their leadership. Ardern had pledged transformational change but could not fully translate it into policies and processes. For example, many of the government's decisions still build on cost-benefit analysis rather than the Wellbeing Framework, many policy proposals were watered down after negotiations within and outside her coalition, and she had to step back from some of her election promises. There was limited information on whether Carole Delga's agency was a barrier to her leadership. On two occasions, former coalition partners and political opponents stated she was dogmatic, discriminatory against other political ideas, and ready to throw others under the bus for her program. Still, I cannot substantiate these claims. Valérie Plante's critique was somewhat the opposite of Ardern's, as she pushed for transformative changes during the COVID-19 crisis and, thus, when the public may not have been ready for change. The media consequently stated that she was unaware of citizens' realities. At the same time, she was unable to fulfill some of her major election promises, such as implementing the Pink metro line. On several occasions, the public and colleagues also questioned her integrity and leadership style, e.g., when she failed to admit that she had broken a significant election promise or when colleagues seemingly quit due to her authoritarian leadership. Overall, however, the cross-case analysis suggests that agency was not a significant barrier to the women's leadership, especially regarding the number of terms they were in office.

To conclude the analysis, all agency factors, ranging from the women's background to traits, competencies, and leadership style, enabled the three leaders to successfully drive political innovations for sustainable statehood and development.

Political innovations are a prerequisite for sustainable statehood

Moving on to the specific political programs and innovations, the practical research supports the theoretical findings that the State and political leaders can play a significant role in driving sustainable development (Meadowcroft, 2011). All three leaders drove political innovations aimed at establishing sustainable statehood. These included a new narrative for sustainable statehood and development (Göpel, 2016; Mazzucato, 2018; WBGU, 2011), the institutionalisation of this narrative within State institutions (Heinrichs, 2022; Heinrichs & Laws, 2014; WBGU, 2011; WWF, 2012), and the enabling of greater leadership for sustainable development within and beyond the State (Braams et al., 2021; Heinrichs & Laws, 2014; Rotmans et al., 2001). The women deliberately created the circumstances and possibilities for these innovations (Selman, 2002) in their efforts to implement innovations in polity, politics, and policies (Sørensen, 2021) with a normative orientation towards sustainable development. Thereby they aimed for socio-institutional transformations that change cultures, structures, and practices (Loorbach et al., 2017).

Moving on to the strategies the leaders employed, the case studies demonstrated that the women used sustaincentric approaches and a taming strategy within the rules of capitalism (Wright, 2019). Based on the research, I cannot tell whether the leaders' ultimate aim was to dismantle or erode capitalism in the future. Still, in many instances, they implemented non-reformist reforms to transition their social systems toward sustainable development. Setting this in perspective, as discussed in Chapter 2, transformational processes take a long time and include different phases. All three leaders may have acted in the pre-development and take-off phases of a transformation towards a more sustainable social order (Mersmann et al., 2014; WBGU, 2011). The initial research on potential cases thereby revealed that they represented frontrunner exceptions rather than the norm. At the same time, the leader's relatively incremental approaches within the rules of the capitalist game enabled them to implement their political programs successfully, thereby potentially forming a new hegemony. That way, as Jacinda Ardern put it, the leaders were able to create changes that "stick" and lead the way toward the acceleration phase. In this phase, political leaders may implement a more significant number and potentially more radical political innovations for sustainable development so that a new hegemony and respective institutionalisation efforts may stabilise, rather than lock in, backlash, or lead to the system's breakdown.

From the sighted materials, there are no signs that the women aimed to change the capitalist social order's foreground characteristics. To recapitulate, these include class division, the institutionalised marketisation and commodi-fication of wage labour, the dynamic of capital accumulation, and allocative markets (Jaeggi & Fraser, 2020). However, all three sought to relieve the effects of these foreground conditions on the background conditions of social reproduction, non-human nature, racism, imperialism, and expropriation (Fraser & Jaeggi) through their political programs.

Finally, looking through an intersectional lens, all three leaders priori-tised relieving effects on social reproduction and the exploitation of non-human nature within their territories. In addition, Ardern and Plante delib-erately tried to support the Indigenous population and immigrants, thereby countering racism, their colonial past, and minorities' exploitation. How-ever, there was no evidence that the women aimed to relieve the capitalist social order's effects outside their geographic location. It thus appears as though they were taking a privileged Western approach to sustainable development, setting their focus within the borders of their territories rather than outside of them, where the capitalist social order continues to exploit both humans and non-human nature.

Overall, the cases demonstrated that sustainable development requires political innovations for sustainable statehood and the power that women political leaders have in driving change in their social systems.

How women political leaders may become agents for sustainable development

To conclude this chapter, women political leaders seeking to become agents for sustainable development face a broad array of structural factors that may hamper their endeavours and it is particularly their agency that lets them succeed. Jacinda Ardern's, Carole Delga's, and Valérie Plante's cases demonstrated the validity of the normative concept of *women's political leadership for sustainable development*, as all three leaders acted as politi-cal entrepreneurs who drove political agendas for sustainable statehood with the goal of sustainable development.

To be successful at their attempts, the literature and cross-case analysis suggest that the following prerequisites support women political leaders in becoming agents for sustainable development:

1 Their childhood and upbringing exposed them to social, economic, or environmental challenges and influential role models, both shaping their political convictions and leadership.
2 Social and ecological conditions are dire enough to promote demand for and leeway for political innovations.

3 Prior governments and administrations on their governance level or above, installed solid political programs for sustainable development for the leaders to build on.
4 The leaders must act in a social context where women's leadership is promoted and sought after.
5 The configuration of the party system must be favourable to their election to leadership, either due to coalition agreements or the positioning of their political party.
6 They should have a positive outlook on feminism that allows them to overcome gender biases and choose a context-sensitive gender positioning strategy to overcome female stereotypes.
7 They must have systemic knowledge of sustainable development challenges and hold and communicate a solid political vision for a sustainable future.
8 Their personality traits should match Openness, Extraversion, Agreeableness, and Conscientiousness, along the Five-factor Personality Model.
9 They should employ collective and transformative leadership styles.
10 They need sufficient analytical, personal, communication, positional, strategic, organizational, and follower empowerment competencies.
11 They must use the right mix of "power with," adhering to the public's demands, and "power over" to do what is necessary to drive a progressive agenda.
12 They must install a new narrative for sustainable statehood and development, institutionalise it, and enable greater leadership for sustainable development both within and beyond the State.

References

Ambler, G. (2005). *Understanding leadership in context*. www.thepracticeofleadership. net/2005/12/08/understanding-leadership-context/

Avolio, B. J., & Gardner, W. L. (2005). Authentic leadership development: Getting to the root of positive forms of leadership. *The Leadership Quarterly*, 16(3), 315–338. https://doi.org/10.1016/j.leaqua.2005.03.001

Avolio, B. J., Gardner, W. L., Luthans, F., & May, D. R. (2004). Unlocking the mask: A look at the process by which authentic leaders impact follower attitudes and behaviors. *Management Department Faculty Publications*, 15(6), 1–35. https://doi.org/10.1016/j.leaqua.2004.09.003

Bass, B. M., & Riggio, R. E. (2006). *Transformational leadership* (2nd ed.). Brighton: Psychology Press.

Battilana, J., Leca, B., & Boxenbaum, E. (2009). How actors change institutions: Towards a theory of Institutional Entrepreneurship. *Academy of Management Annals*, 3(1), 65–107. https://doi.org/10.5465/19416520903053598

Bischoff, C. S., & Christiansen, F. J. (2021). Political parties and innovation. In Sørensen, E. (Ed.), *Political innovations. Creative transformations in polity, politics and policy* (pp. 74–89). New York, NY: Routledge.

Bommert, B. (2010). Collaborative innovation in the public sector. *International Public Management Review*, *11*(1), 15–33. https://doi.org/10.4337/978184980 9757.00032

Borins, S. (2001). Leadership and innovation in the public sector. *Leadership and Organization Development Journal*, *23*(8), 467–476. https://doi.org/10.1108/ 01437730210449357

Braams, R. B., Wesseling, J. H., Meijer, A. J., & Hekkert, M. P. (2021). Legitimizing transformative government. Aligning essential government tasks from transition literature with normative arguments about legitimacy from public administration traditions. *Environmental Innovation and Societal Transitions*, *39*, 191–205. https://doi.org/10.1016/j.eist.2021.04.004

Brooks, D. (2011). Testing the double standard for candidate emotionality: Voter reactions to the tears and anger of male and female politicians. *Journal of Politics*, *73*(2), 597–615. https://doi.org/10.1017/s0022381611000053

Cohen, J., Tsfati, Y., & Sheafer, T. (2008). The Influence of presumed media influence in politics. *Public Opinion Quarterly*, *72*(2), 331–344. https://doi.org/10. 1093/poq/nfn014

Coleman, M. (2011). *Women at the top. Challenges, choices and change*. London: Palgrave Macmillan.

Eagly, A. H., & Karau, S. J. (2002). Role congruity theory of prejudice toward female leaders. *Psychological Review*, *109*(3), 573–598. https://doi.org/10.1037// 0033-295X.109.3.573

Fischer, L.-B., & Newig, J. (2016). Importance of actors and agency in sustainability transitions: A systematic exploration of the literature. *Sustainability*, *8*(476), 1–21. https://doi.org/10.3390/su8050476

Fletcher, J. K. (2004). The paradox of postheroic leadership: An essay on gender, power, and transformational change. *The Leadership Quarterly*, *15*(5), 647–661. https://doi.org/10.1016/j.leaqua.2004.07.004

Fukuyama, F. (2004). *State-building: Governance and world order in the twenty-first century*. Ithaca, NY: Cornell University Press.

Fung, A., & Wright, E. O. (2003). *Deepening democracy: Institutional innovations in empowered participatory governance*. London: Verso.

Gardner, W., & Clevenger, D. (1998). Impression management techniques associated with transformational leadership leaders at the world class level. *Management Communication Quarterly*, *12*(1), 237–251. https://doi.org/10.1177/ 0893318998121001

Göpel, M. (2016). *The great mindshift*. Wiesbaden, Germany: Springer.

Harris, M., & Albury, D. (2009). *Why radical innovation is needed for the recession and beyond: The Innovation Imperative*. NESTA. https://media.nesta.org. uk/documents/the_innovation_imperative.pdf

Heifetz, R. (2010). Leadership. In Couto, R. A. (Eds.), *Political and civic leadership: A reference handbook* (pp. 12–22). Thousand Oaks, CA: SAGE Publications.

Heinrichs, H. (2022). Sustainable statehood: Reflections on critical (pre-)conditions and design options. *Sustainability*, *14*(15): 9461. https://doi.org/10.3390/ su14159461

Heinrichs, H., & Laws, N. (2014). "Sustainability state" in the making? Institutionalization of sustainability in German federal policy making. *Sustainability*, 6(5), 2623–2641. https://doi.org/10.3390/su6052623

Helms, L. (2016). Democracy and innovation: From institutions to agency and leadership. *Democratization*, 23(3), 459–477. https://doi.org/10.1080/13510347. 2014.981667

Jaeggi, R., & Fraser, N. (2020). *Kapitalismus. Ein Gespräch über kritische Theorie* [*Capitalism. A conversation about critical theory*]. Berlin, Germany: suhrkamp.

Judge, T. A., & Bono, J. E. (2000). Five-factor model of personality and transformational leadership. *Journal of Applied Psychology*, 85(5), 751–765. https://doi.org/10.1037/0021-9010.85.5.751

Kingdon, J. W. (2011). *Agendas, alternatives, and public policies* (2nd ed.). New York, NY: Longman.

Klenke, K. (2017). *Women in leadership* (2nd ed.). Bingley: Emerald Publishing.

Körösényi, A. (2005). Political representation in leader democracy. *Government and Opposition*, 40(3), 358–378. https://doi.org/10.1111/j.1477-7053.2005. 00155.x

Künkel, P. (2019). *Stewarding sustainability transformations*. Cham, Switzerland: Springer Nature

Loorbach, D., Frantzeskaki, N., & Avelino, F. (2017). Sustainability transitions research: Transforming science and practice for societal change. *Annual Review of Environment and Resources*, 42(1), 599–626. https://doi.org/10.1146/annurev-environ-102014-021340

Mazzucato, M. (2018). *The entrepreneurial state. Debunking public vs. private sector myths*. London: Penguin Randomhouse.

Meadowcroft, J. (2011). Engaging with the politics of sustainability transitions. *Environmental Innovation and Societal Transitions*, 1(1), 70–75. https://doi.org/10.1016/j.eist.2011.02.003

Mersmann, F., Holm Olsen, K., Wehner, T., & Boodoo, Z. (2014). *From theory to practice. Understanding transformational change in NAMAs*. Wuppertal Institute and UNEP DTU Partnership. https://epub.wupperinst.org/frontdoor/deliver/index/docId/5700/file/5700_Transformational_Change.pdf

Montecinos, V. (2017). Introduction. In Monetcinos, V. (Ed.), *Women presidents and prime ministers in post-transition democracies* (pp. 1–36). London: Palgrave Macmillan.

Nalau, J., & Handmer, J. (2015). When is transformation a viable policy alternative? *Environmental Science & Policy*, 54, 349–356.

Ospina, S. M., & Foldy, E. G. (2016). Collective dimensions of leadership. In Farazmand, A. (Ed.), *Global encyclopedia of public administration, public policy, and governance* (pp. 838–844). https://doi.org/10.1007/978-3-319-20928-9_2202

Ottens, M., & Edelenbos, J. (2018). Political leadership as meta-governance in sustainability transitions: A case study analysis of meta-governance in the case of the Dutch National Agreement on Climate. *Sustainability*, 11(1), 110. https://doi.org/10.3390/su11010110

Patt, A., Reckien, D., Klein, R. J. T., Van Vuuren, D., Wrobel, M., Bauer, N., Eskeland, G. S., & Downing, T. E. (2010). What can social science tell us about meeting the challenge of climate change? Five insights from five years that might make a difference. In Hulme, M., & Neufeldt, H. (Eds.). *Making climate change work for us: European perspectives on adaptation and mitigation strategies* (pp. 369–388). Cambridge: Cambridge University Press.

Prim, A. L., Filho, L. S., Zamur, G. A. C., & di Serio, L. C. (2017). The relationship between national culture dimensions and degree of innovation. *International Journal of Innovation Management, 21*(1), 173001. https://doi.org/10.1142/s136391961730001x

Pullen, A., & Vacchani, S. J. (2020). Feminist ethics and women leaders: From difference to intercorporeality. *Journal of Business Ethics, 173*(2), 1–11. https://doi.org/10.1007/s10551-020-04526-0

Rashbrooke, M. (2021). Jacinda Ardern. Good in a crisis but cautious when not. *IPPR: Progressive Review, 28*(2), 134–139. https://doi.org/10.1111/newe.12258

Roberts, D. C. (2017). Understanding the social change model of leadership development. In Komives, S. R., & Wagner, W. (Eds.). *Leadership for a better world* (pp. 35–37). San Francisco, CA: John Wiley & Sons.

Rosanvallon, P. (2011). *Democratic legitimacy.* Princeton, NY: Princeton University Press.

Rotmans, J., Kemp, R., & van Asselt, M. (2001). More evolution than revolution: Transition management in public policy. *Foresight, 3*(1), 15–31. https://doi.org/10.1108/14636680110803003

Ruderman, M. N., Ohlott, P. J., Panzer, K., & King, S. N. (2002). Benefits of multiple roles for managerial women. *Academy of Management Journal, 45*(2), 369–386. https://doi.org/10.5465/3069352

Schmidt, M. G. (2002). Political performance and types of democracy: Findings from comparative studies. *European Journal of Political Research, 41*(1), 147–163. https://doi.org/10.1111/1475-6765.00007

Selman, J. (2002). Leadership and innovation: Relating to circumstances and change. *The Public Sector Innovation Journal, 7*(3), 1–9. https://innovation.cc/discussion-papers/2002_7_3_5_selman_leadership-innovation.pdf

Sørensen, E. (2020). *Interactive political leadership. The role of politicians in the age of governance.* Oxford: Oxford University Press.

Sørensen, E. (2021). Political innovations: Innovations in political institutions, processes and outputs. In Sørensen, E. (Ed.), *Political innovations. Creative transformations in polity, politics and policy* (pp. 1–19). New York, NY: Routledge.

Sørensen, E., & Torfing, J. (2009). Making governance networks effective and democratic through metagovernance. *Public Administration, 87*(2), 234–258. https://doi.org/10.1111/j.1467-9299.2009.01753.x

Stempel, C. R., Rigotti, T., & Mohr, G. (2015). Think transformational leadership – think female? *Leadership, 11*(3), 259–280. https://doi.org/10.1177/1742715015590468

Walker, B. H., Holling, S. R., Carpenter, S. R., & Kinzig, A. (2004). Resilience, adaptability and transformability in social-ecological systems. *Ecology and Society, 9*(2), 5. https://doi.org/10.5751/es-00650-090205

WBGU. (2011). *World in transition. A social contract for sustainability.* https://www.wbgu.de/en/publications/publication/world-in-transition-a-social-contract-for-sustainability#section-downloads

Westley, F. R., Tjornbo, O., Schultz, L., Olsson, P., Folke, C., Crona, B., & Bodin, Ö. (2013). A theory of transformative agency in linked social-ecological systems. *Ecology and Society, 18*(3), 27. https://doi.org/10.5751/es-05072-180327

Wright, E. O. (2019). *How to be an anticapitalist in the twenty-first century.* London: Verso.

WWF. (2012). *Mehr Macht für eine nachhaltige Zukunft. Politikbarometer zur Nachhaltigkeit in Deutschland [More power for a sustainable future. Political barometer about sustainability in Germany].* https://www.wwf.de/fileadmin/fm-wwf/Publikationen-PDF/WWF_Politikbarometer.PDF

CONCLUSION

The future potential for women political leaders and sustainable development

We are living in increasingly turbulent times. While conducting the research for this book over the course of four years and writing up the final manuscript, a variety of economic, political, social, and environmental events shook people around the globe: Belarus protested for fair and free elections (Lindsay, 2020, December 17); protesters around the globe joined the Black Lives Matter movement against racial inequality; Australia was burning as a consequence of climate change, the United States witnessed historically destructive tropical storms, and the Sahara fell victim to draughts; the United States, under President Trump, left the Paris Agreement; the large-scale systematic repression of the Uighurs by the Chinese was exposed; the United Kingdom exited the European Union; the COVID- 19 pandemic spread across the globe (Lindsay); supply chains faltered due to COVID-19 (Lindsay, 2021, December 15); migration to the United States and the European Union came to all-time highs, as political and environmental events displaced around 84 million people around the world; the Taliban returned to power in Afghanistan; the global democratic erosion continued in countries such as the United States, India, Brazil, Russia, and Hong Kong; the UN called out "a code red for humanity," as countries failed to meet their emissions targets and record droughts, flooding, wildfires, and monsoons ravaged around the globe (Lindsay); Russia invaded Ukraine, starting the first war on European soil since World War II (Zemelyte, 2022, July 8); abortion was banned in the United States and Poland, repressing women's rights (Bryant, 2022, June 25; Zukowski, 2021, October 19); the "Women, life, freedom" protests shook Iran

DOI: 10.4324/9781003507666-16

(Lindsay, 2022, December 6); inflation rose across the world as the COVID pandemic eased (Lindsay, 2022, December 6); climate change effects intensified, e.g., when more than one-third of Pakistan was flooded (The Guardian, 2022, September 3); the global democratic recession continued in Africa, India, South America, and Europe (Lindsay, 2023, December 8); US-China tensions continued to escalate; Israel started a war on Hamas in Gaza, threatening a broader Middle East War; global temperatures broke all records (Lindsay), and scientists established that we crossed seven out of eight quantified planetary boundaries (Rockström et al., 2023).

Whilst this excerpt of events provides but a glimpse at the complexity of today's fast-changing world and plays to the human negativity bias (Pinker, 2018) many are also but a range of "morbid symptoms" (Hoare & Nowell-Smith, 1971) of the Global North's unsustainable social order. These quickly occurring events expose its fragility and contradictions, as the political and economic sphere, social contracts and values, and ecological stability keep faltering. They are a not-so-gentle reminder that the "old" cannot last, and we must transition to a "new". Still, as pointed out in the introduction, the "new" is lingering, and too little appears to be happening too late.

The book argued that the State and politics must move to the forefront of the transition to a "new", steering society towards a sustainable future. We need women political leaders who, rather than managing the immediate, have a sharp sense of reality and a powerful vision of the future, striving to transform the current social order so that humanity and non-human nature may flourish.

The predicaments of the capitalist social order

Exploring capitalism's evolution as an institutionalised social order, the research revealed that we can look back at a mixed balance sheet. Capitalism has enabled remarkable progress for humankind and improved living conditions for many. Still, at the same time, its foreground characteristics had detrimental effects on the entire web of life on which it depends. From Mercantile Capitalism to Sustainable Capitalism, once one regime could no longer solve the crises it had created, a new one replaced it in a dialectical process. Thereby all regimes of this "old" social order are built on ever-increasing growth and an Imperial Mode of Living that goes hand in hand with the expropriation and exploitation of humans and non-human nature. In this logic, the capitalist social order cannot stabilise. Instead, it leads to ever-new instabilities, and it appears as though the capitalist growth model has approached its economic, ecological, and social limits.

The necessary transformation to sustainable development

The counter-notion to capitalist exploitation, expropriation, and ever-increasing growth that may define the "new" is sustainable development. It has been a contested concept because its interpretations and the strategies for achieving it vary significantly along paradigms and the degree to which proponents perceive environmental and social equality concerns to be dire.

Sustaincentric approaches seek to stay within the rules of capitalism and tame it to alleviate increasingly recognised social and environmental problems. The central premise is that we may make our social order sustainable via inclusive green growth once we improve market mechanisms and accelerate technological innovation. The result is the current Sustainable Capitalist regime with its respective reformist agendas and measures from the Paris Agreement to the European Green Deal. To date, these strategies achieved considerable progress, and their estimated potential is significant regarding social inequality and environmental harm. Still, capitalist fractions promote these strategies, seeking to commodify emerging social and environmental problems for capital accumulation, providing few, with higher material wellbeing and not stopping environmental degradation.

The current Sustainable Capitalist regime is still in its early stages. Nonetheless, its internal contradictions are already increasingly exposed, leading to flourishing deficits in the web of life, as argued throughout the last parts of the second chapter and the opening lines of this conclusion. Once again, a capitalist regime is creating more problems than it is solving, leading large parts of society to call it into question in the current era of historical transition and societal upheaval. Considering capitalism's balance sheet, the greatest challenge for societies in the 21st century must be increasing societal standards while protecting the Earth's ecosystem. And once again, we may expect that, in a dialectical process, a new regime, potentially a Regenerative Capitalist one, or even a new social order, will succeed the current one. As pointed out in the introduction, this "new" is lingering, and we must actively promote it.

Proponents of socio-ecocentric views have already proposed several approaches for a more radical "new". They hold that the social order that has driven us into severe economic, social, and ecological crises cannot be their panacea. Rather than taming capitalism, they seek to transform it via non-reformist reforms that significantly alter and ideally dismantle or erode capitalist logics. The steady-state economy, new economics of prosperity, and degrowth upkeep capitalism's fundamental institutions, including, amongst others, markets and price systems. Conversely, eco-socialism aims to overcome capitalist logics and build a new social order.

Opponents may, however, deem these approaches too radical regarding human-risk aversiveness and current institutional configurations.

The overall exploration revealed that sustaincentric approaches could indeed significantly alleviate social and environmental harms, but only a transformation of the current social order may genuinely enable humanity's and non-human nature's flourishing. Yet, this evaluation must consider the bigger picture of transformation processes. Looking at history, societal transformations typically take between 40 to 80 years. Sustainable development has been on the agenda for nearly 50 years and inclusive green growth for around 10 years. Respectively, sustaincentric approaches may be the necessary precondition for socio-ecocentric visions. They contribute to coalition building, regulatory changes, and the anchoring of social acceptance for sustainable development. Thereby the approaches accelerate the move along the transformation path, potentially paving the way for a transformation of capitalism.

In any case, all approaches attest to the vital role of the State in driving respective measures, and a key to understanding how we may promote sustainable development is thus how the State can come true to this task.

Sustainable statehood is a prerequisite for sustainable development

Chapters 1 and 2 demonstrated that the State was and is critical to capitalism's evolution, amongst others, by enabling and guaranteeing property rights and driving economic development. Respectively, I argued that it could also be at the centre of taming or transforming the capitalist social order for sustainable development.

Governance literature reveals that the neoliberal agenda retrenched the State, downsized its institutions, restricted its leeway for action, and shaped public perception to its detriment. Today, the State is not set up to take on its decisive role in driving sustainable development. What further complicates this is the Capitalist State's bind to capital accumulation, which it must maintain for its democratic legitimacy. In this bind, it is important to understand how actors may extend the State's strength and scope to set it up for the pursuit of sustainable development, following the notion that actors have the agency and strategic potential to do so.

A central finding is that political actors must promote sustainable statehood for sustainable development. First and foremost, this includes repositioning the State's public image and replacing the notion that it primarily focuses on economic growth with one of providing public value. Hand in hand with this repositioning, actors must establish a hegemonic vision for why sustainable development is desirable, paramount, urgent, and possible, as narratives play a vital role in forming identities, collective visions, and strategies for systemic transformations. The central successional challenge is implementing this new narrative by altering State institutions and processes that run counter to the requirements of sustainable development. These revolve around innovations in polity, politics, and policies and include, amongst others, creating new institutions, establishing long-term planning, and evaluating measures along sustainable development dimensions ex-ante and ex-post. Finally, this pursuit also requires significant human resource development to build capacities and competencies for greater leadership for sustainable development in the parliamentary, administrative, and public spheres.

A prerequisite for extending State scope and strength in line with this argumentation is sufficient demands from the State's stakeholders, including social, economic, and political actors and, indirectly, the environment. Only if State actors obtain legitimacy for this new hegemonic project can they promote sustainable statehood and thus drive sustainable development. Political leaders are thereby predestined to directly select and channel these demands into the political process as citizens appoint them to defend the public interest. Furthermore, they potentially have the knowledge, resources, and competencies to develop political innovations for sustainable development and drive their implementation. Thus, much of the responsibility for enabling sustainable statehood rests with them.

Women political leaders are vital to the pursuit of sustainable development

Chapter 3 conceptualised the phenomenon of political leadership for sustainable development, which is a prerequisite for sustainable statehood and, thus, sustainable development. Since political scientists thus far neglected the phenomenon in research, the theoretical exploration was extended beyond political leadership literature to include disciplines focusing on transformative leadership for social change, institutional innovations, and transitions.

Political leadership for sustainable development entails said leaders becoming political entrepreneurs who promote political innovations with a normative orientation towards sustainable development, defined as intentional efforts to transform polity, politics, and policies for sustainable statehood. The literature confirms that women political leaders may take on a particular role in driving said innovations because there appears to be a nexus between women leaders and transformational leadership. They are still perceived as a novelty and may thus particularly respond to increasing demands for change.

Understanding how women political leaders can become agents of sustainable development required an in-depth exploration of the various structure and agency variables that may hinder and enable them. The literature revealed contextual factors ranging from the public, administrative, and parliamentary arenas to the leader's gender. Agency factors, on the other hand, ranged from general strategic capabilities to women-specific qualities and leadership styles.

Finally, existing frameworks for analysing leadership outcomes differed along the structure-agency duality. Some emphasised the decisiveness of structures, such as political time. Others pointed to an interplay of structure and agency and the decisiveness of institutional context and political will, skills in context, leadership resources, and external pressures, or a combination of context, skills, individual capabilities, and power.

A framework of women's political leadership for sustainable development synthesises these findings, as shown in Figure 11.1.

Agency is the central enabler of women's political leadership for sustainable development

The research generated many lessons about women political leaders aiming to become agents for sustainable development in the 21st century. The phenomenon of *women's political leadership for sustainable development*, first and foremost, entails acting as a political entrepreneur, in the sense of an orator, persuader, and public-opinion leader. The women explored deliberately created the circumstances and possibilities for innovating polity, politics, and policies to promote sustainable statehood and sustainable development.

Women political leaders seeking to be successful at this attempt should ideally follow a collective leadership approach, creating empowered participatory governance processes to advance shared missions they could not achieve individually. In this, their formal authority allows said leaders to drive their visions but their informal authority may be even more significant in legitimising their actions. Informal authority connects to the traits and capabilities laid out along the Authentic, Transformational, and Social Change models of leadership. These leadership styles generate high levels of trust and inspire and empower followers and stakeholders to pursue shared objectives for the common good. Thereby, women leaders may be specifically prone to transformative leadership styles, implying that they are specially cut out for political leadership for sustainable development.

In all three cases, the women broke with predominant top-down male political leadership styles by following transformative leadership styles,

STRUCTURE

External context
- Historical developments
- State of democracy and legitimation of state rule
- Social conditions
- Economic conditions
- Ecological conditions
- Stakeholder demands for sustainable development
- International prestige of the nation
- Role of supranational bodies
- Dependence on the international economy
- Culture
- Gender equality and women's representation

External actor-related context
- Childhood and upbringing

Internal State context
- Institutional culture & processes
- Configuration of the party system
- Stability of the current government
- Policy legacies
- State responsibilities and tasks
- Stakeholder demands for sustainable development
- Past political decisions
- Gender equality

Internal party context
- Organisational culture & processes
- Alliances
- Political program
- Gender equality
- State of the party and its leadership

AGENCY

Background
- Work experience: career or non-career politician
- Feminist stance on gender

Political agenda
- Political vision for a sustainable future

Traits
- Openness
- Extraversion
- Agreeableness
- Conscientiousness

Power
- Positional/formal
- Power exercise

Leadership style
- Authentic Leadership
- Transformational Leadership
- Social Change Leadership

Competencies
Along meta-governance, IE, CLC
- Personal
- Analytical
- Communication
- Positional
- Strategic
- Organisational
- Follower empowerment

Positioning
- Context-sensitive gender strategy

POLITICAL OUTCOME

Political innovations for sustainable development
- Narrative for sustainable statehood and sustainable development
- Institutionalisation of narrative within the State
- Enabling of greater leadership for sustainable development

FIGURE 11.1 Table showing the framework of women's political leadership for sustainable development.

coupling "soft" qualities such as compassion with stereotypical male ones such as resolve. Furthermore, said leaders had sufficient personal, analytical, communication, positional, strategic, organisational, and follower empowerment competencies. Overall, the case findings substantiated the importance of the transformative leadership models I explored in Chapter 5, first and foremost revealing that agency variables particularly enabled the leader's political outcomes.

These findings go hand in hand with the concept of power. Leaders should mainly employ "power with" to inspire stakeholders to collaborate for shared goals. However, a transformation towards sustainable development requires a fundamental redistribution of values that risk-averse society is typically uncomfortable with. In this case, leaders may cautiously use "power over" and push innovations to raise humanity to their vision of what is necessary for a sustainable future. Retaining legitimation for these actions is of specific importance because society expects political leaders to justify their decisions and actively listen and respond to their demands. They play a decisive role in creating pull factors for innovation. Still, they can equally act as a break if cultural values do not necessarily promote innovative capacities and they do not issue sufficient demands. Thereby, the media specifically exerts pressure on the public via framing and can act as a barrier or enabler to political leaders' pursuits.

The political system and configurations of political parties can be additionally decisive and enabling for said leaders. In consensus democracies, the potential for progressive agendas may be most significant when there is a recent alternation in governing political parties and a substantial ideological difference between past and current governments. Coalitions with a few parties with similar but not opposing positions may be equally favourable to progressive policy changes as are coalitions with more parties representing diverse interests. Concerning election cycles, a shorter time frame restrains the period for leaders to implement progressive policies and the public to perceive its effects. Thus, significant policy changes are easier to implement the longer governments stay in office. However, this only applies if the coalition aims to promote progressive agendas. Otherwise, there may be a lack of incentive to be innovative since there is no fear of alternation.

On an individual party level, parties with top-down decision-making, drawing on collective resources, may have a more substantial innovation capacity if leadership is motivated to drive an innovative agenda. If not, parties with collective leadership and horizontal, open, and democratic decision-making are better suited to the task. Finally, distinct ideologies promote political innovations, while parties with broad, vague, and more centred ones may do the opposite. Overall, the configuration of the party system and the state of the leader's political party and leadership are decisive for leaders striving to promote progressive political agendas.

Regarding the administrative sphere, political leaders need to bear in mind that sustainable statehood is the objective and that State institutions and staff may not yet be equipped to develop and implement envisioned political innovations. Hierarchies, silo structures, and closed-down top-down bureaucratic processes may hinder progressive agendas. In addition, whilst political leaders and heads of ministries typically develop and promote large-scale systemic political innovations, administrative staff can equally do so under the proper guidance and once trust in a shared mission is established. To increase the quantity and quality of innovations, it is vital to make processes more open and collaborative, especially regarding external networks and communities.

For women leaders stereotypes may represent a barrier in all arenas, as society expects them to come true to qualities such as kindness, sensitivity, and compassion. These traits correlate with the outlined transformative leadership styles and capabilities. However, raising societies to a vision also requires determination and resolve to not be perceived as lacking the fortitude to promote progressive agendas. Showing these traits may, however, put women leaders at a disadvantage because they counter typical stereotypes. It is thus particularly relevant for women leaders to choose a context-sensitive gender strategy, which is enabled by current women's representation, the demand for women's leadership, and culture-specific female stereotypes. A feminist stance, trust in one's agency, and the proper positioning strategy will enable women leaders to forgo these gender-based barriers.

Finally, regarding strategies for sustainable development, women political leaders may follow sustaincentric or socio-ecocentric approaches to reform or transform the social order they are embedded in. Whilst the former can significantly alleviate pressures on society and the environment, the latter may be too radical and progressive to convey risk-averse society to promote it. Hence, non-reformist reforms that act within the current Sustainable Capitalist regime may enable said leaders to implement changes that "stick". They can build coalitions along a shared vision of a sustainable future, drive regulatory changes, and anchor social acceptance for a necessary transformation. That way, they may potentially lead society further along the transformation path into an acceleration phase, where they can implement further non-reformist reforms to finally overcome the "old" and establish the "new".

Overall, structures, more often than not, represent a significant barrier to women political leaders' efforts. Only social and ecological conditions, gender equality, in the sense of women's rights and representation, the configuration of the party system, and the state of the leader's political party and leadership appeared to be enabling. Conversely, almost all agency variables, from the leader's stance on feminism to their leadership style and personality traits, were both decisive and enabling. This is particularly important considering that structures typically act as barriers that women leaders can only overcome because of their agency. In this sense, it is also important to stress that I only shed light on women political leaders whose agency enabled them to overcome said barriers. We cannot grasp the number of women who failed but should not neglect to consider them.

In summary, the following 12 prerequisites appear to determine how women political leaders can become agents for sustainable development:

1 Their childhood and upbringing exposed them to social, economic, or environmental challenges and influential role models, both shaping their political convictions and leadership.
2 Social and ecological conditions are dire enough to promote demand for and leeway for political innovations.
3 Prior governments and administrations on their governance level or above, installed solid political programs for sustainable development for the leaders to build on.
4 The leaders must act in a social context where women's leadership is promoted and sought after.
5 The configuration of the party system must be favourable to their election to leadership, either due to coalition agreements or the positioning of their political party.
6 They should have a positive outlook on feminism that allows them to overcome gender biases and choose a context-sensitive gender positioning strategy to overcome female stereotypes.
7 They must have systemic knowledge of sustainable development challenges and hold and communicate a solid political vision for a sustainable future.
8 Their personality traits should match openness, extraversion, agreeableness, and conscientiousness, along the five-factor personality model.
9 They should employ collective and transformative leadership styles.
10 They need sufficient analytical, personal, communication, positional, strategic, organizational, and follower empowerment competencies.

11 They must use the right mix of "power with," adhering to the public's demands, and "power over" to do what is necessary to drive a progressive agenda.
12 They must install a new narrative for sustainable statehood and development, institutionalise it, and enable greater leadership for sustainable development both within and beyond the State.

The findings are summarized in Figure 11.2.

Potentials for future research

While the cross-case analysis confirmed the validity of the normative concept of women's political leadership for sustainable development, there is also significant potential for future research.

The variables of the analytical framework are exhaustive and require extensive in-depth research to grasp truly. This is ambitious and the cases remain limited in that they only touch upon the most critical information. The availability of research materials further restrained the cases' understanding. As expected, most information could be found on Jacinda Ardern since she became the world's youngest woman head of State and was in a national executive political position, thus generating much publicity and interest in her leadership. The second most information was available on Mayor Valérie Plante but rather on her political program than her personal life and leadership style. Finally, the least information was available on Carole Delga's life and leadership. This could be expected since the literature revealed that regional politicians remain the least researched. However, due to the lack of resources, some of the findings could not be validated, and the evaluation of how decisive, hindering, and enabling some of the variables were remains limited. Thus, the cross-case comparability remains restricted by the amount of information found on each leader. Potential for future case studies may thus lie in adapting a broader range of research methods, particularly personal interviews with the leaders, their staff, political opponents, and the public. Finally, the generalised findings build on just three case studies, and conducting further case studies on all governance levels will add to their validity.

As laid out in Chapter 1, countries of the Global North are first and foremost responsible for many of the social, economic, and ecological problems we are encountering today and should thus become role models in solving them. Still, it would be highly insightful to research women political leaders trying to push for sustainable development in other political systems and geographic areas. The structural limitations they face may be even more critical to understand and their agency potentially more

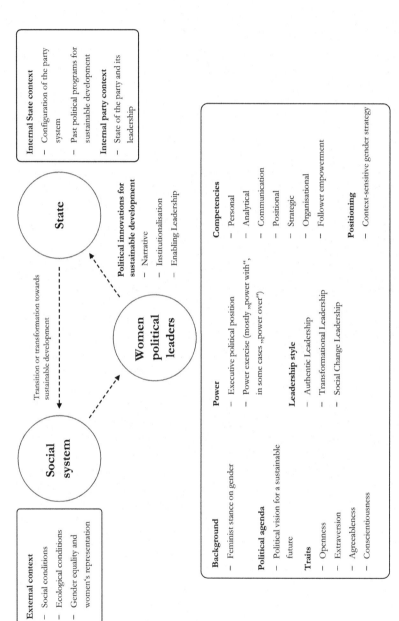

FIGURE 11.2 The agency and structure factors enabling women political leaders to drive sustainable development via political innovations.

limited. Considering the dangers of White feminism (Zakaria, 2022), another potential lies in exploring women leaders who are not White. Leaders such as Barbados Prime Minister Mia Mottley, who has been campaigning and acting against pollution, climate change, and deforestation (UNEP, 2021, December 7); the first woman mayor of the Ethiopian capital Addis Ababa, Adanech Abebei, who is part of the C40 initiative and a champion for inclusive growth (Ndungidi, 2021, September 29); the first woman head of Tokyo, Japan, Governor Yuriko Koike who is also part of the C40 initiative, empowers women, and aims to transform the administration and finance towards sustainability (C40 Cities, 2022); Bogotá City's first woman and openly gay mayor, Claudia López, who strives for a new social and environmental contract for the 21st century (OECD, 2022a); Leila Mustapha, joint President of Raqqa, Syria, who works across complex traditional, tribal, cultural, and religious boundaries and conflicts to ensure societal inclusivity and collaboration in a world dominated by men (O'Connor, 2022); Dang Thi Ngoc Thinh, President of Vietnam, who fights for women's empowerment, sustainable development and economies of shared values (Vietnam Plus, 2018, April 27); Fatima Zahra Mansouri, the first woman mayor of Marrakech and Minister of Housing and Urbanism of the kingdom of Morocco, who is committed to driving the Sustainable Development Goals (Latrech, 2021, December 16); or Fatma Şahin, the first woman mayor of Gaziantep, Turkey, who is an OECD champion for inclusive growth and driving green city development (OECD, 2022b). This list is not exhaustive but pays homage to the many women leaders fighting for the wellbeing of both people and the planet worldwide.

Another opportunity for future research is political leadership research that does not play to the gender binary (Hyde et al., 2019). Leadership literature still overwhelmingly differentiates leadership traits and qualities along gender. This does not come true to the most current notion of androgynous leadership (Blake-Bear et al., 2020), suggesting that all humans possess both traditionally assigned feminine and masculine psychological characteristics and should thus not be differentiated as such (Hyde et al.). Respectively, there lies great potential in analysing political leadership for sustainable development through an androgynous lens.

Finally, the most recent leadership theories stress the importance of shared and collective leadership. Thus, potential lies in analysing how shared leadership facilitates the development and implementation of political innovations for sustainable development, including actors from civil society organisations, media, businesses, administrative staff, and other stakeholders. This would move the focus away from individual leaders and demonstrate the importance of collective leadership for a sustainable future.

A future outlook

As laid out in the introduction, leadership tends to slack in long periods of tranquillity. Only in adverse times do people, out of necessity, turn to courageous leaders who have the potential to transcend the routines of the "old" and lead the way toward the unknown "new". The research demonstrates that our time's social, economic, and ecological conditions gave rise to women political leaders with systemic visions of a more sustainable future. They overcome the traditional approach of politics as the "art of the possible and attainable," and their cases demonstrate the exceeding relevance of the phenomenon of *women's political leadership for sustainable development*.

Activist Rosalynn Carter declared that "a leader takes people where they want to go. A great leader takes people where they don't necessarily want to go, but ought to be" (Kirimi, 2007, p. 165). As pressures on society increase and they transition along the transformation path, we can expect them to turn towards more of these exceptional leaders to drive the transformation towards the "new". Women political leaders, who are already out there, predestined for transformative leadership and guided by their strong visions of what ought to be – namely, sustainable development or a good life for all, within planetary boundaries. Eventually, said leaders may move beyond non-reformist reforms and potentially succeed at a new conception of politics, which Nigerian politician Oby Ezekwesili describes as the "art of the impossible," or what seems impossible today, "made possible" (Guardian Woman, 2018, October 27).

References

Blake-Bear, S., Shapiro, M., & Ingols, C. (2020). Feminine? Masculine? Androgynous leadership as a necessity in COVID-19. *Gender in Management: An International Journal, 35* (7/8), 607–617. https://doi.org/10.1108/gm-07-2020-0222

Bryant, M. (2022, June 25). Abortion banned in multiples US states just hours after Roe v Wade overturned. *The Guardian.* https://www.theguardian.com/us-news/2022/jun/25/abortion-banned-in-multiple-us-states-just-hours-after-roe-v-wade-overturned

C40 Cities. (2022). *Governor Yuriko Koike.* https://www.c40.org/steering-committee/yuriko-koike/

Guardian Woman. (2018, October 27). Politics is the art of the impossible, made possible. *The Guardian.* https://guardian.ng/guardian-woman/politics-is-the-art-of-the-impossible-made-possible/

Hoare, Q., & Nowell-Smith, G. (1971). *Selections from the prison notebooks.* London: Lawrence & Wishart.

Hyde, J. S., Bigler, R. S., Joel, D., Tate, C. C., & van Anders, S. M. (2019). The future of sex and gender in psychology: five challenges to the gender binary. *American Psychologist, 74*(2), 171–193. https://doi.org/10.1037/amp0000307

Kirimi, B. (2007). *Successful leadership. 8 principles you must know.* Jacksonville, FL: ABC Book Publishing.

Latrech, O. (2021, December 16). Morocco reaffirms commitment to sustainable urban development. *Morocco World News*. https://www.moroccoworldnews. com/2021/12/346037/morocco-reaffirms-commitment-to-sustainable-urban-development

Lindsay, J. M. (2020, December 17). The most significant world events in 2020. *Council on Foreign Relations*. https://www.cfr.org/blog/ten-most-significant-world-events-2020

Lindsay, J. M. (2021, December 15). The most significant world events in 2021. *Council on Foreign Relations*. https://www.cfr.org/blog/ten-most-significant-world-events-2021

Lindsay, J. M. (2022, December 16). The most significant world events in 2023. *Council on Foreign Relations*. https://www.cfr.org/blog/ten-most-significant-world-events-2020

Lindsay, J. M. (2023, December 8). The most significant world events in 2023. *Council on Foreign Relations*. https://www.cfr.org/blog/ten-most-significant-world-events-2023

Ndungidi, P. (2021, September 29). Ehtiopia: Adanech Abiebie re-elected Mayour of Addis Ababa. *African Shapers*. https://africanshapers.com/en/ethiopia-adanech-abiebie-re-elected-mayor-of-addis-ababa/

O'Connor, M. (2022). An ancient city, destroyed by war, is being rebuilt. *PES Group*. https://pes.cor.europa.eu/article/interview-concha-andreu-president-la-rioja-region

OECD. (2022a). *Claudia López Bogotá Colombia*. http://www.oecd-inclusive. com/champion-mayors/mayor/champion-mayor-claudia-lopez/

OECD. (2022b). *Fatma Şahin Gaziantep Turkey*. http://www.oecd-inclusive.com/ champion-mayors/mayor/champion-mayor-fatma-sahin/

Pinker, S. (2018). *Enlightenment now. The case for reason, science, humanism, and progress*. New York, NY: Penguin Books.

Rockström, J., Gupta, J., Qin, D., Lade, S. J., Abrams, J. F., Andersen, L. S., Armstrong McKay, D. I., Bai, X., Bala, G., Bunn, S. E., Ciobanu, D., DeClerck, F., Ebi, K., Gifford, L., Gordon, C., Hasan, S., Kanie, N., Lenton, T. M., Loriani, S., ... Zhang, X. (2023). Safe and just Earth system boundaries. *Nature, 619*, 102–111. https://doi.org/10.1038/s41586-023-06083-8

The Guardian. (2022, September 3). *Pakistan appeals for 'immense' international response to floods*. https://www.theguardian.com/world/2022/sep/03/pakistan-appeals-for-immense-international-response-to-floods

UNEP. (2021, December 7). *Barbados PM Mottley leads the charge against climate change*. https://www.unep.org/news-and-stories/story/barbados-pm-mottley-leads-charge-against-climate-change

Vietnam Plus. (2018, April 27). *Vice-President Thinh addresses Global Summit of Women's opening ceremony*. https://en.vietnamplus.vn/vice-president-thinh-addresses-global-summit-of-womens-opening-ceremony/130197.vnp

Zakaria, R. (2022). *Against white feminism*. Munich, Germany: Carl Hanser Verlag.

Zemelyte, B. (2022, July 8). Russia-Ukraine war: 'Not all refugees are treated the same'. *Aljazeera*. https://www.aljazeera.com/news/2022/7/8/russia-ukraine-amnesty-interview

Zukowski, G. (2021, October 19). Poland: A year on, abortion ruling harms women. *Amnesty International*. https://www.amnesty.org/en/latest/news/2021/10/poland-a-year-on-abortion-ruling-harms-women/

APPENDIX A

Key Terms and Definitions

TABLE A.1 Synthesised personal traits and competencies.

Trait / competency	Description	References
Awareness of self	Being aware of ones' beliefs, values, strengths and weaknesses; self-reflection and introspection; living by a code of ethics; evaluating own experiences on a deeper consciousness level; relating ones' own to others' stories; conscious reflection of own mind and actions	Avolio & Gardner, 2005; Bass & Riggio, 2006; Klenke, 2017; Komives et al., 2017
Empowering oneself	Having the ability to inspire oneself; believing in ones' efficacy; self-organising to excel	Künkel, 2019
Congruent values and behaviour	Acting consistently with and according to ones' beliefs and values; demonstrating integrity; self-regulating; reflecting and learning from ones' mistakes; being genuine and trustworthy; leading by example	Bass & Riggio, 2006; Bell et al., 2003; Klenke, 2017; Komives et al., 2017; Taylor, 2007

(Continued)

TABLE A.1 (Continued)

Trait / competency	Description	References
Commitment to the cause and drive for change	Demonstrating and intrinsic motivation and passion towards the cause and concrete actions; fully committing to the cause; taking risks in the face of uncertainty; being reliable, determined, disciplined, accountable and patient; proactive actions for the cause and one's goals and a larger transition; showing moral courage and a positive, visionary mindset	Komives et al., 2017; Künkel, 2019; Taylor, 2007
Connectedness to and agreeableness with individuals and society	Feeling an intrinsic connection to society and actively working towards improving the status quo for the common good; being empathetic, demonstrating care and emotional intelligence, and feeling close and connected to individuals and groups; having low ego needs; acting compassionate and respectful, even in the face of differences and difficult situations; being trustworthy and kind	Avolio & Gardner, 2005; Bass & Riggio, 2006; Battilana et al., 2009; Judge & Bono, 2000; Komives et al., 2017; Künkel, 2019
Striving for excellence	Continuosly striving to improve and achieve excellence through performance, dependability and attention to detail	Judge & Bono, 2000; Künkel, 2019
Agile thinking and behaviour	Flexibility; preparedness to venture into the unknown; risk-taking; seeing obstacles as opportunities; attitude of discovery and adventure; acting beyond comfort zone; transcendence of boundaries, humility, resilience, quick adaptation to new situations	Komives et al., 2017; Künkel, 2019

(Continued)

TABLE A.1 (Continued)

Trait / competency	Description	References
Inner balance and emotional adjustment	Well managed balance between personal and professional life; attention to life goals and spirituality; attention to personal relationships; knowledge on how to operate best; finding our optimal rhythm; cultivation of renewal; uniting and integrating one's varied life roles and having time to pursue them; attention to energy levels; attention to own vitality; ability to renew in places of beauty; Life satisfaction, freedom of depression and mental ailments	Bell et al., 2003; Judge & Bono, 2000; Künkel, 2019; Taylor, 2007
Openness	Being perceptive, avoiding judgement and engaging in deep listening; openness to differences; taking creative actions	Judge & Bono, 2000; Künkel, 2019
Extraversion	Being outgoing, active and seeking excitement	Judge & Bono, 2000; Taylor, 2007

TABLE A.2 Synthesised follower empowerment competencies.

Competency	Description	References
Setting and driving a common purpose	Driving a shared vision and narrative with collective aims and the goal of improving the status quo	Komives et al., 2017; Battilana et al., 2009; Göpel, 2016; Mazzucato, 2018; Westley et al., 2013
Support in self-awareness and determination	Helping the individuals and the group to define their own values and identity; setting standards for themselves and encouraging the assessment of discrepancies with outcomes; encouraging authentic behaviour; encouraging mindfulness and stress reduction; mentoring others	Avolio & Gardner, 2005; Bass & Riggio, 2006; Taylor, 2007; Wakefield, 2017

(Continued)

TABLE A.2 (Continued)

Competency	Description	References
Empowering followers and building relationships	Driving extra efforts in the group to achieve the shared vision; rewarding achievements to generate satisfaction; inspiring and motivating the group; encouraging mindshifts and innovative thinking; distributing leadership among individuals to drive sense of ownership; coaching and mentoring others; facilitating cooperation and bonding; paying attention to individual needs and concerns; building trust through empathy and transparency	Bass & Riggio, 2006; Battilana et al., 2009; Komives et al., 2017; Künkel, 2019; Ottens & Edelenbos, 2018; Taylor, 2007; Wakefield, 2017; Westley et al., 2013
Fostering excellence and iterative learning	Making use of diverse expertise and best-practices; learning from each other; driving cycles of reflection, adjustment of strategies and turning mistakes into progress; regular feedback cycles and impact evaluation	Künkel, 2019
Context-sensitive use of power	Employing "power over", "power to/ with"	Coleman, 2011; French & Raven, 1959; Klenke, 2017; Wakefield, 2017

TABLE A.3 Synthesised analytical competencies.

Competency	Description	References
Systemic thinking	Taking a holistic view at systems and seeing the larger context from different angles	Künkel, 2019
Contextual intelligence	Sensitive interpretation of time and place, including institutional landscapes and networks and one's role and position in them; understanding innovation cycles and windows of opportunities; understanding of political and policy problems and opportunities; understanding stakeholder interests and behaviours; analysing cooperation opportunities	Ambler, 2005; Battilana et al., 2009; Ottens & Edelenbos, 2018; Taylor, 2009

TABLE A.4 Synthesised communication competencies.

Competency	Description	References
Sharing a common vision	Mobilising stakeholders by communicating a shared vision for the future, including values and beliefs associated with the vision	Battilana et al., 2009; Bell et al., 2003; Klenke, 2017; Taylor, 2007; Westley et al., 2013
Interpersonal diplomacy	Bargaining, negotiation, facilitating, negotiating and resolving conflict	Klenke, 2017; Bell et al., 2003; Battilana et al., 2009; Taylor, 2009
Rhetoric strategies	Using discourse to convince others of the need for change; framing solutions in regard to the problems they will solve; employing storytelling and narrative styles that stakeholders can identify with	Battilana et al., 2009; Bell et al., 2003; Westley et al., 2013
Fostering dialogues	Raising the quality of communication by driving dialogic practices, active listening, and clear and frequent communication; allowing diversity in dialogues and fostering constructive communication around it	Künkel, 2019; Taylor, 2007
Spreading knowledge	Sharing knowledge on problems and solutions	Taylor, 2009

TABLE A.5 Synthesised positional competencies.

Competency	Description	References
Expertise	Good knowledge of sustainable development, its challenges and opportunities for transformation; sufficient political intelligence and skills; knowledge of the institutional context; continuously developing new knowledge and resources	Avolio & Gardner, 2005; Battilana et al., 2009; Cole, 1994; Klenke, 2017; Taylor, 2007, 2009; Westley et al., 2013
Position	Obtaining a formal organisational position, level and social position within an organisation to drive change; relevance of prior appointments and dismals	Cole, 1994; Taylor, 2007

TABLE A.6 Synthesised strategic competencies.

Competency	Description	References
Developing a political identity and vision	Defining one's own political identity, purpose, and style; developing a political vision that questions the status quo	Bell et al., 2003; Battilana et al., 2009; Klenke, 2017; Künkel, 2019; Skowronek, 2011; Taylor, 2009
Employing networking skills	Actively developing social capital and seeking mentoring relationships	Klenke, 2017
Future oriented thinking	Having a positive outlook on the future and focusing on potentials and solutions with a clear vision and goals; employing methods such as scenario planning or future search	Künkel, 2019
Using windows of opportunity	Scanning the system to either recognise or create new windows of opportunity to connect and mobilise others; building momentum for change; minimising the experience of loss for all stakeholders and creating win-win-situations	Battilana et al., 2009; Westley et al., 2013
Reflective practices in context	Analysis of trends and developments and adaptation of behaviour to these changing conditions; continuously gaining perspective and sensing what is needed; responding to the needs of stakeholders, cooperative networks, and the larger system of society; choosing short-run vs. long-run policies, and reactive vs. proactive politics accordingly; adapting strategies, plans, processes and routines to new contexts and learnings	Ambler, 2005; Bell et al., 2003; Cole, 1994; Klenke, 2017; Künkel, 2019
Designing networks	Setting clear policy goals, deadlines, and procedures; selecting actors to be involved and mobilising actors affected by the issue	Battilana et al., 2009; Ottens & Edelenbos, 2018; Westley et al., 2013

(*Continued*)

TABLE A.6 (Continued)

Competency	Description	References
Framing networks	Aligning strategic vision, strategies, goals agendas, and actors; framing policy solutions in light of the problems they seek to solve; using prognostic framing in relation to status quo; engaging in motivational framing with convincing reasoning; reframing the existing discourse that led to the problem at hand; bridging differences by focusing on connectivity and collaboration and reducing tensions from differing worldviews, identities, and experiences	Battilana et al., 2009; Ottens & Edelenbos, 2018; Westley et al., 2013
Employing influence tactics	Using influence tactics that are suitable to the context; exemplification, i.e., leading by example; ingratiation, i.e., making stakeholders attribute positive qualities to oneself; supplication, i.e., presenting oneself as vulnerable to secure empathy	Battilana et al., 2009; Gardner & Clevenger, 1998; Westley et al., 2013
Creativity, innovation and risk-taking	Driving new ways of thinking and working; supporting and nurturing creative ideas and energy for innovative solutions; including diverse skills and perspectives for creative and inclusive solutions; openness to risks and associated opportunities	Battilana et al., 2009; Künkel, 2019
Drive for excellence	Seeking the best solutions and results by continuously expanding knowledge, benchmarking and taking a service orientation and high-quality delivery approach	Künkel, 2019

TABLE A.7 Synthesised organisational competencies.

Competency	Description	References
Taking on multiple roles	Developing the capacity to switch between different roles, such as decision-taker, coordinator, or power broker	Cole, 1994
Driving collaboration and collective action	Building a central network position and variety of network connections with ties to and relationships with a diverse range of stakeholders; building cohesion by creating identification within networks, building the community, bridging views, linking actors, and reducing conflicts and contradictions; reducing or actively inducing conflicts within networks; respecting differences and fostering diversity and discourse; engaging in collective sensemaking and sense-giving; actively building coalitions by capitalising on diversity and the strength of relationships; working towards a common purpose and mutually beneficial goals; fostering collective responsibility; sharing authority, responsibility and accountability; gathering support from variety of stakeholders and building multi-level networks of support and external partnerships; creating external partnerships with other leaders and organisations	Battilana et al., 2009; Ottens & Edelenbos, 2018; Komives et al., 2017; Künkel, 2019; Roberts, 2017; Taylor, 2007; Westley et al., 2013
Managing networks	Coordinating and facilitating both formal and informal networks; connecting ideas and resources for the common vision; mediating between actors, organisations and institutions; managing complexity with clear goals; planning and directing activities and resources; monitoring progress; focusing on results and outcomes; establishing authorities, roles and responsibilities; mobilising resources; driving effective communication and processes, incl. governance structures and functioning delivery structures; ensuring the relevance of initiatives for the context and vision; inspiring a thinking environment, nurtured by different perspectives; actively creating settings for constructive dialogues and the integration of diverse ideas, perspectives and solutions; ensuring that all stakeholders drive strategy and implementation; ensuring integration of weaker stakeholder groups	Battilana et al., 2009; Ottens & Edelenbos, 2018

(Continued)

TABLE A.7 (Continued)

Competency	Description	References
Fostering creativity and knowledge	Bringing together different kinds of perspectives and thinking; creating conditions for cognitive, strategic, and institutional learning and collective idea generation	Battilana et al., 2009; Künkel, 2019; Westley et al., 2013
Mobilising for change	Promoting experimentation on a small scale; establishing pilot projects; preparing others for change	Battilana et al., 2009; Taylor, 2007; Westley et al., 2013

TABLE A.8 Synthesised political system contextual variables.

Variable	Description	References
Political system	Type of democracy (majoritarian vs. consensus)	Lijphart, 2012
State and government structures and culture	Governance dynamics, structures and incentives; organisational structures and processes; state strength and tasks; actor constellations; organisational culture and values; degree of institutionalisation	Battilana et al., 2009; Bell et al., 2003; Fukuyama, 2004; Taylor, 2009; Westley et al., 2013
State of the current regime	Resiliency and/ or vulnerability; alternation of governing parties	Bischoff & Christiansen, 2021; Skowronek, 2011
Policy context	Past policy choices and problems; policy processes; current programs and policy options; potential changes in the policy environment; opportunities and constraints of potential policy options	Scharpf, 2000
Electoral politics	Mode of election	Cole, 1994
Judiciary set-up	Constitutional framework; judicial constraints	Cole, 1994

(*Continued*)

TABLE A.8 (Continued)

Variable	Description	References
Political parties	Configuration of the party system; organisational positioning; alliances; heterogeneity of networks	Battilana et al., 2009; Bischoff & Christiansen, 2021
Role of gender	Female stereotypes; gender equality	Eagly & Karau, 2002; Genovese & Steckenrider, 2013; Haslam & Ryan, 2008; Hymowitz & Schelhardt, 1986; Klenke, 2017; Montecinos, 2017; Pullen & Vacchani, 2020

TABLE A.9 Synthesised inner-organisational context (party) variables.

Variable	Description	References
Party (s)election	Process of candidate selection	Rahat & Hazan, 2001; Rahat et al., 2008
Party programme	Radical vs. moderate	Bischoff & Christiansen, 2021
Interactions and alliances	Relations with other parties and organisations	Bischoff & Christiansen, 2021
Conditions within the party	Stability, opportunities, crises, and changes	Battilana et al., 2009

TABLE A.10 Synthesised external context variables.

Variable	Description	References
Historical and current context	Economic, social, environmental, political	Synthesised variables from analysis in Chapters 1–2
Culture	Innovation capacity; social norms and values	Prim et al., 2017
Involvement of citizens in political processes	Degree of involvement in shaping living conditions; interactive forms of governance; public demand for change	Criado et al., 2013; Fukuyama, 2004; Nye, 2008; Sørensen, 2020
Media positioning	Influence on political process and public opinion	Belasen & Frank, 2012; Cohen et al., 2008; Rockman, 1984

(Continued)

TABLE A.10 (Continued)

Variable	Description	References
(Inter)national positioning	Role of the cities, regions, and nations in the (inter-) national system; role of supranational bodies; interdependency with international economy and foreign policy making	Cole, 1994
Role of gender	Female stereotypes; gender equality	Eagly & Karau, 2002; Genovese & Steckenrider, 2013; Haslam & Ryan, 2008; Hymowitz & Schelhardt, 1986; Klenke, 2017; Montecinos, 2017; Pullen & Vacchani, 2020

References

Ambler, G. (2005). *Understanding leadership in context*. Retrieved from www.thepracticeofleadership.net/2005/12/08/understainding-leadership-context/

Avolio, B. J., & Gardner, W. L. (2005). Authentic leadership development: Getting to the root of positive forms of leadership. *The Leadership Quarterly, 16*(3), 315–338. https://doi.org/10.1016/j.leaqua.2005.03.001

Bass, B. M., & Riggio, R. E. (2006). *Transformational leadership* (2nd ed.). Brighton: Psychology Press.

Battilana, J., Leca, B., & Boxenbaum, E. (2009). How actors change institutions: Towards a theory of Institutional Entrepreneurship. *Academy of Management Annals, 3*(1), 65–107. https://doi.org/10.5465/19416520903053598

Belasen, A., & Frank, N. (2012). Women's leadership: Using the competing values framework to evaluate the interactive effects of gender and personality traits on leadership roles. *International Journal of Leadership Studies, 7*(2), 192–214. https://www.regent.edu/acad/global/publications/ijls/new/vol7iss2/IJLS_Vol7Iss2_Belasen_pp192-215.pdf

Bell, D. S., Hargrove, E. C., & Theakston, K. (2003). Skill context: A comparison of politicians. *Presidential Studies Quarterly, 29*(3), 528–548. https://doi.org/10.1111/j.0268-2141.2003.00048.x

Bischoff, C. S., & Christiansen, F. J. (2021). Political parties and innovation. In Sørensen, E. (Ed.), *Political Innovations. Creative transformations in polity, politics and policy* (pp. 74–89). New York, NY: Routledge.

Cohen, J., Tsfati, Y., & Sheafer, T. (2008). The Influence of presumed media influence in politics. *Public Opinion Quarterly, 72*(2), 331–344. https://doi.org/10.1093/poq/nfn014

Cole, A. (1994). Studying political leadership: The case of Francois Mitterand. *Political Studies XLII, 42*(3), 453–468. https://doi.org/10.1111/j.1467-9248.1994.tb01688.x

Coleman, M. (2011). *Women at the top. Challenges, choices and change*. London: Palgrave Macmillan.

Criado, J. I., Sandoval-Almazan, R., & Gil-Garcia, J. R. (2013). Government innovation through social media. *Government Information Quarterly*, *30*(4), 319–326. https://doi.org/10.1016/j.giq.2013.10.003

Eagly, A. H., & Karau, S. J. (2002). Role congruity theory of prejudice toward female leaders. *Psychological Review*, *109*(3), 573–598. https://doi.org/10.1037//0033-295X.109.3.573

French, J., & Raven, B. (1959). The bases of social power. In D. Cartwright, & A. Zander (Eds.), *Studies in social power* (pp. 150–167). Ann Arbor, MI: University of Michigan Press.

Fukuyama, F. (2004). *State-building: Governance and world order in the twenty-first century*. Ithaca, NY: Cornell University Press.

Gardner, W., & Clevenger, D. (1998). Impression management techniques associated with transformational leadership leaders at the world class level. *Management Communication Quarterly*, *12*(1), 237–251. https://doi.org/10.1177/0893318998121001

Genovese, M. A. & Steckenrider, J. S. (2013). *Women as political leaders. Studies in gender and governing*. London: Routledge.

Göpel, M. (2016). *The great mindshift*. Wiesbaden, Germany: Springer.

Haslam, S. A., & Ryan, M. (2008). The road off the glass cliff: Differences in perceived suitability of men and women for leadership positions in succeeding and failing organizations. *The Leadership Quarterly*, *19*(5), 530–546. https://doi.org/10.1016/j.leaqua.2008.07.011

Hymowitz, C., & Schelhardt, T. (1986). The glass ceiling: Why women can't seem to break the invisible barrier that blocks them from top jobs. *Wall Street Journal*, *57*, 4–5. https://www.proquest.com/docview/135185178

Judge, T. A., & Bono, J. E. (2000). Five-factor model of personality and transformational leadership. *Journal of Applied Psychology*, *85*(5), 751–765. https://doi.org/10.1037/0021-9010.85.5.751

Klenke, K. (2017). *Women in leadership* (2nd ed.). Bingley: Emerald Publishing.

Komives, S. R., Wagner, W., & Associates. (2017). *Leadership for a better world: Understanding the social change model of leadership development*. San Francisco, CA: Jossey-Bass.

Künkel, P. (2019). *Stewarding sustainability transformations*. Cham, Switzerland: Springer Nature.

Lijphart, A. (2012). *Patterns of democratic government forms and performance in thirty-six countries* (2nd ed.). Yale, CT: Yale University Press.

Mazzucato, M. (2018). *The Entrepreneurial State. Debunking public vs. private sector myths*. London: Penguin Randomhouse.

Montecinos, V. (2017). Introduction. In Monetcinos, V. (Ed.), *Women presidents and prime ministers in post-transition democracies* (pp. 1–36). London: Palgrave Macmillan.

Nye, J. (2008). *The power to lead*. Oxford: Oxford University Press.

Ottens, M., & Edelenbos, J. (2018). Political leadership as meta-governance in sustainability transitions: A case study analysis of meta-governance in the case of the Dutch National Agreement on Climate. *Sustainability*, *11*(1), 110. https://doi.org/10.3390/su11010110

Prim, A. L., Filho, L. S., Zamur, G. A. C., & di Serio, L. C. (2017). The relationship between national culture dimensions and degree of innovation. *International Journal of Innovation Management*, *21*(1), 173001. https://doi.org/10.1142/s136391961730001x

Pullen, A., & Vacchani, S. J. (2020). Feminist ethics and women leaders: From difference to intercorporeality. *Journal of Business Ethics*, *173*(2), 1–11. https://doi.org/10.1007/s10551-020-04526-0

Rahat, G., & Hazan, R. Y. (2001). Candidate selection methods. An analytical framework. *Party Politics*, *7*(3), 297–322. https://doi.org/10.1177/1354068801007003003

Rahat, G., Hazan, R. Y., & Katz, R. S. (2008). Democracy and political parties. On the uneasy relationships between participation, competition and representation. *Party Politics*, *14*(6), 663–683. https://doi.org/10.1177/1354068808093405

Roberts, D. C. (2017). Understanding the Social Change Model of leadership development. In Komives, S. R., & Wagner, W. (Eds.). *Leadership for a better world* (pp. 35–37). San Francisco, CA: John Wiley & Sons.

Rockman, B. A. (1984). *The leadership question: The presidency and the American system*. New York, NY: Prager Publishers.

Scharpf, F. W. (2000). Institutions in comparative policy research. *Comparative Political Studies*, *33*(6–7). https://doi.org/10.1177/001041400003300604

Skowronek, S. (2011). *Presidential leadership in political time: Reprise and reappraisal* (2nd ed.). Lawrence, KS: University Press of Kansas.

Sørensen, E. (2020). *Interactive political leadership. The role of politicians in the age of governance*. Oxford: Oxford University Press.

Taylor, A. (2007). *Sustainable urban water management champions: What do know about them?* 13th International Rainwater Catchment Systems Conference, Sydney, Australia. https://www.researchgate.net/publication/228623868_Sustainable_urban_water_management_champions_What_do_we_know_about_them

Taylor, A. (2009). Sustainable urban water management: Understanding and fostering champions of change. *Water Science and Technology*, *59*(5), 883–891. https://doi.org/10.2166/wst.2009.033

Wakefield, S. (2017). Transformative and Female Leadership for Women's Rights. *Oxfam*. https://s3.amazonaws.com/oxfam-us/www/static/media/files/Transformative_and_Female_Leadership_for_Womens_Rights.pdf

Westley, F. R., Tjornbo, O., Schultz, L., Olsson, P., Folke, C., Crona, B., & Bodin, Ö. (2013). A theory of transformative agency in linked social-ecological systems. *Ecology and Society*, *18*(3), 27. https://doi.org/10.5751/es-05072-180327

INDEX

Pages in *italics* refer to figures.

Printed in the United States
by Baker & Taylor Publisher Services